HIGH PERFORMANCE
SKIING

John Yacenda, PhD

HIGH PERFORMANCE
SKIING

John Yacenda, PhD

Leisure Press
Champaign, Illinois

Developmental Editor: Sue Ingels Mauck
Copy Editor: Claire M. Mount
Assistant Editors: Janet Beals and JoAnne Cline
Production Director: Ernie Noa
Assistant Production Director: Lezli Harris
Typesetter: Yvonne Winsor
Text Design: Keith Blomberg
Text Layout: Denise Peters
Cover Design: Jack Davis
Cover Photo: Lori Adamski-Peek; Skier: Scott Markewitz
Illustrations By: John Evanko
Printed By: Versa Press

ISBN: 0-88011-288-3

Copyright © 1987 by John Yacenda

Library of Congress Cataloging-in-Publication Data

Yacenda, John, 1947-
  High performance skiing.

  Bibliography: p.
  Includes index.
  1. Skis and skiing. I. Title.
GV854.Y33 1987   796.93   87-4207
ISBN 0-88011-288-3

Printed in the United States of America

10 9 8 7 6 5 4 3

Leisure Press
A division of Human Kinetics
  Publishers, Inc.
Box 5076, Champaign, IL
  61825-5076
1-800-747-4457

UK Office:
Human Kinetics Publishers
  (UK) Ltd.
PO Box 18
Rawdon, Leeds LS19 6TG
England
(0532) 504211

Dedication

To Robin, my skiing buddy, friend, lover, and wife; the author within the author whose thoughts and words have impregnated my own. To Tayesa, my daughter and very special friend; for all she's brought into my life, especially the play, the tears, and her wonderful spirit. And to my father, Sam, my first coach, pal, and idol.

Acknowledgments

This book wouldn't exist if I hadn't tapped into the 400 plus years of skiing amassed by my contributors. They are a fine bunch; my thanks to them all.

First I'd like to thank Mike Iman, Ski School Director at Northstar-at-Tahoe, for believing in the possibility of my pursuit and for agreeing to be my chief expert contributor. Five years a professional racer, Mike's prominence is his involvement in the ski instruction industry for 23 years. At one time he was honored as P.S.I.A.-W. Ski Instructor of The Year. Additionally, he has participated in exchange instructor programs and attended and completed National Academies at Snowbird and Alta, Utah. He presently is a clinician for and serves on the Board of Directors of P.S.I.A.-W., and he is a member of the I.S.I.A. intermittently over the past 16 years, he has been an examiner of instructors seeking associate and full certification.

Special thanks to Christin Cooper for trusting a stranger and then so willingly participating in my dream. Christin is presently a columnist and contributing editor to *Skiing Magazine*. Among other activities, she is a television commentator for national and international skiing competitions, and special coach for the Rossignol Race Camp series, and a ski industry spokesperson. Induction into the Ski Hall of Fame in 1984 was the culmination of a brilliant racing career for Christin. Between 1977 and 1984, she earned six national championship titles (two in slalom, two in giant slalom, and two in combined), was on two Olympic Teams (1980 and 1984), and on two World Championship Teams (1978 and 1982). In the 1982 World Championships, she was a triple medalist (silver in slalom, silver in GS, bronze in combined) —a feat unmatched by any other American woman. In the 1984 Olympics, she won a silver medal in GS. When asked for a personal comment on skiing, she said simply, "Skiing is a dance. The mountain and its ever-changing conditions are the music you dance to. Every run is different—waiting to be carved, to be created."

Importantly, my thanks to George Capaul, Assistant Coach of the U.S. Ski Team (Men's Slalom and GS), for his generous time, encouragement, coaching, and teaching. George's credentials are impressive: three-time ski racing champion in Eastern Switzerland; champion in the Great Ski New England Pro Classic (1977); formerly a Swiss Certified ski instructor; Program Director and Head Coach at Waterville Valley, New Hampshire for 10 years; Level III Certified Coach (U.S.); 8-year member of the Downhill Committee in the East; 8-year Associate Coach for the U.S. Ski Team; and Camp Director and Head Coach for the Rossignol Race Camp at Mammoth Mountain, California. As George puts it, "It's a privilege to be a friend of the mountains."

My appreciation to Jack Rounds for all his time and his readiness to share a breadth of knowledge about racing, skill development, racing strategy, ski tuning, and so much more. A talented racer, in high school Jack was ranked seventh in GS (New England); in college he was an Eastern "A" racer and raced pro for 5 years. As a former technical representative for both Sarner and Rossignol Skis, and with certification for all major bindings, Jack understands ski mechanics and racers' needs. As a fully certified ski instructor and race coach, Jack has taught skiing over the past 16 years, coached and worked with a wide range of racers, and in 1973 was the first American chosen in the U.S./France instructor exchange program. As he sees it, "Skiing is my life, so far. Nowhere have I ever experienced the freedom of expression that I feel in skiing—not in painting, sculpturing, or acting."

Thanks to Mark Tache for his engaging personality, impressive credentials, and enthusiasm for the sport, all of which add richness to what he has to say. A seven-year member of the U.S. Ski Team and twice on the World Championship Team, in his first season of professional racing Mark placed 8th overall. Named Junior Skier of the Year in 1980, he was the overall Nor-Am champion, winning all three disciplines: slalom, GS, and downhill. He was the top ranked American male on the Europa Cup Circuit, and placed in the top three five times during the 1979 to 1985 National Championships. Mark continues to race professionally and among other duties, coaches for the Rossignol Race Camp series (1982 to present). With respect to the expression of the sport of skiing, Mark notes the difference between the relative confinement of a track or court and the "totally unrestricted environment" in skiing. As he says, "The conditions and terrain are always changing, challenging even the best of skiers."

Thanks to Fritz Vallant for his coaching, his enthusiastic support, and his sound advice. A graduate of the Austrian Federal Sports School who specializes in ski instructing and coaching, Fritz has a degree in Physical Education and is a former coach of the U.S. Women's Ski Team. As a young racer, he competed in the Austrian Junior Program for 9 years before a broken leg ended his racing career at 17. Presently, Fritz is the Head Coach at Stratton Mountain School, Vermont. He is also candidly proud of his spouse, Cathy Bruce (Vallant), former U.S. Ski Team member, and presently number one on the Women's Pro Tour. As Fritz puts it, "Beauty is simplicity; skiing is beautiful."

Thanks to Pete Patterson for his spirit of sport, his refreshing attitude toward ski racing, and his willingness to share what he knows and feels. A former U.S. Ski Team member, Pete was the only U.S. medalist at the 1978 World Championships. As a Olympic racer, he placed fifth in the downhill at the 1980 Olympics. "The love for the sport," he says, "contributes most to your success as a skier, because it keeps you out there skiing in all conditions."

Thanks to John Hoffman for his interpretation of the art in skiing and his subtleties in teaching the skills inherent to the sport. Director of the Ski School at Donner Ski Ranch (California Sierras, near Tahoe), John has taught skiing for 20 years and coached racers for 10 years. To him skiing is sport "in search of the perfect turn."

There is a group of fine teachers, skiers, and race coaches, with whom I work and ski at Northstar-at-Tahoe, whose words and advice appear in *High Performance Skiing*, and who add to our understanding of high performance skiing. In alphabetical order, my thanks to Steve Armstrong, former NJCAA slalom and GS champion. Steve has been a ski instructor for 10 years, and says of skiing, "Depending on your mood, skiing can be whatever you want to make it."

Thanks to Brent Boblitt for his teaching and excellent eye for ski technique, and for his encouragement to write this book at a time when I wasn't quite sure I could. A fully certified P.S.I.A. instructor, Brent heads the race department at Northstar and says of skiing, "Skiing is a dance, and the mountain always leads."

Thanks to Dirk Haas, a ski instructor for 8 years who has been coaching young racers on the Northstar Race Team for the past

10 sessions. Dirk is noted for his candor and is praised for his passion for competition and working with young racers.

Thanks to Tom "TJ" Jones, a ski instructor for 3 years who has been coaching young racers on the Northstar Race Team for the past 6 seasons. TJ is praised by his head coach for his dedication and commitment to his young racers.

Thanks to Chaz Kruck for his crisp knowledge of racing technique, motivation, skill development, and for the many hours he spent with me reviewing racing concepts. All-American in the NJCAA Championships (slalom), Pacific Coast Champion Ski Meister, and racer on the Peugeot Grand Prix, Sierra Grand Prix, and Sierra Tahoe Pro Circuits, Chaz also raced "A" class on the Far West Amateur Circuit, achieved Level I coaching certification, and was a ski instructor for 3 years. He has been the Head Coach of Northstar's Race Team for the past 10 seasons.

Thanks to Tony Roegiers for his patient review of key technical material and his suggested changes in chapter 8. A former racer in the Masters Series, Tony recalls finishing the Olympia Downhill at Squaw Valley at age 36: "I was never so scared in my life." Fully certified by P.S.I.A., Tony has taught skiing for the past 6 years and is presently a ski school supervisor at Northstar. Speaking of what skiing means to him, he says, "It's one of those sports where you must learn to control your body movements so you can interact with the forces of nature, such as gravity—always a challenge."

My sincerest thanks to my developmental editor at Leisure Press, Sue Ingels Mauck, for her attention to detail, her willingness to try out new material, and her patience with my time demands. Writers have been known to blame editors for a lot of things, but in my mind a good editor means a good book.

Finally, I want to thank Sharon Parodi for her reliable, often tedious work in transcribing my many tapes, replete with a variety of sound effects backgrounding my conversations with contributors and my on-the-spot (wherever, whenever) notes and commentary. Her patient work made my job measurably more enjoyable.

Contents

Foreword

It's been years now since I've stood in the starting gate, clothed in the armor of a world-class racer and steeped in the intensity that matches the challenge waiting just below. But I can still conjure up the memory like yesterday, complete with jitters and anticipation and more than a little fear. I think no matter how much time passes since I've carved an arc on snow, I'll still be able, in my mind, to feel the wind and choose the best line. I doubt if the closeness of those icy breezes and fallaway turns will ever go away, for once the sport of skiing got in my blood it has flowed freely and ceaselessly. Something tells me it will flow there forever.

But like the lifeblood that runs in my veins, my skiing is not always clean and pure and effervescent. It is too often cluttered up with useless information that, like toxins in the system, hinder its natural flow. I remember waking up on race days skittish and scattered (or equally sluggish and uninspired), all my technical knowledge left under the sheets or shattered by nerves. I used to fight those mornings tooth and nail, neither accepting the reality, nor trying to work with it. Instead I would resolutely try to force a performance that had no business existing, (usually ending up on my rear end in the trees). I would forget, or maybe I didn't know yet, that skiing is much more than a physical endeavor. It is a mixture of mental and physical, of psychology and physiology, of conditions and conditioning, of approach and attitude, and the ever-present forces of Mother Nature. These were realities I had to learn to accept if I wanted to improve, working from there in harmony with the mountain instead of in battle against it. Ours is a sport that need be approached from different angles on different days, according to Nature's conditions as well as our own.

An old coach, way back when, used to take me skiing on only the most miserable days, choosing only the most miserably packed runs on the mountain. He taught me to approach the conditions as a challenge, not an adversary, and to search for the soft heart beneath the surface of every "ugly" slope. He would tell me not to expect to ski a steep, crud-filled chute in the fog the same way I would a smooth trail in the sun, nor to feel as graceful. Simple advice, but so crucial to my enjoyment of the sport. Through the years, advice such as this has helped me build a technique that is adaptable to all conditions and up to nearly every challenge, based on a willingness to try, to fail, and to accept reality.

My most inspired high performance skiing comes when I can filter out all the useless "toxic" input with which I am constantly bombarded ("You can't ski THAT, with THOSE skis") and replace it, before the next mogul, with more appropriate stuff. It's a learning process that comes with time and practice and a good dose of knowledge about what is and isn't appropriate. And it is this concept that John Yacenda so effectively addresses. *High Performance Skiing* may contain information on every technical trick for every slope and condition, but more importantly in my mind is that this book teaches you how to *approach* those varied slopes and conditions with a flexibility of mind and body, to enable you to be prepared to enjoy it all.

I now have a little confession to make. I was never one for skiing by textbook. In fact, you could hardly get me to pick up a magazine on the sport during my competitive years. Feel it, play with it, and learn by experience was my lofty approach.

I'd seen too many mechanical skiers up there doing it all by the book and looking like robots. They were totally missing the point. Well, I've softened my attitude since then (growing up, I think they call it), realizing that it's not the books that are at fault, but the attitudes of those who read them. Not everyone can spend all day every day up on the mountain "learning by experience" as I did. *High Performance Skiing* can provide an invaluable shortcut to a great deal of skiing knowledge, if that knowledge is taken to the slopes with some flexibility and ample room for personal style. And taking it to the slopes is the crucial step. Just reading a book on high performance skiing can indeed make you an expert on high performance skiing—for the bars, and the Jacuzzis, and the drive home from the slopes. But if you want to *be* a high performance skier, then take all these tools to the mountain and turn yourself loose to play. Let no set of words be your god, but only your guideline. And remember, no matter how much improvement you make, skiing will always be as frustrating as it is fantastic, demanding from you a subtle balance between aggression and surrender, between dancing and sparring, between hurrying and waiting. It is this tenuous balance, so elusive and so captivating, that keeps us always coming back for more.

Christin Cooper
Aspen, Colorado

Preface

I conceived of *High Performance Skiing* out of my love for skiing and my appreciation for growth and achievement through sport. I wrote this book for people who want to rev up their skiing by exploring high performance techniques and skills that lead to

1. more consistent performance,
2. less fatigue and more endurance,
3. greater strength and flexibility,
4. greater versatility,
5. greater confidence in the full range of skiing conditions, and
6. the incentive and know-how to jump into serious recreational racing.

The beauty of this book is that I've assumed you can already ski, perhaps quite well; yet I haven't assumed you're familiar with all of the skiing lingo. I don't deal with getting started on skis, and the language of the book is friendly. I'm interested in getting you started on the road toward high performance skiing as it is conceived by expert teachers of skiing, Olympic and World Cup coaches, former skiing greats, professional ski racers, and you. Some parts of this book deal with perspectives, opinions, strategies, and ideas; the majority of time, however, is spent on the snow or in training.

As an athlete and former coach, I dislike the theoretical when it lacks the practical, and prefer to follow my guts. As a 15-year college professor, I have espoused the theoretical to organize the practical and explain my fascination with life. As an author, I use whatever I can to help get the job done. I think you'll find that the athlete first, and coach second, dominate this book; I believe the athlete in you will be glad that they have.

High Performance Skiing is an up-front, how-to approach to the best skiing has to offer to recreational skiers interested in revving up their skiing. The most quoted and most influential contributor to this book is Mike Iman, whose credentials as a skier and teacher of skiers and instructors are a block long, give or take a few large buildings. Mike is the major force in chapters

1 through 4, and 6. These chapters are the product of countless hours of discussing skiing, actual skiing, and exploring technique, drills, and exercises. Over the months, I assembled the information Mike gave me on tape as well as while we were skiing into a format and language that we agree works well in reflecting the heart of high performance skiing from the eyes of both student and teacher.

While I consider myself well-informed in many areas of sport, fitness, athletic training, health, behavior, sports nutrition, and skiing, my expertise is best reflected in my ability to organize knowledge and experience, be it my own or that of others. Most notably in chapters 5 and 8 I organized the 400 years of skiing knowledge and experience provided by my host of contributors. We skied, raced, and drilled together; we also met on the hill to talk about skiing, and taped our conversations about skiing over dinner.

George Capaul, Assistant Coach of the U.S. Ski Team (men's slalom and giant slalom), and I spent a good deal of time talking on the phone, taping our conversations. George put in extra duty taping answers to my questions on his own. Along the way, we had an inspiring weight workout in Mammoth Lakes, California, and at George's invitation, I spent a week with the men's team during their pre-World Cup training camp at Copper Mountain, Colorado. Throughout my work with my contributors, I felt as if I were on a great adventure. I hounded them at times, probing with a barrage of questions, challenges, situations, and contradictions. It was a great way to write a book: lots of candor, laughter, and good times.

The fullest reward for their efforts, I trust, will be in how you, the reader, benefit from their insights, experiences, words of encouragement, and teaching as I have quoted them in the text. To wit, the glory of chapter 5 is that it is replete with quotes from my contributors who collectively have outstanding credentials as amateur, professional, World Cup, and Olympic racers and coaches. Take a careful look at their view of the game. The treatment of recreational racing in chapter 5 is the most versatile and exciting I think you'll find anywhere; it is also in terms that you can immediately put to work for you on the mountain.

Overall, you can expect to find short, highlighted sections of expert advice on a variety of topics throughout the book, with occasional moments of reflection on the experts' careers, or timely tips worked into the text. I enjoyed our discussions, and those who weren't already have become my friends over the course of writing this book.

As to the book's content: The first chapter is an exploration of high performance skiing: what it means to the experts, and how you might interpret its fundamentals relative to your own skiing. Each chapter concludes with a summary of the material covered in the chapter. You might find reading the summary first to be an interesting way to begin a chapter.

Once you're focused on the fundamentals of high performance skiing, we jump right into the steeps in chapter 2, with practical advice for revving up your skiing in different kinds of steep terrain and snow conditions. Chapters 3, 4, and 6 follow the same format as chapter 2, and all involve skiing powder, bumps, crud, ice, and slush.

Chapter 7 is a step-by-step approach to getting ready for a day of aggressive, fun-filled, injury-free skiing by warming up. Though the tendency is to skip this chapter because you're in too much of a hurry to make those first turns and get in a day of skiing, I urge you to take a look at it: It might give you some easy-to-accommodate ideas that will actually add to your joy of, and time spent, skiing.

Reviewed for technical accuracy by Tony Roegiers, chapter 8 will be the most popular for many skiers and instructors alike. This chapter presents, for the first time, an organized look at common technical problems along with detailed drills and exercises you can use on your own to help correct these problems. As a rule, when you have one problem you usually have others to a greater or lesser degree. The drills and exercises are designed to concentrate their effect on the main problem, as well as to address other problems in more subtle ways without paying attention to them. This is a fascinating chapter that could keep you busy for years!

World Cup skiers and coaches agree that ski school lessons are at the core of sound skiing fundamentals, yet the ski school experience is a nightmare for some and an enigma for many. Taking a ski school class or clinic, however, is different from going to school. If you prepare ahead of time, you can get more than you ever expected out of a ski school class. Chapter 9 gives you the ABCs of ski school classes from the student's perspective and shows you how to get your money's worth, what to do when you're unhappy about a class, how to choose the right class, and how ski instructors are trained.

The athlete's biggest supporter and rudest critic reside in his or her mind. Chapter 10 proposes that you use your mind, within bounds, to enhance your skiing and minimize your torture. It's a fun chapter, replete with encouragement to use mental directives, to learn from mistakes, to think light, quick, slow, progression, and fluid, and to set goals. This is a real upbeat approach to skiing, with a High Performance Tip on skiing in Wu Wei!

Finally, chapter 11: The best for last? I've spent most of my professional career promoting health and well-being and, in so doing, have improved my own sports performance, as well as that of my college students and the athletes I've coached. I am clearly passionate about this stuff; in chapter 11 I present progressive principles of training that include the five training seasons, physical conditioning, strength building, flexibility training, food as energy, food and performance, the value of rest, and the importance of fluid intake.

If you run, cycle, mountain climb, swim, play tennis or racquetball, play soccer, or take part in triathlons or other athletic activities in addition to skiing, you'll find this chapter an ideal approach to your own year-round training for glory.

The serious skier will find my work with Jack Rounds on tuning (Appendix) fascinating and helpful. A high performance recreational skier takes care of his or her equipment. Although much is available on equipment care in our skiing magazines, this section provides concise and practical tips for a maximum performance ski tune and vital information on properly fitted boots. If you've been thinking more about the performance nature of your equipment and tuning your own skis, you'll relish this information.

Discounting the long hours, writing this book has been a wonderful experience for me; I have had the opportunity to share my approach to sport with others whom I admire and respect for their talents as well as their willingness to share their knowledge. This interaction has afforded me the opportunity to write a book that will mean something to your skiing and overall quality of life.

Certainly, the most important things I've learned from writing *High Performance Skiing* is that there is no one way to ski correctly. In truth, skiing is as individual as our signatures. Common to us, however, are a number of skills, strategies, concepts, and techniques that each of us interprets in a way best suited to our body type, flexibility, athletic aptitude, physical conditioning, and overall sports attitude.

In all sports performance, we must be realistic and honest with ourselves, particularly when we're pursuing skill sports like skiing. Skill development takes time; rushing it leads to frustration, unrealistic personal demands, and often injury. If you don't try to ski like anyone but yourself, and take a patient, yet purposeful, approach to high performance skiing, you'll enjoy your interpretation of the concepts in this book. Getting better in sports doesn't have to mean all work and no play. In fact, for recreational sports the equation is probably best stated: mostly play, some work. The tools are here. You choose the balance of play and work; I and my contributors will give you ours.

John Yacenda
Truckee, California

Chapter 1

Fundamentals of High Performance Skiing

It's odd, but at times skiing seems to be as much attitude as ability . . .

If you compared the fundamentals of high performance skiing to the cornerstones of your house, this chapter could well be titled "Building a Better Brick House." Skiing is one of the many sports that tempts you to figure out approximately how it's done, so that you can go out and do it. You're apt to progress more rapidly and painlessly toward consistent skiing performance, however, if you take the time required to learn the fundamentals at your own pace.

This book assumes from the beginning that you already ski and have a love for the sport, and that you want to learn the basics not of how to ski, but of how to become a high performance skier. That is what this book is all about. The basics of high performance skiing are a blend of your technical skiing skills, the physical attitude with which you ski, and the powers of your mind. In the chapters that follow, I, along with my contributors, will concentrate on honing your technical skiing skills in the fullest array of skiing situations, while fine-tuning your physical attitude and explaining and exploring both the intellectual and the emotional perspectives inherent to high performance skiing. This three-part concept of the fundamentals of high performance skiing can be stated briefly.

1. *Technical skills*: This includes being balanced over your skis with independent legs/skis; having a muscularly relaxed stance; being versatile in the use of different kinds of turns and the linking of these turns; having edge control in varied conditions; controlling speed (acceleration and deceleration); using poles appropriately; moving efficiently; being versatile in using the whole length of the ski as well as the inside and outside edges; and relying on *ski feel*.

2. *Physical attitude*: This includes being reactional; at times, feeling fearless and aggressive as you really work your skis; at times, feeling very loose and light on your skis with very few inappropriate movements or contractions in your muscles and little pressure on your skis as they actually ride or glide atop the snow; at times, feeling playful and adventurous.

3. *Mental powers*: This includes first, confidence followed by a sense of pride and accomplishment; goal setting and determination; self-acceptance and inner-direction; desire to learn; acceptance of personal growth; control over the fear of failures; and kindness to oneself and others.

In chapter 2 you'll be skiing the steeps and jumping off cornices; and in subsequent chapters we'll take you skiing in moguls, powder, the race course, crud, slush, and more.

High performance skiers ski at all levels and in all conditions. You needn't be an Olympic racer or expert skier to ski at a high level of performance. Rather, you have only to pursue high performance in all levels of skiing, be it your 5th or 500th time through the race course, mogul field, groomed run, trees, or wherever. Unless you have the sense of there being fundamentals to every step toward higher levels of performance, you may be disappointed with your lack of progress, even though you're trying hard to improve.

Regardless of whether you're an intermediate, advanced-intermediate, expert, or super expert skier, there's always that hill, mountain, or mogul run that presents trouble or difficulty for you. If you *perceive* difficulty with a slope or condition, you will *experience* difficulty; you reinforce the difficulty with the power of your mind. (Chapter 10 details aspects of the psychology of high performance skiing.)

Five Questions to Measure High Performance

One of the best ways to find out if you are really advancing to high performance skiing is to test your skills and confidence by returning to those slopes or conditions that intimidated you the last time out. In the meantime, ask yourself these five questions about your skiing.

1. Are you relaxed mentally and physically?
2. Do you feel confident with your turns?
3. Are you able to make subtle adjustments of speed without making erratic moves?
4. Do you keep your attention focused downhill, skiing the fall line without hesitation?
5. Do you experience the feeling of effortless control as you move your skis in a pendulum-type fashion, reaching out side to side beneath you, moving your weight from ski to ski while skiing an efficient line down the mountain?

If you answered ''yes'' to all of the above you're a high performance skier! To those of you who answered ''no'' or ''sometimes'' to at least some of these questions, the information in this book should help you to work on your skiing so that you can eventually answer ''yes'' to all of the above.

Expert Impressions of the High Performance Skier

What you might find amusing, or embarrassing, is how teachers and coaches can read the level of your performance simply by watching certain aspects of your skiing. In a conversation with

Christin Cooper, she gave her impressions of the high performance skiers coming down the mountain. "They're really solid on their skis, and dynamic. They work from ski to ski while playing with the terrain and remaining relaxed. Their basic position," she emphasized, "is balanced over the middle of their skis. This provides the control without the risk of their skis getting away from them." As she concluded, "You can tell when skiers have a lot of miles behind their skiing, and when these miles have included a lot of disciplined training doing the basics."

Curious about this point, I asked Mike Iman if he thought there was an observable difference between a high performance skier and a less passionate skier. He answered, "Simply, the high performance skier's last turn in a series is as relaxed and smooth as his or her second or third turn. All you have to do is sit and watch skiers make a series of turns. This alone will tell you a great deal about their skiing ability." The following discussion is a summary of Mike Iman's ideas on high performance skiing.

Confidence

What enables the high performance skier to remain relaxed until the last turn or the last gate in a race course?

The answer is confidence, built on experience in a variety of conditions. When skiers get enough exposure to, for example, powder, the steeps, the bumps, or racing, they naturally develop confidence in these areas. As they develop confidence, skiers acquire versatility and a dynamic attitude about skiing. They are better able to relax or to ski aggressively according to the demands of the conditions and those placed on the individual.

High performance skiing is an evolutionary development that each skier goes through at his or her own pace. Thinking like a high performance skier early in your skiing will get you to ski with more purpose and dedication. With this sense of purpose, you can progress rapidly to the point where the changes in your skiing are subtle and small. It is at this point in your skiing when the real perfection of certain skills takes place: the refinement of your skiing in varied and difficult snow conditions. Through this development you become reactional in your skiing, no longer needing to think about what you're doing.

Reactional Skiing

Is there really a great need to take the thought out of your skiing and just go with the flow of the terrain, that is, ski reactionally?

For high performance skiing, yes. Of course, you always put some thought into your skiing; the curse of too much thought in your skiing is to become overfocused on one aspect, to the extent that you forget about other aspects and end up fighting with balance. You may find yourself bracing against the environment as opposed to flowing with it, when what you really want to be doing is the latter. When you start down any hill you want to feel as though the terrain is doing much of the work for you, the skis are doing the work they're designed to do, and you're enjoying the ride.

Ultimately, through drills, exercises, and time on skis, you want to get to the point of skiing very *reactionally*; that is, making a very quick read of the terrain. You look at it and see that it's crusty, cruddy, icy, bumpy, or poorly lit. Instead of panicking, you are reactional: Your knowledge of appropriate skills is combined with your sense of how you want to ski this condition. You react and respond to the condition. The result: The skis work for you, and energy expenditure is minimal; you can actually feel the skis do more of the work; and the conditions help your skis to perform at a high level.

Skiing reactionally never involves being in a static position. You flow with the changes in terrain, and your upper body is quiet and very still while your legs do the work. As you keep your upper body relaxed and headed down the fall line, your lower body moves by reacting to the cues it receives from the terrain and the messages it receives from your brain. The brain is instantaneously interpreting the sensory information it's receiving from your hands, face, ears, inner ears, eyes, and feet. When you ski reactionally, you are efficient and ready to attack any situation for which you have the skills to ski.

Being ready to attack any situation sounds exciting, but are all skiers ready for this?

Maybe not at first, but they can be with the right mind-set and technical skills. Assuming the skills are there, it's self-confidence that allows skiers to be relaxed and aggressive in any situation. They're confident when they start down the hill, and often have a mental picture of how they are going to ski the hill. This image is so vivid, skiers can almost feel the run before they physically ski it. Skills development leads to their *knowing they can do with their skis* what they *imagine* in their minds. Confidence, perception, and imagery allow skiers to be aggressive, knowing that they can adjust to any changes in conditions. This mind-set allows skiers to stay in balance while in motion, a critical prerequisite to versatile skiing.

Ski Feel

High performance skiers have keen ski-snow sensitivity: *ski feel*. They have the skills to respond to their perception of how to ski a particular run and feel relaxed doing it. Swimmers who are not relaxed look like tanks going across the water. Runners who are not relaxed have no stride or length in their movements. Look at skiers who are not relaxed in the race course; they can't function. All of these athletes are performing their sport statically.

What does Mike have to say about this concept of ski feel?

Ski feel is a concept like balance, which is instinctual to individuals who are athletic, but which can also be developed by others who approach skiing more socially than athletically. Athletic skiers are naturally light on their feet and regularly engage in a host of recreational sports. Ski feel can be developed, in a sense, through any sport that has to do with angles of balance and the sensitivity of pressure from any outside force, which can be either gravity or the resistance of water, ice, ground, or snow.

A good example of this is running. When runners land on the balls of their feet, they roll their feet forward. The last thing to leave the surface of the terrain is the runner's sensation (feel) rather than the shoe. Through the shoes, the feet and toes identify the terrain and send messages to the brain: The ground is either soft, hard, or rocky, throwing the runner off balance or increasing the length in the runner's stride.

Ski feel follows the same theme. When you compare high performance skiers with first-timers, it is obvious that the latter are not working with feeling. They are inhibited, working against feeling; their feeling is cerebral, which creates physical rigidity. First-time skiers would marvel at stronger, more dynamic skiers who are either natural athletes or skiers who have developed these skills through experience: They seem to float down the hill.

These skiers have more fully developed ski feel and a high degree of *ski-snow awareness*. From years of skiing and thinking about the sport, these skiers instinctively know when to put pressure or when to eliminate putting pressure on their skis, and when to angle their ankles, knees, hips, or shoulders to create or relax the edging of their skis. Their sense of the snow comes in part from their naturally acquired degree of ski feel, time spent experiencing the different sensitivities and pressures of their skis on variable snow surfaces, and time spent manipulating their skis on these surfaces.

Former U.S. Ski Team member and downhill medalist Pete Patterson says you learn to ski by feel and stay balanced over your skis by skiing in the worst of conditions. "Sometimes," he goes on to say, "you can get too involved with the technical aspects of skiing and forget the most important thing is to make sure you get out regularly and have fun. When you have fun, you relax and enjoy yourself—you're much more into the *feeling* of skiing, and you don't make it hard on yourself by being too tense. You can concentrate on having fun by skiing efficiently, but not so technically that you get blown away with the preciseness of it all. Just enjoy skiing, and you'll develop the *feel* for it."

Overall, when you think about ski feel, think sensory: *sight*, the look of the snow and conditions; *sound*, the sound of your skis against the snow reveals much about the conditions and your mastery of skiing skills; *touch*, the tactile messages you receive through the tips of your skis/poles from your feet/hands to your brain; and, of course, *sense of balance*, recognizing that the more relaxed and confidently you ski, the more your *balance* helps to naturally correct your ill-chosen reactions to unexpected snow conditions or poorly executed moves. The result is that you fall less often after making clumsy maneuvers. Ski feel: Work on it!

Is there a way to get the mind and body to work together on the acquisition of skills that will build the confidence required for ski feel and reactional skiing?

Goal setting is not a bad way to set your sights on greater skills acquisition, but skiers' goals must be complemented by a willingness to go through the process of skill development. Probably the two most important factors in this development are patience and fitness. If skiers are patient, their learning process can take its natural course; if skiers are fit, and if they are in skier tone (cardiovascular fitness along with strength and flexibility training), they will have the stamina to persevere with practice. Given these factors, it is easy to develop a healthy mental attitude to complement your physical willingness. You can't have one without the other.

This is like a balance in effort. If skiers ski with an aggressive mental attitude, yet lack physical readiness, they may find frustration. Mental desire and output overwhelm the capabilities of the physical body. If, on the other hand, they are physically strong enough, yet haven't the attitude to push themselves and work toward goals, they will similarly be frustrated with their progress. The best approach is to blend their mental desires and physical capabilities, thereby allowing the natural evolutionary development of their skiing skills through experience and exposure.

Types of Skiers

Mike is fond of saying that there are essentially three types of recreational skiers with respect to their use of muscles, skills, and skeletal bracing. What does he mean by this?

The three types of recreational skiers are the *inefficient skier*, the *efficient but tricky skier*, and the *disciplined athletic skier*. Many of the skiers in the first group are fatigued by two o'clock in the afternoon. This is due, in part, to a lack of conditioning, and in part, to a lack of efficiency (i.e., the overuse of muscle and movement). Instead of using a *skeletal bracing*, or standing tall, and allowing outside influences to help work with the skis, the inefficient skier muscles the ski around the mountain. Without sound physical conditioning, especially when efficiency is lacking, these skiers tire quickly. They expend too much energy, too much of the time. The ill-result is often muscle soreness, strains, or more serious joint and bone injuries.

The second type of skier is at midpoint in skills acquisition, mental perspective, and physical attitude. For the most part, these skiers ski technically well and, with their naturally developed muscles, ski with a blend of muscular control and skeletal bracing along with a collection of technically sneaky tricks. They have an inborn ability to stay in balance and their movement patterns seem very precise. They look very smooth, yet do not really espouse high performance skills.

The third type is the *disciplined athletic skier* who knows how to ski highly proficiently. This skier is technically sound, physically fit, aggressive, confident, and committed to skiing and off-season training. *This is the essence of the high performance skier!*

Skeletal Bracing

Skeletal bracing is what many children use when they first start skiing. If you watch children skiing in a wedge or snowplow position, they seem to be hinged back, their legs straight and bodies bent at the waist: They are braced. Instructors, parents, and

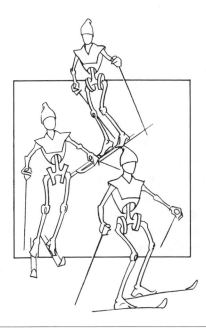

Figure 1.1 Skeletal bracing throughout the turn conserves muscle energy.

friends encourage the children to bend their ankles and knees. Due to their immature muscular development, children need to use structural rather than muscular strength. When the children stand and brace against the skis and hold that position, they are using their skeletal structure. This means that they have their legs straight, forming a natural bracing against the skis and the snow. One of the things that happens with adults is that they stop using skeletal bracing. Skeletal bracing is one skill that, when used properly, allows for most efficient skiing. Skiers who don't occasionally rely on this tax their muscle strength unnecessarily.

If these skiers stood up, kept themselves tall, and used angles from their shoulders to their hips, knees, and ankles, they would ski more efficiently. You can create angles throughout the skeletal structure. (See Figure 1.1.) By using these angles you're not using as much muscle support to hold any one position, or more properly, any series of positions.

Blocks to Becoming a High Performance Skier

What might keep a good skier from ever becoming a high performance skier? How can this be addressed to recreational skiers?

What keeps any skier from becoming a high performance skier is tentativeness and the avoidance of new skiing experiences. A very good recreational skier who can ski most conditions may become stagnant. This particular skier may choose to ski powder only when it's very light and four to five inches deep; or choose only small, developing moguls, only when the lighting is good and there's no real hard pack or ice. This skier prefers the familiar; new situations are often dismissed as too difficult. Because new challenges are avoided, skiers like this keep themselves from the opportunity to express greater skiing potential. It's important to challenge the things that hold you back. Ski the runs that trouble you; ski them the best you can.

Overall, it may seem like you're doing more things awkwardly and inefficiently than properly. If you keep trying those new runs as many times as you ski the familiar ones, eventually those new runs will become your forte; if you continue to add different runs, conditions, and situations to your skiing, you'll break out of your tentativeness. If you avoid the challenges, you're likely to stay in a skiing rut that keeps you from becoming a high performance skier.

Another problem that good recreational skiers have is the low average number of days they are able to go skiing in a season. Infrequent skiing can lead to hesitation and ambivalence; there's little room for either in high performance skiing.

Myth of the Perfectly Carved Turn

Many skiers measure their performance in terms of the carved turn. Isn't the perfectly carved turn really a myth?

There is no such thing as a perfectly carved turn, except in reference to a turn with a very, very long radius. It would take you an entire run to make that single turn. There are, however, relatively perfect, carved turns in which there's a subtle, continuous, and patient steering of the inside ski, and a patient foot guiding of the turning (outside) ski onto its edge until a certain point when it's time to get off of that edge to minimize skidding, and get onto the other ski.

We teach skiers to make *skidded turns* because these help beginner and intermediate skiers control their speed and turn. In a skidded turn, the skier emphasizes rotary, rapid steering first, then pressures the downhill or outside ski, and finally uses the edges of the skis to control movement or speed. As skiers advance to higher levels of skiing we want them to largely abort the dynamics of a skidded turn and embrace the dynamics of a carved turn. In the carved turn, the skier emphasizes pressure and edge control to the skis, and finally rotary motion or ski steering (constant steering with both inside and outside skis) to finish the turn.

When you examine the phenomenon of the carved turn in Figure 1.2, you realize the inside (uphill) ski has to be constantly moving away from the turning ski to effect a truly carved turn. There are many levels of carved turning you can create with inside-ski steering:

- You can accomplish beginning carving with your downhill ski by lightening the inside ski, relaxing the pressure of your leg/foot/boot, and letting the ski glide atop the snow rather than through it.

Figure 1.2 Steer or guide the inside ski into your new turn to increase the carving of your outside or turning ski.

- You can accomplish more advanced carving with your downhill ski by steering the lightened inside ski away from the turning ski, directing the knee of this inside leg uphill.

- You can accomplish extreme carving with your downhill ski by diverging the inside ski away from the turning ski, radically pushing off of your downhill ski and directing or stepping the inside ski diagonally uphill.

Certainly, whether or not your turns are carved, and to what degree, says a lot about your level of performance. (See chapter 8 for inside ski steering drills and exercises.)

Summary

1. If you take time to learn the fundamentals of skiing, you're apt to progress more rapidly and painlessly to the point of consistent performance in your skiing.
2. In high performance skiing, the fundamentals are to blend your technical skills, the physical attitude with which you ski, and your mental powers.
3. High performance skiers are dynamic and really solid on their skis. They work from ski to ski while playing with the terrain and remaining relaxed. Their basic bodily stance is balanced over the middle of their skis.
4. When you perceive difficulty with a slope or condition, you will experience difficulty; like a self-fulfilling prophecy, you've reinforced the difficulty with the power of your mind.
5. Confidence is built up by experience in a variety of conditions. As you develop confidence, you develop versatility and a dynamic attitude about skiing.
6. High performance skiers have a keen ski-snow sensitivity: ski feel. They have the skiing skills to respond to their perception of how to ski a particular run, and feel relaxed doing it.
7. The curse of too much thought in your skiing is that you may become overfocused on one aspect of your skiing at the expense of other aspects and end up fighting with balance.

8. When you ski reactionally, you react and respond to changing conditions; you're never skiing in a static position.
9. The high performance skier is technically sound, physically fit, aggressive, confident, and committed to skiing and off-season training.
10. The key thing that would keep any skier from becoming a high performance skier is tentativeness and the avoidance of new skiing experiences.
11. When you think about ski feel, think sensory; sight, sound, touch, and sense of balance. Look at the snow, listen to the sound of your skis moving across the snow, feel the sensations you receive through the tips of your skis/poles to your boots/hands, and relax to be able to respond to off-balancing occurrences.
12. The carve of a turn is influenced greatly by the action of your inside ski, whether it's lightened, steered, or diverged away from your turning ski.
13. It may be that we're incapable of being in perfect balance, and the best of skiers are constantly making subtle adjustments to maintain balance and rhythm.

High Performance Tip #1

John Hoffman: Another Look at Skiing in Balance

Is it skiing in balance or is it learning to keep your balance while in motion? My idea is that we're never actually in balance when we're in motion. Of course, the body is designed physiologically to create balance in itself, and to right itself to maintain its physiological equilibrium. But when we're aware of our motion, I like to think that we're incapable of being in perfect balance. A more dynamic concept is to think of us as constantly attempting to balance ourselves through the tiny and subtle adjustments we make as a means of correcting our movements too much forward, too much backward, or too much to one side or the other.

Good skiers realize they are out-of-balance when only a small degree off center, and have the skills and know-how to subtly correct themselves without so much as a slight interruption in their rhythm. Beginning skiers don't realize they are out of balance until it's too late, and they fall. As we get better and more adept at skiing through experience and learning, we can get to the point where a person observing us can't really detect when we're out of balance.

Someone may watch you ski down a run and say, "You were great—in balance all the time." Not true; you know better, and wonder aloud, "Gee, I was catching edges all the way." Indeed, but your adjustments were so subtle that to anyone but the professional skier and expert, they looked normal. Think about this sense of dynamic balance: that when in motion, the best of skiers are constantly making subtle adjustments to maintain balance and rhythm. When working on balance, I like to teach people to recognize when they are out of balance so that they can learn ways to correct it, rather than teaching them to be in balance, or to feel what it is like to ski in balance. It's just a different way of looking at it.

Chapter 2

Skiing
the Steeps

**This is the kind of stuff
that keeps your juices
flowing . . .**

Indeed, there are refinements in the application of basic skills to different conditions, but the basic mechanics of skiing change little from condition to condition. What changes is our interpretation of the conditions, and the application of our skier sense to changes in terrain, snow texture, wind, temperature, wet, other skiers, and ourselves. With this in mind, let's ski the steeps.

Very Steep Chutes

Situation: Very steep chute with 45-degree drop.

Conditions: Snow is wind-blown pack with 3 to 6 inches of loose, good snow covering the chute. No obstacles; it's cool and calm, and the lighting is good.

Slope Traffic: Only a few of you.

According to Mike, if you're intimidated by this situation, it's inevitable that you'll have to deal with your fear to be able to ski a steep chute with confidence. Although overcoming your emotional fear is highly individualized, most skiers find that a necessary ingredient to successfully overcoming fear is developing skills most suited to skiing the condition that troubles them. In very steep terrain, these skills include a solid pole plant, sound edging and angulating skills, good upper and lower body separation, extension and flexion, the active steering or guiding of your skis, and the ability to rhythmically link your turns.

You need a solid pole plant to stabilize your upper body and thus to momentarily block its movement (momentum) downhill across the path of your skis. Blocking your upper body with a pole plant accomplishes another very important goal—getting

Figure 2.1 First, practice establishing a platform on intermediate terrain.

your upper body in a *countered* or anticipated position as shown in Figure 2.1. Once established, this countered position allows you to control all other movements necessary to safely and confidently ski the steeps.

From a countered position, it is easy to form a platform in the snow beneath your skis that gives you a measure of stability and edge control. Specifically, you want to create a platform by standing over the center of your skis, knees and ankles flexed, with the inside edge of your downhill ski and outside edge of your uphill ski set firmly in the snow. We call this instant of edging control an *edge set*. When accompanied by a blocking pole plant, the edge set creates the *three-point platform* crucial to skiing the steeps (Figure 2.1). In fact, in steep corridors or chutes, you must think platform after platform, turn after turn. (Chapter 8 presents a detailed discussion of platforms and edge sets, along with a host of drills and exercises to explore their use.)

When you ski into this chute, look down the hill and seek the fall line, but do not attempt to pick up speed and then turn. As soon as you get into the chute, make a *preturn* with a slight uphill steering of your skis (see chapter 8, "Lack of speed control") in combination with your pole plant to establish your first platform.

The critical factor here is commitment: You must make a commitment to follow the lead of your first turn and continue to look down the hill and *make turn after turn until you get to the bottom*. This commitment to a series of three-point platforms will help to ensure consistent upper and lower body separation—your upper body stays countered down the fall line in an anticipated position. This position prepares your body to use its natural skiing resources to execute a quick, smooth change of direction once you release the pressure on your skis and pole.

Take a look at some of your natural skiing resources useful in the steeps: coiling and uncoiling of muscles; extension, flexion, and rotation in the joints; kinesthetic awareness; balance, and a sense of *integrated rotation* of all appropriate turning/steering forces needed to execute a turn without the overrotation of any of these. Applied to the steeps, you extend your legs (knees, ankles, and hip joints) as an expression of the uncoiling of your countered upper and lower body, and you use a rebound-type

Figure 2.2 Head down the fall line.

pushing off your pole to help direct your body mass into and down the fall line. Simultaneously, you actively steer or guide your skis into the new turn, and you use the flexion of your knees and ankles to make an edge set platform that controls and serves to complete your turn, leaving you in an anticipated position for the next turn (see Figure 2.2).

Your Pole Plant

Although in much of skiing we use the *pole touch* as a timing device to add rhythm, as an additional terrain, as a condition and balance sensor to the brain, and as a *signal* indicating the transfer of weight from the old turning ski to the new, in the steeps we rely especially on a blocking pole plant, often referred to as a defensive pole plant. While the defensive pole plant aids your rhythm in the steeps, the solid planting of your pole downhill momentarily blocks your upper body from moving into the new turn before your legs have uncoiled, adds stability to your platform, and helps keep your upper body facing down the fall line in a countered or anticipated position (Figure 2.1).

Edging/Angulation

When in the steeps, you want to ski the edges of both skis effectively, keeping the majority of your weight on the inside edge of the downhill ski as it firmly grips the snow. Your outside hip and knee are *angled* into the hill (some refer to this as angling into the turn). The uphill ski is edged on its outside edge with just enough pressure to give you balance and control over both of your skis. The risks of not using angulation and a countered upper body are (a) *inclining* or leaning into the hill, with the likelihood of having your skis break loose and slip down the hill out of control; (b) lack of balance; (c) lack of versatility and poor turning power; and (d) lack of speed control.

Rotation in the Steeps

In the very beginning or preparation of the turn, you are in a flexed and coiled position with your ankles and knees bent forward, your skis together and edged in the snow. As you uncoil, your legs extend (straighten) and your body projects down the fall line, creating a feeling of free-falling down the mountain in the direction of your pole plant. To effectively ski the steeps, you must learn to trust this extension outward and down the fall line with each turn. Use what the conditions give you, and in the steeps constantly allow your momentum to travel downhill.

Turns in the steeps have a dramatic preparation (the platform), a short initiation (during extension) where the skis are very light and follow the body around, a very brief control phase where the skis are steered with both feet (beginning flexion), and an abrupt finish (maximum flexion), which leads to new turn preparation.

Your uphill leg is short until you extend. As you extend and change direction (i.e., steer), your former uphill leg becomes your downhill leg and becomes very long and braced against the edged ski. Use the rhythmic sequence discussed here when skiing the steeps, and work to avoid the signs of static skiing: being timid, leaning back, locking the knees and hips, and using the poles little or not at all.

Figure 2.3 Feel the angles, as if in the steeps.

Figure 2.3 illustrates something fun to try. Stand about a foot from a secure counter or wall and imagine you're sitting on a bicycle that's parallel to it. Think about the position of your feet and legs when pedaling this bicycle: One foot and leg are up (an uphill ski), while the other foot and leg are extended down (a downhill ski). Now extend your right foot, and bring your left foot up as if pedaling the bicycle. The counter is about a foot away from you on your left. Imagine letting your bicycle fall against your left leg. What's your natural reaction? To seek balance.

To seek balance, you throw your arms and upper body over your right hip (down the fall line). In real life, your bicycle leans to the left as you shift weight to the right. In this example, you fall into the counter with your left hip and fully rotate your upper body over your right hip, arms extended as you settle your left hip into the counter (steep terrain), just like you'd do in the steeps, coiled and all. Your right leg is longer than your left, and you've just set a platform for a right turn.

Turn yourself around and do the same with your right foot up; set a platform for a left turn in the steeps. Ever wonder about angles in your skiing? Take a look at yourself with your hip planted against the counter, your feet parallel to the counter and your arms and upper body facing away from the counter. Look at the angles formed by your hips, knees, and ankles.

Machine-Groomed Steeps

Situation: Steep run that's been machine groomed, offering plenty of room and plenty of thrills and challenges for skiers in search of high performance.

Conditions: It's cold and crisp, not a cloud in the sky, and the snow is freshly groomed and firm. No wind or flat lighting.

Slope traffic: Heavy; consider safety.

According to Mike, these are some of the most invigorating ski conditions there are. Above and beyond powder, crud, and moguls, a groomed steep is a type of slope on which you can really draw on and engineer all the skill concepts you have. The best type of turn for you to use in these conditions will vary depending on your skiing ability and interests, but, if you'll follow my lead for a moment, the turn to do on this slope for getting the thrill of acceleration is the medium-radius turn.

With the medium-radius turn you are able to ski in a more upright position on your skis for longer periods between turns than with the short-radius or short-swing turns. And even though your period of relaxation between turns (i.e., the time you are skiing upright) is not as long as in long-radius turns, medium radius turns allow you to ski longer in these conditions without having to confront the issue of fatigue.

In the medium-radius turn you predominantly ride your downhill or outside ski, applying foot and ankle pressure through the angles created by your ankle, knee, and hip as they are pressed or flexed forward and into the mountain (into the turn). Thus, in the medium-radius turn, you flex and pressure the downhill ski gradually until the end of the turn, where there is a brief point at which you become compact (a point of maximum pressure/ flexion to your skis and in your legs). Once the ski is released, or relaxed, you will feel yourself being deflected or slightly rebounded in the direction of the next turn from the energy that had built up in the skis.

The momentum of your upper body mass travels directly over the end of the old turn to the center of the new turn. The key here is to work independently from foot to foot, leg to leg, just like the bicycle: As one foot increases pressure, the other relaxes until it must apply pressure (pedal), at which time the foot that was previously working decreases its pressure (relaxes).

As you use one leg more predominantly than the other moment to moment, so too are you using one ski more predominantly than the other, *steering each to an edge* (chapter 8 contains many drills to acquaint you with the concept of steering both skis into, through, and out of turns). Skis have several technical characteristics built into them that enable you to ski them independently and with different pressures applied throughout turning. Of particular importance here is a ski's camber, which is put on the ski to equally distribute the skier's weight (pressures) over the entire length of the ski, giving it sensitivity at its ends for turning, stability, and holding. Your skis have the built-in ability to flex in several different directions. In the medium-radius turn, you can really sense what ski design is all about.

Using Your Angles

One thing to think about when you are working with your skis on this type of terrain is to first *focus* on your upper body and then transmit a portion of this focus to your skis. Think of it like this: Your upper body *seeks* the new turn, your skis follow its lead. For example, in a long-radius turn, you angle your outside hip into the mountain to get things started, then angle your outside knee into the turn to increase the amount of edging on your downhill ski, and finally, angle your ankle subtly into the turn to complete the edging of your turning ski. This sequence of angles adds precision to the shape of your turn. If you want

Figure 2.4 Use hip, knee, and ankle angulation to effect dynamic turning.

to shorten the radius of the turn, instead of moving the hip in first, move your knee in first; in this way, you can steer your ski to edge more quickly. When on edge, skis insist on turning!

Try this exercise on groomed terrain. If you're already comfortable in the steeps, use this terrain for the exercise, but be forewarned that some aspects of this exercise may produce very fast speeds. You may want to go to a gentler slope. Ski down to a place where you can safely stop, out of the way of other skiers, yet still on the slope. Pick up some speed and make three turns, being sure to first angle your hip, then knee, then ankle. STOP! Next, make three turns being sure to first angle your knee, then ankle. STOP! Do you feel the difference? It's huge, because angling in your hip alone is not enough to get your turning ski onto its edge without the aid of distance. On the other hand, angling the knee will quickly set your turning ski on edge, and in a much shorter distance. Now take the same run, and without stopping, make a series of turns in which you go from hip angle, to knee angle, to ankle angle, back to knee angle, then hip angle. (See Figure 2.4.)

Which angles would you want to use in the steeps if you felt you were traveling a bit too fast? Knee and ankle, of course. As a rule, knee angulation (knee-in) creates sharper turns; hip angulation (hip-in) creates turns with a longer radius. To tighten a medium-radius turn, check your speed or move to a shorter radius or short-swing turn, get on the edges very quickly, and angle the knee. In actuality, you use many angles both to turn and to subtly change aspects of the turns. Use the rule on knee and hip angulation only as a guide.

When you create a long-radius turn, all the processes of a medium-radius turn are slowed down. The hip goes in much slower and gradually. You progressively tip the ski onto its edge. For tighter turns in the steeps, your knee is angled in. To radically create angles for extremely tight turns in the steeps, however, you want to get your hip as close to the hillside as possible with your uphill leg very short and your downhill leg fully extended and long, with your ski edged in the snow.

Using Your Pole Touch

In the earlier example of the steep chute, we explained the technique of the blocking pole plant. When the turn is necessarily tight, requiring you to use the pole to block your body from crossing too far over your skis, the pole plant should be used because it's a far more forceful and dynamic way to keep your momentum under control. When using this pole plant, the blocking of your body's momentum may lead to a rebounding of your skis off the snow. Use this, but control it; on the groomed steep slope, you want to keep the skis in contact with the snow as much as possible.

For most of your skiing, however, the more rhythmic and less abrupt offensive *pole touch* serves as a recontact with, or sensor point on, the snow and accentuates the perpetual turning of your skis. Overall, it enables your body to move across the skis while you're turning them, creating new angles that help you transfer your weight from one ski to the other without losing ski-snow contact. Use the pole touch to establish and maintain rhythm and timing in your skiing. As the pole is touched on the snow, move from the old downhill ski and ski the new downhill or turning ski. This pole touch rhythm eventually becomes an internal rhythm. (Chapter 8 has a number of drills for refining your use of poles and pole touch rhythm.)

Leaping Off Cornices

Situation: On the edge of a cornice with a 3 to 6 foot drop.

Conditions: Celestial: Snow has firm base with a 3 to 4 inch give; very steep for the first 50 feet after your landing, graduating out for 100 yards of challenging terrain. It's warm, calm, and the lighting is good.

Slope Traffic: Polite and cordial: "You're next."

According to Mike, here we are atop a cornice that's quite pronounced though tame by many standards. For you, it's a first, but your friends are all here and you feel like it's time to take the leap.

Let's imagine we're all rookies and establish safe habits for taking this and other leaps. Foremost, the way to approach this is *not to jump off* the particular cornice area where you're standing, but to position yourself to *ski off*. You want to be able to ski off the cornice to ease yourself into this new situation and be able to adjust more comfortably to the slope conditions. Further, you get the feeling of actually falling and reuniting with the snow below you.

For your first few times off, the angle you choose in leaving the cornice should be one that doesn't put you directly down the fall line. Think of skiing off the cornice in a *fan progression*, which plots your progress in getting to know the cornice and ensuing terrain and represents the different angles at which you have skied off the cornice. Think of every higher angle of descent as represented by the rib of a fan, your goal being to ultimately ski the middle portion of the fan where the rib is straight: the fall line. The repetition of the fan progression builds confidence as you learn to control your speed on the steep terrain below the cornice. (See Figure 2.5.)

Start by taking the shallowest line and then decrease its angle until you are skiing in the fall line. In other words, if you still aren't comfortable about skiing down something steep, traverse

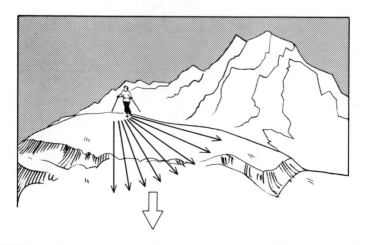

Figure 2.5 A fan progression can help build confidence and reduce fear.

across it first to get accustomed to the texture of the snow and the look and pitch of the slope. This will help you determine the kind of line in which you'd ski down this hill. Then ski the hill at progressively steeper angles, or at least the steep part of the cornice area, until you can point your skis straight down the hill and make turns to the bottom. Although this is a method of getting comfortable with the steeps, it also cuts up the slopes for others who'd rather just point their skis and go. Use a bit of sensitivity when in the steeps. If you really want to ski off cornices, but are unsure of yourself, don't hesitate to use the fan progression.

Unquestionably the most difficult aspect of cornice skiing is standing on top and making that decision to go off and make a first turn. If you aren't familiar with the terrain or snow conditions this is doubly complicated. To be safe, you should always know the kind of snow you'll be turning in once you land; to this end, some sampling of the conditions is advised.

If the direct approach to takeoff (i.e., skiing straight ahead for maximum air-time) is foreboding, you have two basic options for getting down: (a) Ski off the cornice at an angle so that when you land you're already edging (you must be strong to control this and have good independent leg skills); (b) use a fan progression and ski off the side of the cornice first, getting progressively closer to a more direct takeoff.

Let's consider the second option: First you want to get the feeling of what it's like to go off, so take the cornice where there's a shorter drop-off, move right up to the edge, and slide off. Next time, go off a little higher point of the cornice and follow that leap with even higher places. These are basic fan progression tactics.

Consider adding an accelerated dimension to your fan progression: a more aggressive takeoff. Once you're comfortable with going off the cornice, move further back and pick up more speed before getting to the edge. Do this repeatedly until you sense a little spring in your legs and feet/boots when you leap off the cornice. The *spring action* prevents the tails of your skis from dragging over the cornice. Once you've added spring to your leap from the cornice and feel comfortable with the conditions in which you land, you will fully experience the exhilaration of cornice skiing.

After you leap off and land, the first turn will be out of the fall line to check your speed and establish a platform, followed by a series of rhythmic platforms and turns (recall the steep chute discussion). Remember also that the fan progression takes time and some cornices take more than a few minutes to get to (many require hiking). Plan to spend a day at it, especially the first time around.

Summary

1. The essential perspective to have when skiing the steeps is a blend of edging skills, a blocking pole plant, and an aggressive attitude.
2. Think *platform* when skiing the steeps: platform after platform, turn after turn, especially when you are required to make short turns in a corridor or chute.
3. Look down the hill, and ski to that point. Do not hesitate. There is no room for hesitation in very steep chutes; the steeps have to be skied!
4. Plant the poles to block the upper body and set the edges.

Once set in the above position, your body is coiled and ready to extend down the hill and into the fall line to execute the turn. As you uncoil, experience a full range of up-out-down motions during this very brief midpoint of your turn; coil or sink again to set your edges for the next platform. Use subtle steering to control your transitions between full extension and your new platform.

5. Static skiing in the steeps leads to being timid, leaning back, locking the knees and hips, and using the poles too little or not at all; in other words, a lousy time.

6. In the steeps, the mountain gives you momentum. Keep the momentum going for more effortless skiing; constantly allow your momentum to work for you, and use your rhythmic extension and flexion motion to create platform after platform down the fall line.

7. As a rule, knee angulation (knee-in) creates sharper turns; hip angulation (hip-in) creates turns with a longer radius. When you create a very long-radius turn, all the processes of a medium-radius turn are slowed down.

8. On the groomed steep slope, keep the skis in contact with the snow.

9. The pole touch rhythm becomes an internal rhythm.

10. After you leap off of a cornice and land, your first turn will be a preturn out of the fall line to check your speed and establish the platform from which your turns will follow in a series of rhythmic platforms and turns.

Chapter 3

Taming the Bumps

The condition of your body changes the condition of the terrain; the shape of your thoughts changes the shape of everything . . .

A good part of mogul skiing involves attitude and perspective. For many skiers, developing an attitude about mogul skiing according to which they look for moguls rather than avoiding them takes an adventurous appetite for more challenging skiing. As in many other sports and challenges in life, overcoming mental barriers often allows your body to move more fluidly and naturally in response to various tactile, auditory, and visual stimuli. Skiing bumps often involves reacting and responding to the tactile stimuli, communicated through your feet, from the snow and terrain. Overcoming the common intimidation of moguls allows you to enjoy and appreciate skiing, not surviving, the bumps.

Attitude

There are days when we ski bumps aggressively; fast, in the fall line, and in control. There are also days when we get mad at ourselves for skiing the bumps; putting on a show under the chairlift, we ski awkwardly, clumsily, and downright terribly.

But we return to the bumps day after day, knowing that there's enjoyment to be found in those bumps, somewhere.

An important theme in revving up your efforts to ski well in the bumps is that, in one way or another, it can be fun for you. Approach the bumps with enjoyment in mind. You'll find it easier to be patient with your self-paced approach to learning and happier with the style of skiing which you feel works best for you. This chapter is designed to help you discover enjoyment in the bumps.

Your attitude about the bumps helps you and keeps you in the right frame of mind to learn to ski moguls, but attitude alone is not enough. There are skills and tactics to skiing the bumps. These are often best learned on packed runs and then taken into the bumps or are practiced in the bumps in the form of specific drills or tasks. Importantly, going into mogul fields time and time again to try to learn to *ski* them, when you end up merely *surviving* the bumps, is likely to teach you more about your endurance and strength than about efficiently skiing moguls.

Two common obstacles for many would-be bump skiers are their fear of injury and their desire not to look like a fool—both apparent in athletic endeavors that present a degree of risk to limb or self esteem. Unfortunately, these obstacles cannot be easily remedied in a universal way. Some skiers gain more confidence by focusing on their basic skills and staying with these in the moguls, viewing the terrain as just "more bumpy." Other skiers rely on a host of psychological "self-talk" ploys to literally ease their minds. Still others use relaxation techniques like those used by firewalkers, while others explore new bump-skiing techniques and strategies by taking classes or working with skilled teachers.

Whatever your disposition, it's critical that you address both your mental perspective toward the bumps and the skills you utilize to ski them. Thinking of learning to ski bumps as an adventure is one way to add enjoyment to moguls. Just as you would take runs of increasing challenge in preparation for a marathon, an adventurous attitude in the bumps means that you begin applying your skills to small bumps and build toward the size of bump you find most enjoyable, yet still challenging, for your level of skiing. At least this is one way to edge the fear out of moguls.

Next, you must focus on your skills. Tops on the list are the ability to *absorb* bumps—''sucking up'' and retracting your knees toward your chest (and then extending your legs to be able to turn in the fall line)—and a solid blocking pole plant. Hand in hand with these skills are the ability to make a short-radius turn in the bumps, the appropriate application of *integrated rotation* to control steering, and a readiness to respond quickly to terrain changes. Additionally, remaining countered (i.e., your upper body facing down the fall line as your skis are traveling and pointed across the fall line) helps you to control your speed, turn more precisely, and maintain a balanced, anticipated, and ready position over your skis.

Guide and Ride

Skiers approach moguls in many ways. They ski the tops of the bumps, the troughs in between, or any of the sides of the bumps—front, side, or back. In truth, you can ski any combination of the above on any run; depending on the shape of the moguls, their height, snow conditions, terrain, and your energy level, you'll want to employ every option open to you. Consider a *guide and ride* approach to skiing the bumps.

The essence of *guiding* your skis in the bumps is *momentarily steering both skis* to the position on a bump where you want to turn, and then following through by *actually steering* your skis into your turn. *Riding* your skis in the bumps is the action of extending your down hill leg to establish dominance of your turning (carving) ski, while continuing to *steer* your resting uphill ski through the turn. Your uphill ski may be gliding along the side of a bump while your downhill ski is *riding* through the trough.

Thus, as one leg works, the other one rests, until that instant when both skis momentarily meet to be *guided* into the next turn. In effect, you *guide* briefly with both skis, and *ride* your downhill ski through the bumps.

Relax and flow with the movements you know best. It's not all that easy, but keep the enjoyment theme in mind and recognize that, rather than one perfect way to ski moguls, there are a number of ways to approach the bumps by using various skills like those highlighted in this chapter. (Chapter 10 discusses many attitudes and mental perspectives helpful in understanding and accepting our fear and reluctance to forge ahead in our skiing.)

Steep, Difficult, Large Bumps

Situation: Steep, difficult, and large bumps.
Conditions: Sunny, warm, and good lighting; solid moguls with soft edges; well-spaced.
Slope Traffic: Sparse.

According to Mike, in skiing this situation, allow yourself to sneak into skiing directly down the fall line. First consider *garlands*, a turning maneuver that carries you toward one side of the hill. In doing garlands, you make a series of short turns that end/begin with turning uphill, slowing down, and turning again downhill. Importantly, you're always moving in only one direction across the hill. When you finish a series of garlands to your right, for example, you stop, reverse directions, and do a series of garlands back across the slope to your left. If you could erase the bumps, your tracks would look like the garland on a Christmas tree. (See Figure 3.1.)

This sidehill, uphill turn helps you to comfortably traverse a slope without having to ski down the fall line at speeds you can't handle. Skiers use garlands to get the feeling of bumps and develop their confidence in them. As long as you know you can stop at any time in big bumps, you'll feel a lot more comfortable with trying other exercises to get you closer to skiing them in the fall line.

For example, try skiing across the terrain by going up and over the top of one bump and then going down the other side of it; then immediately turn uphill onto the top of the next bump. Do this until you get the feeling of contact with the snow while in balance. Try this same exercise, but this time use your legs as shock absorbers in order to keep your head on the same plane.

Figure 3.1 Use garland turns to develop confidence skiing bumps.

Imagine having a book on your head. As you get across the slope, make a full turn on the biggest bump and ski to the other side using this garland-type exercise. You won't be carrying much speed so it will be easy to stay in control. Just keep turning uphill until you become very comfortable with the terrain.

As you progress gradually down the slope, try to shorten the distance you travel from side to side until you get the sense of skiing near the fall line. If you could erase the bumps again, your tracks would fit within the outline of the upper half of an hourglass (see Figure 3.2): Your garland-type traversing represents the upper globe of the hourglass and your skiing in the fall line represents its narrow neck. Complete the outline of the hourglass by gradually skiing out of the fall line. Then repeat traversing within the hourglass until moving in and out of the fall line in big bumps is not the least bit intimidating. Repetition of this hourglass approach will ease you into skiing the fall line in no time at all.

If, however, skiing in the fall line means too much speed for you, start turning uphill and you'll slow down. (Chapter 8 provides exercises that develop your sensitivity in making subtle adjustments in your skiing to affect greater control in varied conditions like the bumps.) At any time in the bumps, you can resume hourglassing until your confidence returns and you're again able to ski the fall line.

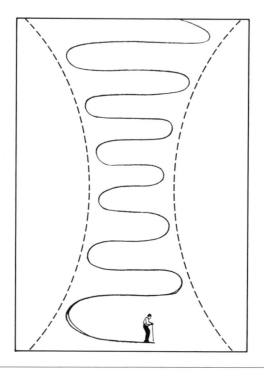

Figure 3.2 Another exercise for the bumps: Ski an hourglass pattern on intermediate terrain.

Erratic Bumps

Situation: Erratic bumps with no rhythm.

Conditions: Gusty winds, clear, and cold; variable snow depths in the troughs; good lighting.

Slope Traffic: Sparse.

According to Mike, vacate the area and ski the conditions of the day on a slope that's more comfortable. Get the feel of the snow and work with some short-radius turn exercises until you

Figure 3.3 Add some playful action in the bumps.

feel comfortable skiing in these conditions, then return to the original situation with renewed confidence.

Traverse across the slope and get a feel for the snow. Use your legs to absorb (suck up) the top of the mogul. Extend your legs into the trough of the upcoming mogul using them much like shock absorbers. Take a moment to catch your breath and think about these two elements of mogul skiing: the top of the mogul, and what's between the moguls; relate these to what you felt during the exercise. Try this exercise again across the slope; this time hop a little bit off of the top of the mogul and extend into the trough so that you blast through that loose snow in the troughs.

Here's how to hop off a mogul: When you are at the top of the mogul, point your skis in the direction away from where you want to go. Begin your turn by taking a little hop and then turn your skis in the air. To end your turn, travel through the loose snow in the trough. Continue to do this until you shorten the radius of your turns and are skiing the fall line. At this point, eliminate the hopping action and flow in and out of your turns, beginning at the top of the mogul and then skiing through the snow between the troughs. (See Figure 3.3.)

The intent of this hopping drill is to add aggressiveness to your mogul skiing. It is best used in beginning moguls. It helps you to push your legs and body off moguls as you hop with some retraction of your legs as you turn, and to push your legs into and through the trough, landing on both skis as you fully complete the turn. The more you do this hopping exercise, the more aggressive you become. To execute this drill you must be aggressive!

Windblown Snow Between Moguls

There are a number of problems with windblown snow and moguls. One is psychological. You can't see the trough or the depth of the loose snow. The mogul is likely to be firm and the trough soft. This creates resistance in the trough as well as a significant change in conditions when skiing mogul to trough.

Too often, skiers go into the moguls, skiing straight at them, without making a turn. By the time they get to the trough, they're carrying too much speed and react by turning through the trough. There's so much resistance in the soft snow that skiers find it deflects their skis, and some skiers experience being thrown in toward the mountain.

If, however, you are well into your turn as you enter the trough, you've already engaged the strongest part of your rotary skill to take you through the trough. In this way, the skis brush the loose snow out of the way and spray it downhill. Again, if you wait too long to turn (i.e., begin your turn in the trough) you will run into trouble.

The remedies to windblown snow and moguls discussed here are applicable to all difficult mogul situations. As a rule, it's important to keep skis a hip-width apart rather than pasted together so that each can be worked independently. Using this stance, try this exercise: Open the tails of the skis to form a very narrow, short-leg, long-leg wedge. Your downhill leg is longer than your uphill leg; the uphill leg is bent and pulled in slightly for balance as it would be if you were walking across a steep hill.

Figure 3.4 The rhythm of mogul skiing: independent leg action in the bumps and troughs.

(See chapter 8, "Lack of edge control," for a more complete description and application of the short-leg, long-leg wedge.)

In a short-leg, long-leg wedge turn, there is (a) a pinching in the waist (on the long leg side of your body) somewhat like you feel when doing side bends, and (b) pressure on both skis. As you turn through windblown snow between the moguls, you are turning with your downhill (long-leg) ski and giving your uphill (short-leg) ski a nicer, smoother line through the snow that your downhill ski has brushed away. Turning in this way makes it possible for the downhill leg to work while the uphill leg rests. The uphill ski is guided through the turn with less pressure even though it may be riding along the side of the mogul. Such is the rhythm of mogul skiing: One ski works while one ski rides, back and forth, leg to leg. The downhill works, the uphill rides: This is independent leg action. The action flows like a musical beat. (See Figure 3.4.)

Initiating the turn starts very early. While the uphill ski is riding, it's already being set up to make the next turn; as it turns, the other, now uphill, ski is setting up to make the next turn. It's all in the rhythm you establish. Think about running or pedaling a bicycle. Left foot, right foot; one works and one rides, over and over again. When one foot completes its cycle of effort the other begins its cycle of effort. There's no lag between. Develop this sensation and you'll develop rhythm in the moguls.

Hard, Icy Bumps

Situation: Hard, icy bumps.

Conditions: Cloudy, very cold; variable lighting; icy to crusty patches through the moguls.

Slope Traffic: Heavy.

According to Mike, the skier should start by going to the side of the run and making short-radius turns. The importance of short-radius turns in this situation is two-fold: (a) to control speed; and (b) to safely maneuver among other skiers who under these conditions may be standing on the sides of the run. Why ski the side of the run? Because snow is being crushed and pushed from the center to the sides of the run, the conditions are more favorable here when skiing the fall line.

Although there are bumps on the side of the run as well, they are likely to have more snow in between the troughs. The key here is to ski, rather than jam, the skis to an edge. It's a subtle, but critical, difference for skiing in these conditions.

After you come off hard, icy moguls you feel the sensation of skidding. The first instinct is to hit the edges of your skis to stop yourself. Instead of slowing you down, this only serves to drive your skis to their edges, where they break loose, skid, and cause you to lose control. It's like skipping a stone on water. The stone hits the water and skips repeatedly until its momentum dissipates. Whereas the skidding of your skis is propelled by the weight of your body, and little decrease in your skidding is likely until you do something to control your movement and speed.

My advice is to go into the icy mogul easily: Roll back your speed, round out your turn, and gradually guide or turn your skis (primarily the outside ski) onto an edge. As soon as you feel the ski's edge bite (grab the snow), move your weight off this turning ski and onto the other ski to begin the next turn. In situations that offer very little resistance to turning forces (e.g., icy), anything more than quick on-off motions will create too

Figure 3.5 On ice, use just enough edge to get the skis to change direction.

much pressure. The unfortunate consequence of too much pressure against very little resistance is skidding uncontrollably. (See Figure 3.5.)

To review: When the ice is on the crest and downhill side of moguls, the troughs are probably the best place to ski as they are more likely to be filled with brushed, loose snow. Try to ski these conditions edge to edge, foot to foot, starting your turns with very light pressure on the turning edge of your ski. Gradually build up this pressure. Placing too much pressure on the edge will cause your skis to skid away from you.

If you continue steering and pressuring, gradually tipping the ski onto an edge, the ski is going to carve like a knife. If you hop your ski it's going to lose the characteristics that help you to turn effectively in ice. When skiing icy moguls, you can use the platforms that they create to help you move very lightly onto your next ski. So, you let go of one ski (the turning ski) and step onto the other (the riding, now turning ski). Don't hit it; just step onto and stand on it.

Difficulty With Moguls

Many skiers in ski school classes have trouble with moguls. Should they be concerned about that?

According to Mike, not at all, because *moguls are only one aspect of skiing*. Unfortunately, the problem for many recreational skiers is that they don't get enough skiing time to fully develop the skills necessary to efficiently ski moguls.

The advent of more aggressively groomed mountains has made moguls all the more intimidating because they're not a common part of recreational skiing. Few recreational skiers look at moguls as skiable terrain with predetermined turns. As you begin to develop skills that allow you to flow down a mogul field in a relaxed state, the turns become more and more obvious. If skiing bumps is not a part of the fun or drilling in your skiing, the very sight of moguls may mean only one thing: obstacles.

It's the time spent in the bumps that makes a difference. Remember at first that you may flounder in the bumps. The more time you spend developing basic skills and doing exercises in the bumps the less floundering you'll experience, and the more you'll view bump runs as an alternative for leisure skiing and as a boost to your versatility.

Nine Ways to Rev Up Your Performance in the Bumps

Anticipation

Ski the bumps by drawing on the benefits of upper and lower body separation. As your skis extend into a trough, look down the fall line with your upper body already planting the pole and casting its weight in the direction of the next turn; your skis will follow. As they do, anticipate each next turn all the way down the slope. By using upper and lower body separation, you stabilize your speed, increase your ease of turning, and turn early. Keep your body in proper alignment thereby increasing your balance and force yourself to keep looking ahead. (See also chapter 8, ''Overrotation of upper body.'')

Retraction-Extension

Indeed, the concepts are mentioned a fair amount in this book because they form the essence of high performance skiing. Importantly, understand that retraction and extension are used in the bumps to neutralize them, allowing your upper body to ski along as if the bumps weren't even there. It's not easy to ingrain this into your skiing, yet when retraction-extension becomes as natural as bouncing is to walking, you've got a powerful force working for you on the mountain in all conditions. Invest time in using retraction-extension in your free skiing and eventually it will join you in the bumps.

A simple exercise you can use to work on retraction-extension in your free skiing is *prejumping* knolls or natural terrain jumps. Instead of blasting over these, use them as opportunities to retract and extend. Just before you reach the takeoff point, retract your knees, keeping your skis in as much contact with the snow as possible. As soon as you pass this point, fully extend your

Figure 3.6 Sometimes you want to control ''air time.''

legs down the knoll to maintain contact with the snow. (In a race course, the less time you're in the air the faster your time!) (See Figure 3.6.)

Short-Radius Turns

Tony Roegiers puts it simply: "You're not going to teach a person much about really skiing moguls until they have a solid short-radius turn." Tony's not saying that you can't get through the bumps or be coached down a mogul field unless you know how to ski a short-radius turn, but if you really want to ski moguls with rhythm, speed, and muscular efficiency, you need to make not one, but an ongoing number of linked short-radius turns. The short-radius turn is considered by many to be the essential complement to retraction-extension in bump skiing.

You don't learn to make short-radius turns in bumps. Learn them on smooth terrain, and then take them into the bumps. A drill you can use just for fun is to start a series of rhythmic short-radius turns on a smooth terrain that leads into an easy mogul field. As you ski into the mogul field, see how long you can maintain the rhythm. To rev up this drill, start a rhythm in the bumps and see how long you can maintain it. In both varieties of this activity, you're skiing your rhythm first, and thus you may find you have to ski over, around, even through bumps that get in the way of your rhythm.

Matching Lines
(or Making a Commitment to Turning)

There's no one perfect line through the bumps. There may be more efficient lines, but even this depends on your skiing ability, strength, mood, and snow conditions. In the end, bump skiers who enjoy their runs take the line that most suits their approach to the hill and their preference for the types of bumps they enjoy skiing. Your line is the one you'll trust most, but try other lines as well.

Try this: Stand atop a bump run and identify as many lines as you can through the bumps. Look for the most obvious lines laid by skiers who've skied the hill before you. Pick out a line that's a bit different from how you think you'd ski this hill and

Figure 3.7 Pick a line through the bumps and ski it.

match that line by skiing it. Here's the catch: You must commit yourself to making four to six turns before stopping to assess how it felt. At this point, you can either continue matching the same line another 5 to 10 turns, or match another line with a four to six turn commitment. (See Figure 3.7.)

Attack Bumps in a Series

Except for specific drills, when skiing bumps follow the instructions for matching lines, commiting yourself to skiing a series of at least four turns or bumps; don't ski bumps one at a time. This is particularly helpful to new bump skiers faced with a half mile or more of bumps below. At first, the hill may look impossible, but by segmenting it into series you not only ski better but also counter some of the intimidation of the bumps. Instead of skiing bumps as far as you can see, approach the bumps by perceiving them in series of 50 feet each. As you feel more comfortable with each subsequent segment, the bumps lose their intimidating quality and you're ready to go back for more, assured that you can ski them better the next time. Start with a four-turn commitment and build up to a 20-turn commitment.

Be Loose, Flexible, and Fluid

If, while skiing the bumps, you find yourself thinking a lot about technique rather than just skiing, you are working too hard. Drills are for thinking; bump skiing, on the other hand, requires being loose, flexible, and fluid. You must be highly reactional and able to rely on the skills you've perfected through drills and during your free skiing.

Establish Rhythm
(and Build Confidence)

Losing control in the bumps is a nightmare that keeps many skiers from skiing them at all. You can avoid getting out of control by establishing a rhythm that allows you to talk to the mountain and be the one in charge. Whether it's very slow and deliberate skiing, or goofy and loose, each successive turn builds confidence so that you can actually enjoy the bumps because you're skiing in control. Why ski bumps if you can't enjoy them?

Try this: Make a four-turn commitment. Ski up to a bump and stab it right on top with your left pole. Imagine that this stabbing triggers a punching bag to sprout up in the trough below and to the side of the mogul. Immediately punch this bag with a good *right cross*. As you complete the punch, look ahead for another mogul to stab with your right hand and a punching bag on which to land a *left cross*.

Continue this stab and punch exercise to complete your turn commitment. Do it again and again; you'll be so busy stabbing and punching that you won't even recognize the bumps. Don't think about turning; allow your natural turning skills to operate on autopilot. If, however, this leads to getting tripped up, you're probably not accustomed to rounded turns in your skiing and need to work this out on smoother terrain. (There are many drills that will help you ski more rounded turns. See chapter 8.)

Arms Forward

That's where they belong in skiing, particularly in the bumps where arms forward and down the fall line represent a proper upper body alignment. The exception is when arms are dangled out front in the defensive posture of a skier who's hunched over at the waist and holding on for his or her life. The stab and punch exercise will help you to keep your arms down the fall line. If you are not getting them away from your body and out ahead of you, they're probably hanging aimlessly at your sides or dangling behind you, pulling and tugging your upper body back into the hill. This is not the way to ski bumps. (Chapter 8, "Over-rotation of the upper body.")

Free-Dogging and Other Approaches to the Bumps

Indeed, there are many ways skiers get through the bumps. The perspective presented in this chapter is based on concepts learned from World Cup racing techniques and refinements of older, less aggressive methods of skiing bumps. Of course, *doggers* are a breed in themselves, blasting down bump runs for speed with a few serials thrown in for effect. You've got to admire their aggressiveness, though I'm not sure you could ever teach free-dogging to anyone. Still, some recreational skiers try to mimic this style of bump skiing, even though they have too little experience, too little strength, and poor reactional skills; these skiers are frequently injured.

In addition to the above, some people ski bumps by swiveling their skis from the top of one bump to another; sliding through the troughs, bump to bump, without ever making a clearly defined turn (carving is not in their vernacular); skiing bump to bump by bouncing off the tops of the bumps; or skiing bump to bump by banking off the sides of the bumps. There are certainly many ways to ski bumps. The skills and techniques discussed here to improve your bump skiing, however, are a further elaboration of high performance skiing highlighted in chapter 1.

Summary

1. A good part of mogul skiing is attitude and perspective: Your attitude about the bumps keeps you in the right frame of mind to learn to ski moguls.

2. There is not one perfect way to ski moguls, but there are a number of more efficient skills you can employ when in the bumps.
3. Get the feel of skiing big bumps by traversing across the bumps using garlands—sidehill, uphill turns that allow you to ski across the slope in control without skiing down the fall line before you've learned to control your speed in the bumps.
4. Ski moguls by retracting (sucking-up) your legs when on top of the mogul, and extending your legs into the trough of the upcoming mogul.
5. Your turns in the moguls are often 90% completed as you enter the trough.
6. Ski moguls with independent leg action and more dynamic turning.
7. There's a rhythm to mogul skiing: One ski works while the other rides, back and forth, leg to leg. It flows like a musical beat.
8. The new turn begins as soon as you've stood on the ski that's turning you; while the uphill ski is riding it's actually being set up to make the next turn.
9. In icy conditions, gradually ski your skis to an edge; don't jam your skis on edge! If you hit the edge of your skis hard and too abruptly on ice, your skis break loose and skid. Go into icy moguls easily; roll back your speed a bit, round your turns, and gradually steer your skis to an edge. Once the ski has come to an edge, get off of it and step onto the edge of the other ski and begin a new turn. In ice, it's a quick but subtle transition between turns. Carve the icy snow; think about carving around the bottom side of a mogul.
10. The primary obstacles for many would-be bump skiers are fear of injury and looking like a fool. You needn't be concerned if you're intimidated by moguls. To most recreational skiers, moguls look like obstacles. The problem for most recreational skiers is that they don't get enough skiing time to develop the skills that are necessary to ski moguls. The obvious solution: Spend a good part of your skiing time doing drills and exercises in the bumps. Your overall skiing will improve!

The fear of injury is real and no one should tell you not to be afraid of being injured. Rather than being super tough, you're encouraged to focus on applying basic skills in comfortable terrain and gradually working up to more challenging terrain. Don't ski a difficult run when you're feeling tough enough; ski it when you're feeling technically ready.

Knowing you're ready will do a lot to quell your fear; incremental challenges to your mogul skiing will build this readiness. Unfortunately, the fear of looking like a fool in the moguls is equally ruinous while concomitantly increasing your risk of injury. Striking the proper balance is between you and your ego!

High Performance Tip #2

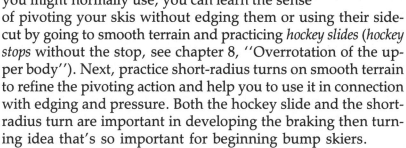

Brent Boblitt: A Short Course on Mogul Skiing

You don't learn to ski bumps by skiing only in the bumps. Rather, you first build skills such as pivoting and turning and then take these into the bumps. Even though there's more skidding than you might normally use, you can learn the sense of pivoting your skis without edging them or using their sidecut by going to smooth terrain and practicing *hockey slides* (*hockey stops* without the stop, see chapter 8, ''Overrotation of the upper body''). Next, practice short-radius turns on smooth terrain to refine the pivoting action and help you to use it in connection with edging and pressure. Both the hockey slide and the short-radius turn are important in developing the braking then turning idea that's so important for beginning bump skiers.

Assuming the drills were done correctly, the steeper the terrain the more dynamic your use of hockey slides and short-radius turns. Now you're going to rev it up somewhat and ski to a varying cadence. This will sharpen both your timing and your ability to react to changes in conditions as well as other surprises in the bumps. Staying on smooth terrain, begin by making short-radius turns, then go to long- or medium-radius turns, and finally back to short-radius turns, making dramatic shifts in direction. Be quick! Be reactional! If possible, ski to the rhythm set by another skier and ask that person to vary the rhythm. (See chapter 8, "Tense and static skiing"; *cadence skiing*.)

A key element to bump skiing is to stay centered over your skis while your lower body flexes (retracts) and extends to seek a line through the bumps that seems to be the most effortless. As you practice absorbing the bumps (retraction and extension), you want to keep your upper body as still as possible and your center of mass level, with arms relaxed and poles ready to be planted either to set and maintain rhythm, to serve as a defensive stabilizing force in difficult terrain, or to help reestablish your line. (See chapter 8, "Tense and static skiing"; *using bumps*.)

Once you can absorb the bumps smoothly at low speeds, turn your skis down toward the fall line to increase your speed and experiment with the slope. On some traverses head for the top of each mogul; on others relax and let your skis find the line of least resistance. As your familiarity with the bumps increases, you'll be ready to try different tasks on bump runs. All along, though, continue to use smooth terrain to perfect your basic skills, especially the short-radius turn.

Try this two-part drill: *Part one.* Stand atop a bump, pointing yourself and your skis down the fall line. Focus your attention on only two bumps, the one upon which you are perched and the one ahead of you. Not too scary, right? Okay, now allow your skis to slide (as in hockey slides) down the side, not the front, of the bump and while you are sliding, twist your feet in the direction of the next bump, coming to a stop in the widest part of the trough. Don't dig in your edges on the side of the bump: Slip to the trough and stop in it.

Part two. Move yourself up the hill on an angle from any bump you want to use in this part of the drill. You need to be higher so that you can carry a little speed into the bump. Let go. When you get to the bump, retract your knees, pivot your skis, and glide (slide) them into the trough. At the widest part of the trough, check your speed with an edge set and stop.

Try to incorporate all of the pointers I've mentioned and ski a line of your choice in the bumps. To control your speed and protect your rhythm, you might want to check your speed before each mogul by employing a *braking action* in the widest part of the trough. This braking action might include an edge set or check platform, where your edges are set and your pole is solidly planted an instant before turning. Find a pivot point on or near the next mogul at which you will begin your next turn. Look ahead to plan not only where you'll ski, but where you'll brake, pivot, absorb, and so on. (See chapter 8, "Lack of speed control"; *check platform*.)

Although this discussion has centered on a very basic application of skills in the bumps, by approaching the bumps in this friendly way it's easier to get acquainted with their nature and your ability to manipulate your skis through them. Of course, you've got to give your body plenty of freedom in the bumps. As your skills develop to the point where you enjoy a bump run every now and then, allow yourself to play around with the slope. Ski bump after bump, turning around each bump you encounter; ski around each of three bumps in succession, then skip a few bumps before turning; or traverse and change your line without too great a loss of rhythm. Whichever your choice, have fun in the bumps!

Chapter 4

Powder Skiing

When God gives us light, new-fallen powder, we are given a glimpse of heaven . . .

There is something wonderful about skiing in snow where you cannot see your skis, boots, or even legs. The dream of skiing effortlessly through light, new-fallen powder, like most dreams, omits the reality of what you must do on your skis to accomplish this. Skiing powder requires a different application of basic skiing skills. Powder skiing is momentum skiing down the fall line. If you're undaunted and want to realize your dream of skiing powder like the rest of those skiers in the trees, come along with us on our powder adventure.

Deep, New-Fallen Powder

Situation: Deep, new-fallen powder on steep, very skiable, tree-covered terrain.

Conditions: Two to three feet of very light snow fell overnight. It's chilly (around 10 degrees), and the skies are sunny and clear. No wind and excellent lighting.

Slope Traffic: A few of you in the trees.

According to Mike, skiers without powder skills shouldn't go into the trees, especially when it's deep. A lot of good yet inexperienced skiers find the deep stuff very intimidating. You've really got to think of new-fallen snow as a *fresh element of the conditions* with neither tracks in it nor direction to it. If you've got powder skills, however, the opportunity to inscribe your feelings and abilities, your skiing signature, into new-fallen snow is most appealing!

You can approach powder skiing from at least three different perspectives: beginning, more advanced, and expert. Here's an outline of what each embraces.

Beginning

Set up a series of tasks for yourself in 5- to 10-inch deep powder. First, ski down a gentle slope, skis together, just to get the feeling of the following four characteristics of powder: (a) texture; (b) depth; (c) resistance against your skis; and (d) balance point (i.e., where you stand on your skis). Try to center yourself over both skis, balancing yourself as much as possible. Be very deliberate about this so that you're moving along in balance with your skis, the snow, and the terrain.

Now, add retraction-extension movements to your skiing; at first make these rapid movements, then slow them down and make them more subtle. When you look back at your tracks in the snow they may show compressions from your extension and

Figure 4.1 Get a feel for the characteristics of the day's powder.

higher areas from your retraction. Repeat this several times until you become so used to the powder's characteristics that you feel relaxed in this condition. (See Figure 4.1.)

Start to feel the skis retracted up and extended down, the down motion of your legs creating a type of platform beneath your skis. In the powder, you and the snow (you are your skis) do the work together: retraction-extension *in balance*. As you consciously retract your skis, the snow will project them up toward the surface where they will have less resistance and be easier to turn.

Second, you're ready to add some basic rotary movements (i.e., the simultaneous pivoting of both skis). At this point, you're comfortable with the characteristics of the powder and ready to approach a more challenging fall line. Pick a place in the trees that looks open. Begin retraction-extension movements, adding a rotary movement as you retract your legs and pivot both skis together, turning them in the direction of your next turn. As you extend your legs continue steering both feet through the completion of your turn, letting your momentum counter the resistance the snow will exert against your boots and skis at this point. Then you retract again with a new turn accomplished through rotary movement. (See Figure 4.2.)

Third, you're ready to add pole rhythm. Ski as usual, only add an exaggerated pole touch at the end of your retraction (and beginning of your new turn) and follow the pole touch with your retracted legs. When you've put all three together you'll be

Figure 4.2 Steer or guide both skis into your new turn as you retract your legs.

Figure 4.3 Ride and continue to guide both skis through the turn as you extend your legs.

producing slow vigorous extended movements accompanied by light retracted rotary movements. Your pole is used not as a brace upon which to lean but as a prop that provides rhythm to your turns as well as some deflection and balance in more aggressive powder skiing. (See Figure 4.3.)

More Advanced

Apply the beginning principles but rev them up by adding the following adaptations. *First,* during your retraction movements, add more emphasis to your outside ski's rising and dipping, thereby allowing your inside ski to actually be lighter in the powder. In doing this, you will be more aware of the weight, pressure, and steering action of your outside ski, independent of your inside ski, in the powder. This is definitely a more dynamic approach to powder. (See Figure 4.4a.)

Second, consciously lighten your feet at the end of your down movement. As you flex down, let your feet come slightly toward you: Let them float up. Although deliberate at first, these movements will soon become subtle aspects of your powder skiing. (See Figure 4.4b.)

Third, along with the rotary movements of your feet as you come up, project your hip to realign your body to the fall line (i.e., left turn, right hip; right turn, left hip). Do so by thrusting your hip to the outside and forward, allowing your body to fall

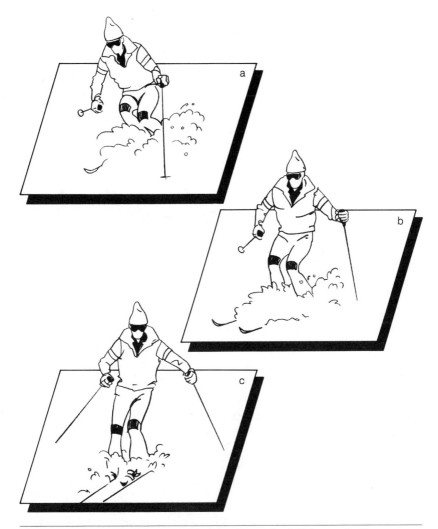

Figure 4.4a,b,c Chase your pole plant down the hill by projecting your outside hip into the fall line.

diagonally down the fall line and into your next turn. (This technique is particularly important on steeper runs with deeper snow.) (See Figure 4.4c.)

Expert

The expert skier skis outrageous powder: steep, difficult, chopped, heavy, or light. There are four characteristics this skier

Figure 4.5 Ski the powder as if there are moguls beneath you.

must possess: (a) strength and physical conditioning; (b) well-developed technique; (c) condition exposure, plenty of experience in these kinds of conditions; (d) an aggressive and committed attitude.

The development of expert powder skiing involves taking the skills of the beginning and more advanced powder skiers and isolating them as if one were skiing big, steep, and difficult moguls! It's a matter of skiing powder aggressively and effortlessly (that's the magic of it). (See Figure 4.5.)

At the expert level of powder skiing, the legs are dynamically moving up and down while the upper body remains relatively still; the upper body is not twisting around to help turn the body but riding atop a very active lower body. At the same time, the center of mass remains relatively square with the fall line while moving laterally side to side to accommodate the turning action of the legs. While the lower levels of powder skiing require you to ski over your skis, expert powder skiers move the skis out from under them, their retraction and extension movements reaching side to side, turn to turn like a pendulum. This is very exciting skiing! (See Figure 4.6.).

Some professionals advocate the use of the upper body to help turning in powder. Is the upper body being used this way?

According to Mike, there are a number of skiers who use their

Figure 4.6 Project your hip forward.

upper bodies to help them turn in powder. What they are doing is creating *rotational force*. Although rotation is the primary turning power in skiing deep powder, it's not necessary to use the upper body to provide rotation. You can, however, practice using the upper body to assist rotation by swinging your arm into the turn to help rotate your body around.

As you are extending to complete a right turn, touch the left pole; as you retract to turn left, thrust your right arm down the fall line to create greater rotational force. After thrusting forward (downhill), the right arm/pole swings through, and as your legs extend to complete the left turn, your right pole is placed in the snow to initiate your next right turn.

As you spend more time in the powder, you will become more familiar with the function and necessity of rotation. You will ski with the necessary rotation without having to create it by overusing your upper body. Rotation will follow naturally when you learn to ski with your upper body separated from your lower body.

Guide and Ride

While there are many approaches to powder technique, *guide and ride* is a natural evolution of sound parallel skiing. The latter is based on independent leg action led by active inside ski steering.

The key to powder is hinging the knees to the motion of the lower body. This can apply to both the more vertical retraction and extension of the legs in beginning and advanced powder skiing or to the lateral retraction and extension seen in the elite powder skier. Keeping your knees "hinged" or as close together as possible while retrieving your skis out of the snow during retraction allows you a more controlled and problem-free initiation of your new turn with the simultaneous *guiding* of your skis in the direction you want to go.

As you continue into your turn, your focus changes to *riding* your skies as they bend, arc, or plane through the loose snow until a platform is formed from the compression of the snow beneath the bases of your skis. In active powder skiing with slight to more overt independent leg action, there are actually two interrelated platforms formed beneath the snow. This is true even as the knees are held close together, moving up and down to correspond to the independence of your legs.

Whether one or two platforms are formed, the critical matter of *guide and ride* is to continue to *guide* or steer your skis throughout the turn as long as your legs are extended—particularly through (and against) the powder that's above your boots. It's helpful to visualize turns in powder as continuous maneuvers that begin as you *guide* your skis into a first turn, *ride* them momentarily as they platform in the snow, and then continue to *ride and guide* your skis to the completion of this first turn and into the initiation of your second turn. In effect, *in powder as in pack, to link your turns and maintain ultimate control of speed and to ensure maneuverability, you guide into a new turn by guiding out of an old turn.*

Common Mistakes

Skiers make at least four classic mistakes in powder. First, they carry too much speed into the snow with their legs (and knees) too far apart. Second, they try to abruptly change directions with little retraction of their legs. The ill result of both mistakes is often falling; the resistance built up on the skis when they're compressed against the snow (from going too fast and trying to turn in an extended "static" position) is too great to allow these skiers to use the design of the ski to *ride and guide* through the turn.

Third, when skis get "locked" in the snow, instead of changing technique, skiers rely on forcing their skis into a turn. Not only will this lead to excessive fatigue and aching thighs and calves, these skiers will find their mass traveling in one direction and their skis in the other, with no sense of control.

Finally, the fourth mistake actually compounds the first. It's simply forgetting to continue to *guide* the skis after *riding* them to a platform. In many ways, this is the same kind of mistake that skiers with poor parallel turning skills make—they turn their skis fine, but they forget to *ride and guide* their skis through the completition of the parallel turn. Coincidently, the better your parallel skills on packed and groomed slopes, the easier it is to learn skills on powder.

Heavy, Wet Powder

Situation: Heavy, wet powder.

Conditions: It's bright and just below freezing, with the temperature rising. This snow will deteriorate rapidly, but this is good early morning snow, especially at the higher elevations and in the shade of the trees. There's no wind and excellent lighting in this advanced area of the mountain.

Slope Traffic: Traffic in the trees is sparse.

According to Mike, heavy and wet conditions are probably the most difficult for any skier regardless of skiing ability. Unlike dry powder and groomed slopes, the consistency of heavy, wet snow presents challenges to all levels of skiers.

When most recreational skiers encounter these conditions, they seek areas where there has been a lot of traffic. In these areas it is as if the skiers themselves have groomed the slopes: This

Figure 4.7 Steer your knees into the hill for more dynamic turning.

is called *skier pack conditions*. You know these areas: those *channels* created by constant use, which after a while are prone to develop bumps and ridges. Yet, these channels offer many skiers the only way in which they feel comfortable getting down the mountain (i.e., packed condition).

Why does this situation occur? Because a good many recreational skiers are intimidated by heavy, wet powder and would rather ski something with a firm look to it.

Venture out in these conditions. Don't spend an entire day in these conditions, but go out and play a while. You have to be a bit more aggressive in these conditions because your ability to turn, move, push, or press the snow out of the way of your turning ski is going to be more difficult; wet snow offers a great deal more resistance. In order to overcome this added and unusual resistance, you can actively steer your knees into the hill (uphill) with each retraction movement (see Figure 4.7), or you can use *leap and land turns* which are quite vigorous. You begin with slight retraction and extension movements and advance to more vigorous movements. Next, on the up side of the bounce, simultaneously turn both feet and skis to create a hopping turn. Doing this several times creates a degree of fatigue. In order to use this and other exercises functionally in heavy, wet snow, you must have sufficiently steep slope to provide less resistance against your skis and greater momentum for turning. (See Figure 4.8.)

Figure 4.8 You can leap and land in heavy wet powder.

Acquaint yourself with the resistance you will experience on a slope. In other words, first traverse the slope at different angles to feel where you are on your skis and feel the characteristics of the snow. In this way, you develop a kinesthetic appreciation of the elements you are working with or against in heavy, wet snow. Once the feeling of the characteristics become ingrained you can assume a very aggressive attitude.

If you take a positive and aggressive attitude about heavy, wet snow and use it to become proficient in this condition, you'll add to your overall skiing ability by building greater confidence and skill. For versatility, go out and ski these conditions, leaving a signature in the untracked snow.

Look for opportunities to experiment with different kinds of turns. Try *leap and land*-like hop turns. Extend off the platform beneath your skis and leap out of the snow, retracting your legs and rotating your skis in the direction of the intended turn. Use your landing to complete that particular turn by extending your legs. As you gain proficiency you'll find that it's just like skiing in lighter powder; you take the raggedness out of your exaggerated movements and let your legs do the movement up and out of the snow with a still upper body.

The primary goal of perfecting this hop turn exercise is to retract your legs to lessen the resistance of the snow and use the greater strength in your legs to press or bend your skis through the snow into the completion of the turn. This is an active retraction-extension turn: one you achieve rather than begin with. One rule: When you retract, retract both legs and feet simultaneously; as you extend, extend both legs and feet with the same amount of force.

Another turn that works well in heavy, wet snow that's not too deep is the *uphill stem christie*, a very functional one in these conditions. The uphill stem christie is actually a skidded turn where your turning ski sets the arc of the turn and the inside ski matches it. Imagine how this kind of turn would work in difficult, hard-to-move snow. You push the turning ski out, stand on it, release the pressure from the uphill ski, and match it to the turning ski to create a turn in heavy, wet snow. Once you gain confidence in this, you will begin to understand the importance of starting your turn early to establish a good base and completing the turn throughout to maintain rhythm and control in these conditions. (See Figure 4.9.)

Figure 4.9 Sometimes a stem christie type turn in crud is effective.

Ego Fluff

Situation: Ego fluff powder: three to five inches of new fallen, dry, light snow (even medium-light snow) covering previously groomed and packed terrain. This stuff is ideal for powder novices.

Conditions: It's cold and a little hazy, but there's no wind and overall conditions are ideal.

Slope Traffic: Crowded. If you're late getting out, you might head for the outer edge of the trails.

According to Mike, these are great conditions in which to become acquainted with powder skiing. The main reason is that there are no technical nuances that you need to apply assuming you're skiing confidently and efficiently already. The significant change occurs in your mind.

Go out onto your favorite slope early. Ski as you normally do right down the center of the slope. If you feel that you are having some difficulty, look back at the tracks you have created and see if they are rounded like a series of the letter *s* or sharp like a series of the letter *z*. (See Figure 4.10)

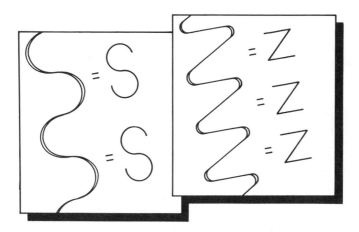

Figure 4.10 Study the shape of your turns.

If they are rounded you're skiing better than you think. If they are sharp you are not doing at least one thing that you probably omit in your everyday skiing: *finishing your turns*. If the z is apparent, return to the slope and try lengthening your turns. Ski a long- to medium-radius turn. Steer your skis through five or six turns, making them as rounded as you can (i.e., gradual pressure through the arc of the turn).

Look at your new tracks. If they are rounder than before, continue to ski rounded shorter-radius turns and pick up the cadence of your skiing. Make shorter-radius turns by increasing the tempo of your pole touch. Don't sit back and don't lean forward; stay centered. You don't have to put equal weight on both skis; stand more on your downhill ski. Touch with your poles as you usually do.

Most importantly, enjoy this kind of snow when you can. The elements of powder that make skiing more difficult are wetness, pitch, and depth. Ego fluff offers a tremendous opportunity for beginning powder skiers to practice, even if they are experienced packed-snow skiers.

If you're having difficulties with the ego fluff, it is possible that it is too wet or that there is too little pitch to the slope, causing far too much drag against your skis. (At this point, the ego fluff is crud.) Another cause of trouble skiing any powder is that it is psychologically foreign and intimidating. This reason is, in most cases, a small part of the real problem of turning ability. If you can't create a rounded turn on packed slopes, either short- or medium-radius, then work on your technical skills out of the powder.

The problems you encounter in this kind of powder are just an exaggeration of the problems you have when skiing on any groomed slope. If you have technical problems with basic skiing skills, they will show up more dramatically in these conditions. Perfect your skiing on packed or groomed slopes; ego fluff will be the greatest introduction to powder skiing.

General Tips
for Powder Skiing

1. Your power in the powder comes from momentum: Always carry the momentum of your body down the fall line. Versatility in powder comes from your manipulation of this momentum with ankle flexion, knee steering, and hip projections by which you direct your outside hip down the fall line. Rely on your lower body to rotate while compact or retracted and continue this rotation all the way through the extension and completion of your turn.

2. Go into powder with the attitude that you're in charge and take command of the conditions. If you go into the powder feeling intimidated, you'll ski in a cautious and tentative manner. You can't derive flowing rhythmic movements from a muscularly tentative body. To be in charge, you dictate the radii of the turns and ski with the attitude that you're lighter than the powder. Feeling light in powder will allow you to ski close to the surface because of the buoyancy of your skis.

3. The complementary perspective to tip 2, above, is the attitude and sensation of letting go in the powder. Let go and experience effortlessness. This is not an easy proposition when you're intimidated by the fluffy stuff; rather, it's impossible. So, let go; once you've worked on your powder skills, go out into the powder and ski loose. This will help you to let go and as you allow your body and mind to ski without restrictions, your skiing will become effortless. Momentum and attitude will find a perfect balance.

4. The essence of deep, light powder, beyond the sheer ecstasy of skiing untracked snow in the trees, through open bowls, and down chutes, is the quality of its expression as dynamic skiing in slow motion. For a moment, consider skiing a groomed run very smoothly and effortlessly. Your turns are crisp, rhythmic, rounded, and well-sequenced. Now, imagine that same perfect feeling in the powder, only in slow motion: nothing abrupt, nothing aggressive; you're truly flowing with the powder.

5. Not all powder is slow-motion powder. Recall how the heavier and deeper powder require more aggressiveness and determination. Still, the sense of your skiing has a very subtle and quiet component. For example, as you ski more aggressively you must exaggerate your pole rhythm, extension-retraction, rotary steering, and hip projection. The subtlety comes into play when you float between turns from the down/extended position to the up/retracted position. During this flotation your center of mass crosses over the path of your skis; actually your skis cross under your stable upper body. This interaction takes the harshness out of skiing powder.

6. A powder skier is a centered skier. The powder skier skis over the center of the skis, not the tails as you often hear. You don't need to ski on your tails because your ski is built to bend up against the force of the snow. Skiing on the tails puts you out of balance with the turning forces of your skis (the mid-portion) and makes powder skiing quite fatiguing. Some good powder skiers appear to be sitting back at times, when they are actually standing upright, square with the fall line, their skis beneath them, poised, and ready to move in either direction.

   A revealing centering exercise on smooth terrain is to ski with your boots unbuckled. If you don't stay centered over your skis, you will neither be able to turn as well nor subtly control the speed of your skis.

7. Overall, powder skiing demands absolute commitment to the first few turns, pole rhythm, projection down the hill, continuous movement, looking ahead, being in charge, staying light, letting go, and staying in the powder and exploring the mountain. A helpful exercise for building commitment is to decide that you will make a certain number of turns in succession without stopping. Start with 4, and as discussed with regard to bump skiing, progress to 20. Ski around the mountain and hunt up new powder adventures.

8. Finally, hinge your knees together. Doing this will help focus the attention of your feet/skis on turning as one unit.

Summary

1. Think of new-fallen snow with no tracks in it as an opportunity to inscribe your skiing signature into the snow!
2. Get to know these three characteristics of powder: texture, depth, and resistance against your skis.
3. In powder, center yourself over both skis.
4. Feel your skis moving up and down: The down motion, which results from extending your legs, creates a type of platform in the snow; the up motion, which results from retracting your legs, represents the action of your skis floating through the snow.
5. During the up motion turn your skis; during the down motion complete your turn.
6. The upper body is useful in helping to create rotation in the powder, but it's not necessary once you've perfected powder skills. Until then, you can practice using the upper body to assist rotation by thrusting the arms down the fall line.
7. Skiing heavy, wet powder requires the application of certain turning skills and an aggressive attitude. Two kinds of turns you can use in heavy, wet powder are hop turns and stem christie turns.
8. When skiing ego fluff there is nothing you have to do differently, assuming you're skiing confidently and efficiently already. The significant change is in your mind.
9. The shape of your tracks in ego fluff can tell you a great deal about your skiing. Your tracks may reveal weaknesses and deficiencies in your basic skiing skills.
10. Enjoy ego fluff when you can; it's a wonderful introduction to powder skiing. Problems other than undeveloped skills may be due to the snow being too wet, the slope being too flat, or the powder being psychologically intimidating.

Chapter 5

Recreational Racing

If you're naturally athletic and competitive, recreational, club, and league racing may light fires in you that will be difficult, if not impossible, to extinguish.

That's at least part of it; as you'll discover in this chapter there's a great deal more. For all it entails, properly running gates forces you to ski more precisely, perhaps more aggressively, use many skills, and employ your skiing senses (e.g., sight, sound, touch, balance, proprioception) as well as your kinesthetic memory. Overall, properly running gates teaches you to ski more reactionally.

The issues don't exclusively concern how you properly run gates, whether it really helps your skiing, or how you get access to gates. These are important, but the bigger question concerns whether recreational, club, or league racing is for you. Club and league racing are more organized and competitive forms of recreational racing. Amateur racing is yet another step in competition. After reading this chapter, you may find yourself looking for any opportunity to be a racer.

The first step is to get access to practice gates. For the average recreational racer the availability of gates depends on the resorts that you frequent. Although most resorts have regularly scheduled races, if you're looking for practice gates you have to find pay-as-you-go practice courses or coin-operated courses (usually a dollar a run). Also, most resorts have recreational racing clinics that provide expert coaching and practice gates.

Many would-be recreational racers are obsessed with the drive to get in the gates. This is true despite advice from the pros that it's far more beneficial for recreational racers to free-ski and do training exercises and racing-related drills on the mountain than to rely on banging gates on a practice course, or running as many races as you can on a public course to learn racing techniques.

You must run gates some of the time, however, so it's good to assess the two kinds of courses available: the *practice* course (coin-op courses); and the *race* course (standard races, league races, resort races, tour citizen races, etc.). Both practice and race courses are set by experienced course setters; most cover intermediate slopes and are friendly to ski.

Practice courses allow you to perform drills and experiment with different techniques at your own pace for as long as you'd like. When the course gets too rutted, you can continue to ski it for technique or pull the poles and set up another less-rutted course nearby. Race courses are far more restricted, providing you limited exposure to the gates, and usually operate on a pay-per-run basis. Although coin-operated race courses can be used for practice, most people allow technique to take a back seat to ego by racing as fast as they can.

Of course, fast doesn't always mean velocity. In racing, fast involves "skiing smart": skiing the fastest line, using proper technique, making effective recoveries, and concentrating on the course. I'm sure you'll find that the advice and coaching of my contributors will help you to fully appreciate skiing smart in a race course and provide you with useful insights and practical advice on how to make recreational racing an important part of your skiing.

Value of Free-Skiing

Like learning to ski bumps, you don't learn to ski gates by running gates. Instead, you work on basic technique while free-skiing, drilling, or exercising. According to George Capaul, the amount of time spent racing versus actual time free-skiing and training is very small. Speaking of the academy at Waterville Valley, New Hampshire, where he was Program Director and head coach for 10 years, he said, "We trained approximately 400 hours on the snow. Out of this, skiers raced approximately 50 minutes of total time for the whole winter. You figure it out: You practice 400 hours for one hour of racing."

Of course, practice includes running gates, racing drills and exercises, and plenty of free-skiing. Dirk Haas, who in addition to coaching for Northstar-at-Tahoe's junior race team, conducts summer racing camps in Oregon, advises: "Recreational racers should spend a good 60% of their time free-skiing with *purpose*; that is, with certain tasks in mind and a generous amount of pure "get-out-there-and-shred" driving them down the hill; 30% of their time on specific racing drills (includes practice courses and gates); and only 10% of their time racing."

Only 10% for racing doesn't seem like much until you follow this prescription and discover that all of your purposeful free-skiing to become a better racer is making you a better overall skier. As you begin to have better racing times while experiencing once-difficult runs as easier and more fun to ski, racing and free-skiing become more complementary. Your time spent on the race course helps you to understand what you need to do in your free-skiing; your accomplishments in your free-skiing give you the confidence to take something new into the race course. Successes in either can build on the other; seeing failure in either can have the opposite effect.

Mark Tache is adamant about the importance of free-skiing for racers, especially newcomers. "Too often when people start getting into gates, they go overboard. All they want to do is run gates. They think free-skiing won't accomplish anything, but this is where you build your base. Free-skiing is where you work on correcting your technical problems, then when you're in the gates, you ski more naturally. If you try to correct technical problems in the gates, it's disasterous."

So, what about preseason skiing? Mark insists people spend 100% of their time free-skiing during the preseason. "I don't think you should touch a pole until you've free-skied a couple of weeks." To this Christin adds, "Think of free-skiing as training also."

To keep this in perspective, take a look at what the U.S. Ski Team slalom and giant slalom racers do on an average, early-season, pre-World Cup, training day. According to George, "We take five to seven training course runs maximum in the morning when everyone's fresh and reflexes sharp. We wouldn't ski more than 300 slalom gates, and 250 giant slalom gates, but these would be skied very intensely at high speed. After lunch, we go out and free-ski for 1-2 hours, or as long as the snow is good. Then, we usually go in and play a game of basketball."

It is late November, well into the ski season for many skiers, yet these racers are just beginning their racing season. In fact, if you're intrigued with figures, consider this: George estimates his racers run approximately 12,000 gates before they start racing. Broken down, this represents 6,000 slalom, 4,000 giant slalom, and 2,000 super-G gates. This is what they've done and will continue to do in preparation for the 1988 Olympics. Says George, "Yes, about 12,000 gates; then we feel that we're ready for the season."

Fritz Vallant, former coach of the U.S. Women's team, and presently head coach at Stratton Mountain School, Vermont, says European racers ski 400 gates a day before the World Cup season. It's not at all uncommon to get in over 10,000 practice gates before their first race. The World Cup season is the culmination of months of practice courses, drilling, and free-skiing.

Most of my contributors agree that the stronger your basic skills, the more proficient a skier you become. Further, they echo the sentiment: *Recreational racing should be a reward*, even a focal point for achievement. Use the race course to review your progress as a high performance skier through the quality of your performance, but don't train so hard for racing that you cease to enjoy free-skiing.

Mike related a story to me about a discussion he had with Jean Claude Killy concerning the differences between European and U.S. racing programs. Mike asked Killy to identify the most important factor that helped him gain prominence in the world of skiing. Killy's response: "I first learned how to like to ski by skiing with a group of kids for years. We skied all over the mountain in all kinds of conditions. After this, we raced."

George related a similar story about his early development as a racer during his childhood in Chur, Switzerland. "We, all the boys in town, always skied in the same place even before we had a lift. As soon as the first snow fell, we packed the hill and continued to ski it all season. Just before we were teenagers, we had volunteer teachers who came out with us every Saturday afternoon and taught us the basics of skiing: traversing, straight run, sideslip in every direction, pole plants, different turns, and so on. They set up obstacle courses and drills for us. There were seven or eight maneuvers we had to master, and for which we were graded. If you did the maneuver perfectly, you earned a '4' and a red patch to put on the sleeve of your jacket. What distinguished the good skiers were not points earned in races, but patches earned for mastering basic skills.

"When we started training for racing, we went out in the forest and cut about 200 hazelnut sticks for use as slalom poles. We got an old rain gutter, sealed both ends, and dipped the sticks in the gutters full of paint: three colors (yellow, red, blue). It was the thing to do, to have three colors of poles. We had to carry all the poles and our ski gear up the mountain. Sometimes I think we were idiotic for all we did to our bodies: hiking, skiing, and then playing soccer or running, but we believed in it as our training program for racing, and it made us strong."

Practical Value
of Running Gates

Jack Rounds, former pro racer and technical rep for Rossignol, presently ski school supervisor at Northstar-at-Tahoe, is high on the benefits of racing to improve your free-skiing. As he says, "Properly running gates can really improve your rhythm and help correct rotational problems which lead to skidded, rather than carved, turns. But more importantly, it makes free-skiing seem easier. Imagine being able to turn anywhere you want! Your line through the moguls can simulate ruts, and the more you do of each, running gates and skiing bumps, the easier each becomes."

Mike feels running gates encourages you to be more versatile in your skiing by "forcing you to create angles and quickness in your turning. Racing makes you turn, and depending on the course and circumstances, you must respond with the appropriate turn radii or you'll ski off the course." And, like Jack, Mike sees the connection between moguls and slalom skiing: "I find that skiers who run slalom gates for an hour and a half, say five runs of 20 to 30 gates (100 to 150 turns), who are then taken to a mogul field will ski way above their normal ability in the moguls. In fact, it's a great exercise for teaching bump skiing: Ski gates first, and then jump into the bumps. You'll be quick, aggressive and surprisingly relaxed."

Taking full account of the practical value of properly running gates, the list of conditions it helps to correct includes: sluggish skiing; excessive skidding while turning; sloppy mogul skiing; rotational problems of the upper and lower body; timidity while skiing under adverse conditions (ice, slush, crud, etc.); fear of speed and speed control; slow reaction times to obstacles and other skiers; erratic turning; lack of, or decreased excitement about, skiing; self-doubt as a skier; and most notably, the fear of falling.

Falling

If you're inclined to examine your skiing and racing from the mind down—not a bad idea for the serious recreational racer—consider this:

> A ski race is like a sprint in track. The difference between winning and losing is measured in hundredths of a second. But unlike a sprint, falling is common, even likely, in skiing. Based on this analysis you might think that the primary objective in ski racing is to avoid falling. Wrong. Making that the primary objective would be a mistake for two reasons: First, as we have explained before, if your primary goal is to prevent a fall, you will reflexively be stiff and tense and will not ski well or fast. Second, in order not to fall, even if you are not tense, you must ski more slowly than your peak performance level. And since races are won and lost by fractions of seconds, you will be out of the running if you are skiing slowly enough to guarantee that you will not fall. (Loudis, Lobitz, & Singer, 1986, pp. 160-161)

Indeed, falling in a race course or while free-skiing or drilling has purpose and intention, even though at times you'd rather it had meaning for someone else. Nevertheless, falling gives you the opportunity to take yourself to the edge, that wonderfully scary, and exceedingly exciting place where the "juice" is free, and where you're going as fast as you can. At this point you are still skiing smart, in touch with yourself just enough to stay in control, and remaining responsive to changing conditions and those it-could-never-happen-to-me surprises.

If you can't take yourself to the edge, you won't overcome the competition; those skiers are likely to be taking it to their respective edges. In racing, it is literally and figuratively an edge-to-edge shoot out. Falling helps you to discover the dimensions of your edge in varied conditions and teaches you to get up and go for it again.

"One thing is for sure," George nods, "you have a hard time learning anything if you're afraid of speed or falling down, because this means you're likely afraid of the fall line. You've got to overcome your fear of speed and falling down to progress in ski racing. The first thing you do is practice skiing fast on slopes you can ski without fear and then gradually move up to more challenging slopes retaining the speed." (Chapter 10 explores a number of perspectives helpful for keeping fear under control.)

When Dirk's kids fall, he says simply, "Hey, no one is perfect. There are going to be a lot more races. And besides, it's not a big deal to fall down in a ski race. It would be a big deal if no one else did it, but considering how often it happens, it's part of the sport. Look at the 1984 Winter Olympics, Men's Slalom. There were 104 of the best skiers in the world and only 47 didn't fall in one of their two runs. When you fall in a race, you just get back on the horse and go for it the next time out of the gate."

As Fritz says, "The best slalom skiers know they're going to fall at some time. They don't dwell on it, nor is it a written law, but most figure it's not out of the ordinary to fall two out of every five slalom runs." Of course, most hope the falls come in practice.

Use your falls to teach you to race better and faster:

During practice your attention should be on your falls. Because peak racing performance means that you must be carrying your speed right up to the limit of the forces of physics, you need to find that limit. To know where that limit is, you must exceed it some of the time. If you do not fall very often in practice, you are not close enough to that limit. Conversely, if you are falling frequently in practice, you are too far over the limit. This limit is equivalent to the peak in your performance/arousal curve; for purposes of this discussion, speed replaces arousal. (Loudis et al., p. 161)

Let's Go Racing—A Short Plan of Attack

Ever hang around the top of a race course? If so, you're well aware of the many emotions evident in everyone present: excitement, competitiveness, friendliness, guardedness, and quietness. The atmosphere is both intimidating and exhilarating. There are a lot of egos waiting to race and each wants to be its definition of the ultimate racer! On the recreational circuit it's mostly fun stuff; but when sponsors add prizes, racing becomes much more serious. For pro racers, it's a job.

Before going into more detail here's an overview, or a short plan of attack, on racing that you might want to stash in your pocket. Go into the race to have fun. At the starting gate take a deep breath and look ahead. When you start, push off hard and look ahead. Ski smart, stay early, and aim for speed. Be sure to drive through and past the finish. This last item is particularly important, yet at times it's taken to its extreme while at others it's completely ignored.

Something humorous happened to a friend's daughter. Her skiing had been getting better and better and she wanted to start racing. Her dad and I took her over to the race course and signed her up to run a real open GS course. She's a sharp young woman, and we talked about the race beforehand. My general advice was to go and have some fun with the course. My two points of strategy: Relax and look ahead to the gates coming up, rather than the gate around which she was skiing. If she wasn't sure where to go, I added, she should just follow the tracks in the snow where others had skied. I reminded her I would be waiting for her at the bottom of the course.

She had a fine first race, a little tentative on the steeper part, but well done overall. Her dad and I were proud of her. I was standing right at the finish next to the timing light. Instead of skiing through and past the finish, she made a nice stop in front of me on the uphill side of the finish and never actually went through the timing light; she wanted to ask me how she did. When I realized what was happening, I kicked my boot through the timing light so she would get a time. I had forgotten to tell her to drive through and past the finish.

Let's Go Racing—A Long Plan of Attack

For the remainder of this chapter, I'll examine the views of my contributors and share their advice and other racing-related information, exercises, and drills.

To be sure, there's a great deal to recreational racing, and I apprepreciate the description of the passion it can ignite in the citizen racer out for the challenge of the gates, as described by Horst Abraham (1983): "Part of the addiction to racing gates is the vicarious feedback that is provided instantly and continuously. . . . The fact that a skier finishes a course and the speed in which he completes that task will provide him with an intoxicatingly clear picture of his performance and progress" (p. 166). There's definitely a hook to recreational racing.

Once the more serious recreational racer eclipses the high provided by the "intoxicating" personal experience, he or she seeks refinement in skills and technique. This skier trains year-round to be a racer, thinks of him or herself as a ski racer, and goes to racing camp in the off-season. Still, this skier may race only 10% of the time, even less for racers who free-ski 4 to 6 days a week.

Mental Attitude

Jack offers practical advice: "There are many mental states that can help the recreational racer, particularly relaxation, concentration, and the ability to focus on strategy, goals, and your line.

The critical mind-set for the recreational racer is the sense of being calm, and staying focused on the important changes in the course's rhythm. To do this, the racer must be able to ignore outside stimuli. The more the racer carriers a dead serious nervousness about racing, the more difficult it will be for the racer to have a positive and confident attitude about his or her racing."

Christin maintains the origins of her confidence as a skier, and then as a racer, grew out of her passion for the sport. As children, she says, "We loved skiing, and spent a lot of time working at it, slowly but surely. Figuring out that skiing wasn't a fight between me and the mountain was a critical step in my progress to higher levels of performance.

"When you're first learning, there's a lot of fighting and struggling to keep yourself together. As you get more miles behind you, you begin to realize you can work with the terrain and really play with the mountain. This is when your skiing makes big leaps, and you approach the feeling of being a high performance skier; a skier who's in control, and who's able to enjoy playing with the mountain. This same attitude carries into your racing."

Former pro racer and head coach of Northstar-at-Tahoe's Junior Race Team, Chaz Kruck, expresses a similar view: "Unless you're physically unable to race, it's your mind that hinders your racing, because it's your mind that gets down on your body for not being able to learn the same skill Joe Blow learns easily. This is unnecessary because sometimes Joe Blow's going to have problems learning new skills that are easy for you. Each individual is different; each racer is different. The most important things are that you remain dedicated and keep trying, and never give up!"

Pete Patterson feels that by seeking challenges in your skiing you acquire an adventurous mind-set and become more versatile. "Unfortunately, a lot of young racers learn to race before they can ski properly, and they just don't have the mind-set for wanting to ski a variety of terrain. As soon as they get out of their comfort zone (e.g., a smooth race course), they often shy away from it and become static. They practice the easy things, but don't work for challenges.

"Would-be racers ought to look for challenges in their skiing: crud, ice, powder, steeps, poor lighting, and stormy skiing. In fact, some of the best days are those stormy days when very few skiers are out on the mountain and you find those places in the trees with good snow and decent lighting and have a great time. Without challenges, you may lose interest in free-skiing, and you need plenty of free-skiing to perfect your racing skills.''

Mark says simply, ''If you have an attitude to challenge yourself every day of skiing, overcoming challenges is going to become natural for you and translate into higher levels of performance. Then, when it's time to race, you're not afraid. You accept the challenge and go with it. That's important. That's high performance skiing.''

Both Mark's and Pete's comments reminded me of Christin's second run in giant slalom at the '84 Olympics at Sarajevo. In great position to win the gold, she began the course skiing like a winner. Then, five gates later, she slipped, her hip slamming into the ground, but up she sprang, righted herself, and skied the course in championship fashion, finishing just 0.4 seconds behind the leader, teammate Debbie Armstrong, and winning the silver medal. This is an example of a brilliant run set up by Christin's versatility and history of challenging skiing.

Physical Conditioning

Top recreational racers are skillful and strong both in legs and upper body, whereas the vast majority of weekend recreational racers have a broad range of skills and different levels of strength and conditioning. These differences are most evident when the difficulty factor in courses is increased. This occurs when the terrain gets steeper or the gates are set either closer together down the fall line or back and forth across the hill to effect a curvy course. In these instances, technical skills are essential to maintaining speed in the course.

Another variable that increases the difficulty of late season courses is the softening of snow to slushy conditions in which ruts easily develop, especially late ruts (ruts that have developed from too many skiers beginning, rather than finishing, their turns at the gate). And finally, there are hard, icy conditions, which may bring smiles to the faces of some racers and tears to those of others.

Mike emphasizes the importance of physical conditioning to the recreational racer by contrasting a fit racer with a racer who lacks conditioning: "On very hard, icy conditions, the fit racer uses his skis like razors and doesn't drift sideways during his turns. This racer looks strong and stable. A recreational racer who lacks conditioning, however, is a much different story when you put him on the same course: His legs wobble, his skis chatter, and he drifts all over the course."

Mike continues: "Lack of physical conditioning makes the biggest difference when the conditions get tougher, even when the snow is softer. The racer who lacks conditioning loses his ability to effectively ski ruts (actually use the ruts), because he lacks the strength required to ensure he has the quickness demanded of him to use the ruts. In the most basic of languages, recreational skiers benefit from being able to hold a ski on its edge for longer periods (like riding the downhill ski through a rut). To do this, the racer must be physically conditioned."

"You've got to train for racing," says Pete, "especially at the World Cup level. Through your dryland, off-season training (i.e., running, hiking, weight training, gymnastics, climbing, cycling, etc.), you seek to become physically and mentally stronger, quicker, and better balanced: all the things you need for high level competition. There's no easy way around it; it's a tremendous amount of work. You do it to get yourself ready and tough enough to compete at the level you must be to win."

He adds: "I think the most fun I had with off-season training was hiking into the mountains and knowing that after I came out, I wanted to go back in. It was great fun for us carrying weight around the mountain and not even looking at it like training, but more like something we really looked forward to doing. Pretty soon, we realized how good it was for us."

Christin, who grinned as Pete spoke, added, "There's something meaningful in enjoying pushing yourself and not seeing this as a drag. Rather, you see it as something that's fun and valuable, even though at times it hurt and was a lot of hard work."

A World Cup perspective? Perhaps. Alternatively, consider Jack's friendly perspective on the connection between recreational racing and physical conditioning for the infrequent recreational racer: "Although being in good shape is essential to the top few recreational racers, racers running on more nationally standardized races can be quite successful on shorter courses while carrying a few extra pounds and not having strong quads. This is particularly evident in ex-racer types whose technical skills often compensate for the aggressiveness of a less-experienced racer.

"Still, any recreational racer who wants to get a powerful start," says Jack, "needs good arm strength and a strong back plus, of course, the desire to leap a foot up into the air to better dive at that first gate. And, if you're going to skate all the way through some of the flatter courses, it takes a lot of strength."

Chaz offers similar advice for novice racers, but sees a need for a bit more "juice" for the serious upper level racer: "You don't necessarily have to come into the sport in racing fitness, particularly if you're learning basic skills. As you progress to the middle of your potential, and especially to upper levels of racing, you need a year-round program with different types of training. This program includes summer conditioning, more intensive cardiovascular work in the fall, and a weight-training program to build the bulk you need for upper level moves like you see in World Cup technique.

"For example, you see Ingemar Stenmark go down onto his right or left arm in a turn and then bounce back onto his outside ski. Think about the kind of conditioning he does: He jumps up and hits a basketball hoop 150 times consecutively to train for this sport, and that's only one of the exercises he does. Fortunately, there are many different exercises you can do for the same muscle groups to help break the monotony of training.

"If you don't train, it's going to show in those difficult situations in upper level racing where you get off the softer pack and onto some hard ice. This is where you will discover what your muscles are all about and why you need them to keep your skis from skidding all over the place."

George views the training needs of the recreational racer in basic terms. "Even they must keep up with some sort of off-season training. There are many sports they can perform as well as the running, weight training, and aerobics. They should do all of them; anything they enjoy, just keep moving all summer and fall. It needn't be as vigorous as the training we do, but even if they can do something three or four days a week, consistently, this is the key. Hiking in the fall is great. It strengthens your calves, ankles, and legs. The whole body is involved in hiking, and if I could give one recommendation for the recreational skier's dryland training, hiking would really be the one."

If you've been athletic throughout your life, you already know that training is probably the area of greatest commitment in athletics, competition the most personally rewarding—still, they do go hand in hand. Chapter 11 presents overall physical conditioning concepts; briefly, at the heart of any conditioning program is the amount of heart you put into it.

Conditioning involves doing activities that make your heart pump harder for an extended period of time by working your large muscles (i.e., those in your legs and upper body). The secret to a successful conditioning program is to see it as something that directly contributes to your dreams and aspirations. Don't ever do a conditioning program for anyone but yourself.

Tom "TJ" Jones, coach for Northstar-at-Tahoe's Junior Race Team, says he harps on his kids to get into better shape. "Given equal skills," he says, "the one that's in the best shape usually wins."

Skiing Skills

One-time Olympic hopeful in the decathlon, expert surfer, and a top-flight racer, Steve Armstrong has over the years offered me many tips on upper level recreational racing. Although Steve is a man of few words who does most of his talking on the race course, I coaxed him into giving me a contribution that he felt would be most beneficial to serious recreational racers.

The Three Hs. "The keys to advanced recreational racing are the three Hs: hands, head, and hips, plus the inside ski and outside arm. *Hands*: Keep them forward, pointing toward the next gate; this keeps you headed in the right direction. *Head*: When turning, keep your head over your outside or turning ski; this gets your ski where it's supposed to be, on edge. *Hip*: Place your inside hip into the hill when turning; this keeps your ski on edge throughout your turns. *Inside ski*: The more you lift it when turning (exaggerate if you must by bringing the knee of your inside leg up toward your chest), the easier and more natural it is for your hip to fall into the hill and your outside ski to hold its edge. *Outside arm*: Drive your outside arm around and

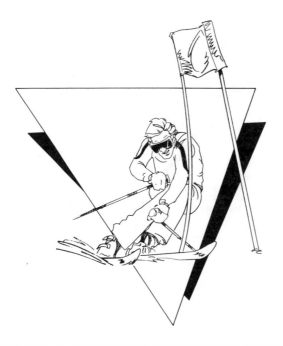

Figure 5.1 A dynamic GS turn.

through the turn; this gets you ready for the next gate and keeps you early." (See Figure 5.1.)

Developing Efficiency. Sometimes when you watch top racers move on skis, you know they're doing something incredibly efficient but exactly what it is is a mystery to you. This is how Bill Shaw, former pro racer and head of the racing department at Heavenly Valley, California, impressed me when I took a racing clinic from him at Squaw Valley this past season. Bill emphasizes using quick foot action, flexible ankles, and knee movement to initiate turning, along with taking a slight or more exaggerated lateral step out at the finish of one turn (in giant slalom), then immediately extending your legs and upper body into the new turn by directing them down the fall line in the direction of the next gate. (See Figures 5.2 and 5.3.)

As in most skill sports there are slightly different versions of efficiency. "In general," says Christin, "you want to be standing on the downhill ski, have a good pole plant, be relaxed, and ski relaxed. The latter will lead to flexibility, alertness, quickness,

Figure 5.2 Take a lateral step to adjust your line to the next gate.

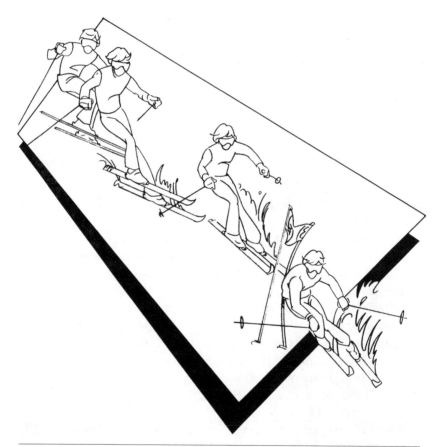

Figure 5.3 Stay on line by extending your legs and projecting your upper body toward the next gate.

Figure 5.4 Patiently ride the downhill ski until it comes around beneath you.

and the ability to recover from unexpected positions by instinctively utilizing basic skiing skills at high speeds.''

She regards the decision to go fast as one that should be made only after the basics are soundly ingrained in your skiing. ''Surprisingly, many recreational racers leave behind the basics when they think about going fast. They want so much to go fast that they come around and step off their downhill ski too early, instead of standing on it and letting it come around beneath them. They end up thrashing about and trying to go faster instead of calming down and using the basics to generate speed down the hill.'' (See Figure 5.4.)

Flexion and Extension.   Dirk's view of important skills for recreational racing is decidedly aggressive. He speaks about the importance of *flexion* (down pressure in the turn) and *extension* (getting up and away from your skis by moving your center of mass down the fall line).

Figure 5.5 Flexion and extension create angles and encourage the independence of legs—important factors in racing.

"Learn to use flexion and extension to control the weight on your skis so you can move from ski to ski. Phil and Steve Mahre say that ski racing is like running: one foot then the other. This is pressure control. Edging is a skill that develops when you learn to angulate (using ankles, knees, and hips). The biggest problem most people have is not being able to apply the above principles in their skiing because they ski with their feet too close together and sit too far back on their skis. They don't have the dynamic balance looked for in racing, and if the skis aren't apart, you can't create the necessary angles needed in racing." (See Figures 5.5 and 5.6)

"You've got to be able to move your skis around," says TJ. "Flexing and extending prevents you from skiing statically because even though you can get through widely spaced gates without a great deal of flexion and extension by using angles, unless you're relaxed enough to flex and extend your knees and ankles and use them as shock absorbers, you'll be bounced all over the course if conditions have gotten rutted and bumpy."

Jack's words of advice for both *novice* and *serious recreational racers*: "Novice: To enjoy skiing a race course, you need only have the ability to manage the hill it's on . . . with ease. Serious competitive racers: To actually do well in a recreational race, it's

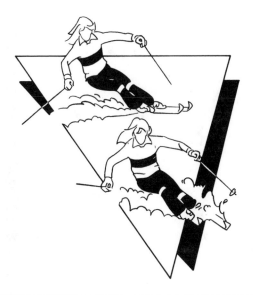

Figure 5.6 Use flexion and extension to control the weight on your skis so you can move from ski to ski.

important to be able to ski without skidding in your turns, pick the fastest line through the gates, and make scissor steps or diverging steps at the end of each turn to begin your next turn. This will add a whole new level of speed to your racing.'' (Chapter 8 contains drills that emphasize diverging steps; see ''Lack of carving.'')

The Fastest Line. Jack describes two kinds of lines: ''On a flat GS course, a late, straighter line is often faster; on a steep course, an early rounder line is often faster.'' By a late but straight line we mean the flag (gate) is where you begin your turn. Aim right at the flag and then turn. In this kind of course, your line gets straighter and straighter up to the last gate in the course. If there were one more gate on the course, you couldn't make it in time because by then you'd be so late in the course, skiing too straight a line. (See Figure 5.7.)

Skiing a straighter line on a flat course, you never really complete your turns. Rather, you leave your turning ski in the fall line as much as possible and step off of it to your new turning ski just before the original turning ski completes its turn. What

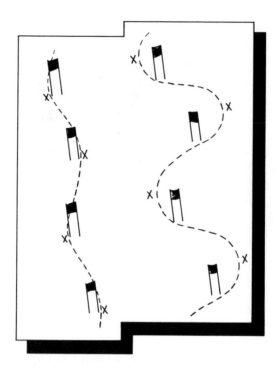

Figure 5.7 The fastest line through a course is the most efficient; it varies with the steepness or flatness of the course.

you're doing is riding a flat ski between gates and rolling it onto an edge to effect directional changes right at the gate. In effect, you're making long-radius turns through the race course.

"Importantly, when skiing a flat course," Jack says, "you want to have maximum edging while in the fall line. To avoid slowing down when you leave the fall line, you want to decrease your edging, that is, ride a flattened ski. Staying on a maximum edge as you leave the fall line leads to skidding. A good way to make the transition from your edged ski to a flattened ski is to *feather* the edging pressure to your skis by relaxing this pressure a little at a time as you leave the fall line. To maintain your line in progressively steeper race courses, you need increasingly more edge pressure as you cross the hill."

Chaz emphasizes the importance of being patient with your line in a GS-type course; in fact, one of the signs that you may indeed be skiing the correct, smooth, round line is the sensation that you're moving very slow. With a smooth, round line in such a course your speed is going to build turn to turn because there's no resistance due to a lack of jerky moves or skidding. Don't ski a smooth, round line by aggressively attacking the slope if conditions and course rhythm don't call for this tactic.

"Instead of trying to ski a good line," says Pete, "a lot of recreational racers get into a course and all of a sudden think they have to go much straighter than they have been in training to go fast. They think the straighter they are, the faster they are, but this isn't necessarily true. In fact, the fastest line is a steady line and knowing where you want to be on the course. It's important to look over the course, to study it. In a lot of recreational racing, skiers get up on the course, look down, and ski off with little idea of where the best line is."

Some Skills Are Tougher to Learn Than Others. I was curious about which skills my contributors felt would be the most difficult for the new-entry recreational skier to learn. Certainly, some of you reading this chapter aren't yet out there racing, whereas others of you have run a course or two with marginal or no success, but before I highlight their observations, I think it's valuable to consider George's perspective on learning: "Muscles tend to memorize certain moves, and to teach them something new by first having the muscles *unlearn* a movement pattern is extremely difficult. I would rather have skiers learn something new without thinking about changing old habits; the old habits will fall away if new, more efficient, and satisfying ones are learned." With this in mind you'll find that the following observations of difficult-to-acquire skills challenge you to learn rather than unlearn.

According to Mike, turning the skis on command or in relation to the line being skied through the gates is one of the toughest skills for the new recreational racer. "If, for example, I start skiers down a very easy slope and out of the woods comes an elephant, believe me, they won't hit it. If, however, I remove the elephant and put a gate in its place it's a whole different story.

"The problem is really an inability to change direction without skidding; it's the weakest skill in many recreational skiers. While good racers steer their skis to an edge, novice racers put their skis on edge. By steering a ski to an edge (gradually changing body angles and correctly using flexion in relation to the hill), you bend the ski and thereby engage its design to direct your ski through the turn. Just putting the skis on edge and expecting them to turn leads to skidding." (See chapter 8, "Skidded turns.")

Many top racers and coaches agree: Most skidding in the race course is undesirable and the result of inefficient turning skills and a poor or inappropriate line. It's difficult to accept that skiing a curvy line may actually be faster than skiing a straight line through a race course. "Personally, I fought it for years," says Mark. "I thought the fastest way between two points was straight, from gate to gate. Once you learn how the ski works and how to use those gates to your advantage, it starts to click that a smoothly skied line is fast. On a good line, there's no fighting with the course; it's like slow motion."

Christin elaborates on this theme: "Line is so difficult to learn because it goes against all of your natural instincts to try to go fast. You want to go straight down the hill, but you can't, regardless of your technical skills; you're on the wrong line and you can't fight the mountain. Things go wrong when you're off line; skiers fight it at all levels, including World Cup.

"I was involved in a Pro-Am Skiing event one year where I helped Danny Sullivan, the race car driver, learn to ski gates. He was just learning to ski, but was a great learner. I told him all these things about how he'd have to start his turns above the gates and so on, and he understood immediately. He said it was just like race car driving: 'You don't go into a turn at 150 mph, you have to bank out first and then come underneath, even slow down sometimes in order to gain more speed afterwards.'

"From there on teaching him was pure fun. He really had the picture of rolling into a turn. He knew from driving that you don't go into a turn cranking it. As in auto racing, in ski racing (giant slalom) you actually begin the turn well before turning, accelerate once in the turn—not to begin it—and apply pressure and power to control the turn. This is a difficult concept for new racers to learn . . . but they must if they want fast times."

Jack is in agreement on the importance of skiing the most efficient line, yet adds, "the ability to lift the tip of the inside ski and drop the inside hip into the hill at the end of the turn, while staying real square (upper body) to the fall line [recall Armstrong's comments] is tough for recreational racers to learn. When they do, their race times and overall performance improve." (See chapter 8, "Lack of edge control," *long-leg, short-leg;* "Over-rotation of upper body," *inside ski steering.*)

"It's the ability to balance on one ski and turn it in both directions, the effective use of lower body rotation, and understanding the difference between slalom and GS turns," says Chaz, "that are tough for the recreational racer." There are drills that address the first two problems in chapter 8, *single ski skiing* in "Lack of variety in turning," and the section on upper body rotation. With respect to the third, Chaz has an interesting way of discovering this difference. "It's all in the length of the turns. In a slalom course you will make short-radius turns with less time on your outside ski. In GS, it's just the opposite: You spend more time on your outside ski, thus, a longer radius turn.

"A good way to practice the difference of the two in your free-skiing is by counting and keeping the steady cadence one, two, three. You have a one-count turn, a two-count turn, and a three-count turn. Your slalom turns would be: 1, 1, 1, 1; right, left, right, left, each count being a turn. Your GS turns would be 1, 2, 3 right turn; 1, 2, 3 left turn.

"Try your GS turns as round and smooth as possible, realizing that in GS instead of in slalom, you'll feel your outside ski accelerating as it is coming to the number two in the count (the middle of the turn). Toward the number three count of the turn, you'll feel more work on your outside leg as you are fighting gravity and the force at the end of this turn. Then, at the number one count of the next turn, you'll feel relaxed as your ski flattens and glides.

"A good way to develop a sensitivity for these differences in turns is to go out free-skiing with the task of making a combination of count turns. Do four turns with a three-count; then four with a one-count; back to three-count. There's also a two-count turn. Your task is to count aloud or to yourself as you turn, allowing your counting cadence to dictate your skiing. You don't want to be counting in a race course, though, unless it's a practice course. There's plenty else to concentrate on."

Try to incorporate these techniques into your race-specific skiing: (a) Ski bumps for a couple of hours and then use the race course for running practice gates to test your endurance and ability to ski the course with a measure of precision; (b) ski powder for several hours and then try the race course to test your versatility; and (c) free ski until the race course is about to close and its ruts are fully developed, then ski the ruts hard for practice.

Sometimes, maybe too many times, I move into the starting gate of a giant slalom course, thinking speed and aggressiveness; it's a wild feeling that comes over me. I light off down the course looking for the underside of that edge, ignoring the fact that an efficient line might well be a faster way from start to finish.

Taking this same attitude of madness into slalom racing doesn't produce the same results. According to Fritz Vallant, "You need patience in slalom. In fact, it's one of the hardest things to develop. You just can't rush it in slalom; you can't be in too much of a hurry."

Indeed, there's plenty to concentrate on in racing: starting; maintaining momentum; focusing on the first two gates; watching your line; recovering; looking ahead; adjusting to rhythm changes in the course; and finishing. In general, you have to concentrate on your *racing strategy* while maintaining a large measure of patience.

Racing Strategy

"Look ahead!" says TJ. "That's the only thing we'll say on race day; look ahead so you'll have an open mind and see what's ahead of you."

Dirk elaborates, "When you look ahead, you get that early line [i.e., turn well ahead of the gates] and achieve better balance. An early line is the key and by looking ahead you'll know when you don't have it. Even more, by looking ahead you won't hook your tips."

Look ahead, not to the gate in front of you, but to the gate beyond the gate you're approaching; how it is set will determine the line you take through the gate immediately in front of you. Further, looking ahead involves focusing your eyes on the fall line, hanging tough, and not being distracted by Mike's elephants.

Tactical Advice. While all coaches and racers agree that looking ahead is paramount to good racing, a good deal of tactical advice is offered as well. For example, Jack says, "If you want to win, you've got to think about your strategy. If it's a one-run race where you run in the order of your sign-up, you might want to consider the snow. If it's soft, you might want a few skiers to go before you to scrape away the loose snow. If it's a two-run race where both runs count, the order of running in the first race will be reversed in the second. You've got to think about where you want to run with respect to the snow conditions.

"There's something else to consider, and that's the toughness of the hill and course when both runs count. You might want to take it easy on your first run, and then punch it on your next. There's no fun in blowing-out in the first run in a two-run race."

Confidence in Your Plan of Attack. To Chaz, racing strategy is all in the line you take and the self-confidence you take with you into the race, especially when it's head to head racing. As Chaz sees it, "You have to have a heck of a lot of self-confidence if you're going to run head to head. When standing in the start, you've got to build yourself up to make your best run. Your concentration level should be high, and directed to the first and second gates. From here, you rely on what you have previously learned about the course from studying it.

"Even if you haven't done it before, you should try studying a course by at least 'slipping' it [sideslipping your skis through the course and around each of the gates]. Study its steepness, check for any rhythm changes, and determine how you'll go into and come out of these transitions. In time and with practice, you gain the ability to retain what you see on the course and use it.

"You see, there's a war going on down there, and you're going to attack that course with all the strategy you can muster. Your knowledge of the course and the line you'll being skiing are going to govern your plan of attack. If you take too straight a line on a course that seems any bit steep to you, it's going to be way too fast and way too late. You'll probably skid through most of your turns. While the rounder line will feel slower, it may prove to be a faster line."

Fine-Tuning Your Plan of Attack. "Another consideration in your plan of attack," Chaz continues, "is how aggressively you're going to skate out of the start. If you skate right up to the first gate, you've got no time to set a line. If, however, you can blast right by the first gate before needing to set a line for the second gate, skate like mad, but remember that skating is only efficient up to a certain speed.

"If the start is very steep, you might get only one skate after your start and be best off letting the skis run to prepare yourself for your first turn. Depending on how fast you are traveling, skating may not do you any good at the finish either. Sometimes the best thing to do is get into a tuck and sit back on your skis to allow them to run as fast as they can to the finish. If the snow is slow, however, or it's a flatter course, skating is going to be very important and you've got to fight all the way to the finish.

"A last strategy to consider is skiing the knoll. Any course is going to be steeper on the downside of the knoll, and whoever set the course is going to make this area of the course more turny than the rest of the course because it's going to put racers on a suicide mission if the gates are set too straight. So, a real good strategy to use as you approach a knoll, before you're at the knoll, is to start making your turns a little rounder than you had made earlier on the flatter part of the course. If you wait too long to change your line, you're going to skid a lot on those first couple of turns over the knoll, and whenever you're skidding, you're losing time."

Training Strategy. Other areas of concern for the serious recreational racer are the kind of strategy to employ in training for a particular race and the general strategy you embrace throughout the racing season. Mark has an excellent perspective on this: Slowly work up to races, taking each day's runs close to where they need to be on race day but stopping short of it. "In this way," Mark says, "I'm hungry each day I train. I get to the point of being satisfied with my training runs, tired, but not having skied that perfect run. This keeps me sharp when I go back out the next day.

"It's important to stay fresh all season. I think a lot of it's trial and error. For me, there was one year when I had trained a lot early in the season and by March, I didn't have anything left mentally. My skiing was okay; I was solid, but I was just going through the motions. There was no spark, no life in me. I was flat.

"I have blown a couple of races because of inappropriate training, thinking I hadn't done enough coming into the races. I didn't have that feeling of being ready, of being sharp. A couple of days before one race, I thought I should get in one more hard stationary bike ride, and frankly, I burned out my legs. I got into

the dual start and knew I wasn't going to beat that other guy;
I just didn't have it.''

Too Much Training. You hear World Cup skiers as well as
recreational skiers talking about overtraining. It's easy to suc-
cumb to the inclination to overdo it; it can happen with activities unrelated to your training. Pete speaks whimsically about
great powder days that led him astray; days when the fun of
powder led to hours of play and stiffness a day later. Christin,
too, remembers overtraining and says you can do it easily, ''By
simply skiing your buns off.

''You get so psyched up for a race and come out during practice thinking there are some things you've got to work on; thinking that you're not quite there but you desperately want to be
there. So, you absolutely fry yourself by going out, training, and
getting in the gates. Sometimes it really works, and you seem
to ski a little better the next day. I can remember a lot of times
when I got my skiing to be much better, but physically burned
out my legs. All the technique and improved skiing that had
resulted from the extra work was useless because I was drained.

''It's really a fine line where on one side you have plenty of
energy to go take a run or ski all over the mountain, but as far
as having that spark in your legs that's going to help you make
the recoveries and win the race, you don't have it. If you're just
a tiny bit over the line, it makes a difference.''

''It's true,'' says George, ''just a little extra training can throw
you off. A lot of racers overtrain physically to compensate for
being undertrained mentally. They lack confidence. They feel
doing more is better. The confident racers take a couple of runs
and know their timing is there. Those who doubt their timing
go out and ski 10 runs trying to find it. When it comes to race
day they've lost their sharpness.''

Be Confident and Have Fun. ''The key to racing strategy,''
George continues, is confidence. When you're sure of what
you're doing, and capable of doing, you perform well because
you're able to train with minimum effort, thus conserving energy
for varied training that will keep you fresh for each different
event. The key to prerace training is getting the maximum confidence out of the minimum training runs.''

Indeed, all racers can overtrain, though it may be that novice racers overtrain mentally and emotionally in addition to physically. Many feel unrealistic pressures to do well their first time out or to progress rapidly without training, coaching, or strategy. Fully cognizant of these struggles in beginning racers, Christin advises: "Seek your own level of performance on the race course. It doesn't matter if you go slow, it's fun just to make it through the course. You don't have to get out there and tear it up. The speed and your time are not the point at all. Having fun is the point, and negotiating the turns will provide it."

Starting. Skills aside, being relaxed in the start is important for many racers, whereas others use a reverse approach. "The way I get psyched up and ready to step into the gate is a bit unconventional, perhaps," says Chaz, "but what works for me is to think about something that makes me angry to the point where I feel fighting mad. Of course, I don't, but if you could imagine feeling like getting into a fight right there at the start, you'd know what I mean.

"It's that pumped up feeling where your eyes are open, adrenalin is flowing, and you're getting ready to fight. Think about something that's going to get you fighting mad, and take that adrenalin rush right into the starting gate. When you blast out of there, let that adrenalin propel you, never once letting up on the concentration you're directing to establishing your line by the first or second gate."

If you're more of an occasional recreational racer who comes out of the start rather tentatively, it might be that you are allowing this lack of momentum to set the pace of your race; this will most likely result in a lot of skidding because of a late line and a fear of carrying too much speed between gates. Why the tentativeness? A good deal of the time it's due to fear and intimidation of the starting ramp; unfortunately no strategy in the world can take away that fear. Increased exposure, on the other hand, will.

You'll never assume the attitude Chaz suggests unless you're over the fear and intimidation of the start. It's hard to get worked up only to step up to the wand and look fearfully down the starting ramp. You need to get out there and do some starts full blast by the first gate until you overcome this fear. Then, you'll be ready to look into specific starting strategy as suggested by Jack: ''If the start is steep, pole two or three times *quickly and forcefully*. Make sure your poles are stuck in the snow at your heels as you push off of them, not in front of you. It's essential to make this poling extremely quick: 1-2-3! When the start is flatter, double pole and skate, making sure you're pushing off an edge and propelling yourself with each skating step.''

If you observe ski racers, you know how they kick themselves up and project out of the start. They're using *kick starts* to build up as much forward momentum as they can before actually hitting the starting wand and triggering the timer. Kick starts aren't something you automatically do the first time, or first several years, in the gates; for the novice racer, this kind of start is definitely far less important than learning proper racing technique on the course itself.

Jack describes two kinds of kick starts. Both begin from the *ready position*: a low stance, knees flexed, your poles set firmly in the snow just the other side of the wand, and your shins approximately four to six inches from the wand.

1. Lift either leg approximately eight inches off the snow, keeping this ski parallel to the snow and the other ski in firm contact with the snow. When you're ready to start, stomp down very hard with the elevated ski. Use your ski's hitting the snow to trigger you to lift straight up and forward, simultaneously using your arms to push you out onto the course. (See Figure 5.8.)
2. Kick one foot back until it's extended behind you (knee relaxed) and only the shovel of the ski is in contact with the snow. When your leg is fully extended your arms straighten and push off to support your forward moving weight. At this point, you extend the stationary ski to match the kicked ski, which is actually on its way down. The swing of your two skis toward the wand provides complementary momentum to the work of your arms. (See Figure 5.9.)

To elaborate on number two, it's important to straighten your back and lift your chin to maximize the pushing effect of the arms and poles that propels you through the wand. Further, when

Figure 5.8 Make a decisive start.

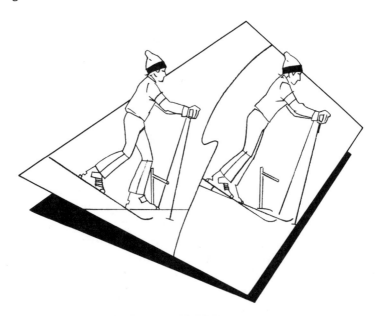

Figure 5.9 Jump starts are an option for the more experienced racer.

using this more active kick start, you want to use your kick to align your skis with the steepness of the ramp: The steeper the ramp, the higher your kick; the flatter the ramp, the lower your kick.

Figure 5.10 A time-efficient start involves pushing off down the ramp.

Time-Efficient Start.   As you might imagine, race day is no time to practice your starts. In fact, if you haven't practiced a kick start of one kind or another, there's no sense in using a poorly developed one in a race. It'll only slow you down. Instead, get out quickly by making sure you have a *time-efficient start*. To do this, assume the ready position, inching your shins a bit closer to the wand. When you're ready to start, extend your body by pushing off with your arms, and straighten your legs, pushing out down the ramp, not up. The weight of your body should be on your arms.

You lose time by going through the wand "flat" (i.e., standing tall and moving your skis through the wand and then down the ramp) and waiting until you're on the ramp to push with your poles. If you feel yourself tripping the wand before you've actually engaged your arms in pushing off with your poles, you're starting late. The clock has started timing your race before you've really started down the ramp. Pole yourself through the wand and if the course and your chosen line allow it, pole down the ramp nonstop for a time-efficient start.

You might want to try this variation of a time-efficient start: Do everything according to the preceding two paragraphs, but

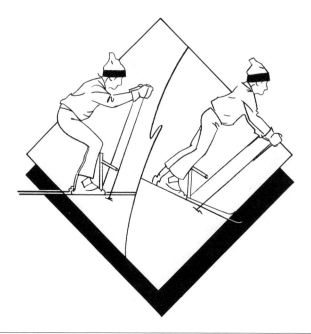

Figure 5.11 Snap your lower legs back to add more zip to your time-efficient start.

when you push off down the ramp with your arms, snap your lower legs back and let your legs follow your upper body down the ramp. (See Figures 5.10 and 5.11.)

The Psyche-O-Drama

Recreational ski racing has been marketed as social racing for the friendly competition it inspires among skiers of diverse skills. Yet, ski racing at any level is still sport, although the word *recreational* softens the sports ethic of racing, which is bluntly, competition and winning. Whether you're competing against yourself, the clock, a buddy, or a group of strangers who all want to win the same prizes as you, physical performance during recreational ski racing is still subject to the influence of your psyche and the games it plays.

From many years of coaching and competing in several team and individual sports, I have developed these postulates regarding the *negative effects of the psyche on physical performance*.

1. If you feel fearful, frightened, or insecure, your body will be tense, static, and less responsive to unexpected stimuli.
2. If you're unable to concentrate on what your body must do, you may give it confusing signals and cause it to react unpredictably.
3. Each time your ego negatively questions or challenges your body's performance, your body is bound to falter.
4. Each time you must think about what you're about to do based on factors outside of yourself (e.g., your coach, other racers, the weather, the course, what you're wearing, the skis you're skiing, etc.), you're vulnerable to actually forgetting what to do.

The postulates regarding the *positive effects of the psyche on physical performance include*:

1. If you feel confident, your body will respond more naturally and spontaneously.
2. If you can focus your attention on the task at hand before ever attempting it, you will perform better without ever giving it a thought.
3. If you can focus on the essential character of your capabilities (e.g., skiing loose, skiing fearlessly, etc.) you will more readily execute movements that complement this character.
4. It's usually best to compete with an empty mind.

A good example of the latter two positive effects is Mark's World Cup slalom race at Vail in 1984. "I had a pretty good first run. At the start of the second run, I felt myself really getting worked up. I just backed up at the start, seconds counting off, and shook my head and said to myself, 'I'm doing this for fun; loosen up!' You're racing because skiing is fun. If you get to a point where you get so worked up over it that you're nervous and tight, you're losing the fun of the sport. I just relaxed that day at Vail, and it was the best I've ever performed."

Mark prevented the occasion of the race from becoming his psyche-o-drama. Instead, he took charge. Unfortunately, most of us, particularly inexperienced racers, seem to engage in psyche-o-dramas that diminish our ability, rather than improve it. (Chapter 10 addresses many concepts that are helpful in preventing psyche-o-dramas in your racing.)

The psyche-o-drama occurs when we allow the fullest array of inputs (like those noted in the negative postulates) to cause us to question ourselves, mistrust our aspirations, and doubt our ability to execute the skills we know we possess. The psyche-o-drama does not occur when we use the positive influences of our ego, helpful mental directives, and the comments of others to uplift our physical performance.

It can be disguised in a lot of ways, but let's be candid: Racers on a dual course are there to compete. I have always raced in dual courses against people who want to beat me and the feeling is mutual: I do all I can to beat the racer next to me.

Dirk identifies the bottom line of competitive racing: ''In a ski race you're not competing against anyone but the mountain. In a way, this is really the best way to race, not thinking about what anyone else did. In reality, though, it gets competitive up there after a while. At these times there's no friendliness at the top of a race course. When the race is over and they've beaten you or you've beaten them, you can be pals again. Next race: It's just like climbing into the boxing ring again. After all, why bother going out to race if you're not going for it? You don't have to race; no one's making you race. Go out there and go for the best time you can, yet ski within your own limits until you're ready to experiment with that edge.''

To be sure, recreational racing is a competitive sport, but for all that I've noted about its competitive nature, it's often the after-race and awards ceremony antics that make the competition friendly. Similarly, the help and advice offered to new-entry racers at the top of the race course in the more standardized, nonprize races are both friendly and recreational. As TJ suggests, ''When new at racing it may be best for you to think about being friendly at the top of a race course. You'll be more relaxed and probably ski better than you would if you were worried about everyone who might beat your time.''

Some Typical Psyche-O-Dramas

I've seen the psyche-o-drama effect in operation at recreational races on several occasions. Here's one example: Kathy knows she is a better skier than Jill, and Jill agrees but is reluctant to admit it. Still, Kathy won't jeopardize this understanding by accepting Jill's challenge to race (Jill is a better racer). Jill actually believes that beating Kathy means something. Of course Jill should win, because Kathy doesn't even like running gates. Taking advantage of Kathy's insecurity, Jill chides Kathy about the results of their race. Kathy is put on the most uncomfortable spot of defending her skiing. Jill is put in the uncomfortable position of living up to her claims the next time they go skiing. Unreasonable tension has been placed on their skiing friendship by their skiing egos.

Here's another example: You're at the top of a race course, and Joe Jock (a good racer, but not great) is riding you about your new padded racing sweater. Jokingly (his ploy), he says things like "Do you ski as good as you look?" "Well, you look hot." If you're at all insecure about your racing, you might smile and shuffle away, wanting to avoid this guy; if you're "hot" and competitive, you might totally ignore him; or if you're inclined to a psyche-o-drama of your own, you might say, "Do we get to race each other?" "How do you keep from getting your arms bruised?"Or, "More appealing than your rags." Finally, if you're totally cool and secure, you'll converse with him about how much you like your new sweater and ask him how he's doing.

Understand, Joe Jocks are at every recreational race. You can usually locate them with your ears. Better to listen to a favorite fantasy or thought, and then go attack the race course.

Chaz offers a good example of a self-inflicted psyche-o-drama. "There's little as terrible as trying to ski a course when you've psyched-out yourself. There's a risk in watching too many other racers race. Somebody falling isn't a good image to let into your mind just before you're going to run. On the other hand, you might see somebody else who makes you take a second look and say, 'Wow, that guy can race! I think he's going to beat me.' That's another bad thought to have in your mind in the start."

Clearly, whatever we let into our psyche can have an effect on our racing. This is likely why Jack says, "Watch the best; ignore the rest." I'd add only, "Fantasize, don't fatalize." Jack continues, "The ego is prominent in many racers, and problems can always occur where the ego is involved. If you are at a race where you know only a few racers, watch the best. Be aware of the guy who's a pretty good racer, real well dressed, yet who loudly complains about the race, starting ramp, course, something [probably Joe's cousin]. Stay away from this racer; don't listen to him, he'll only be distracting. For sure don't watch weaker racers making mistakes. Be friendly with the good guys and your friends; they'll tell you things that may really help your racing."

Feeling Ready to Race

If it's not already obvious, you don't race against another person in a dual course; though you start at the same time, each racer is timed separately by timing devices set up for each course. "Nevertheless," as Mike points out, "racing head to head adds a positive complement to racing against the clock. A racer next to you, especially a little ahead of you, provides incentive to go faster because you'd like to beat the other racer due to your competitive nature. Maybe you'll even take a few chances; instead of taking it to the edge, you may go beyond it. In this way, competition is healthy!"

The most important part of getting ready to race may be in feeling ready to race. Of course it's relative, but I'd imagine few feel the pressure of the start of an Olympic or World Cup downhill. Pete is a proponent of the *empty mind* concept when it comes to being ready for a race. "By the time a race has come around, you definitely know if you're ready. You can feel it. It's sure not the time to start thinking about the technical things you need to do. It's too late for that. That's what you work on in training.

"Once the competition is here, you focus on the race and on trying to bring yourself to a level where you're excited about the race. You feel concentrated and ready, and avoid dwelling on any negative aspects of your racing. You don't think about having problems with anything, including other racers. You just don't put any energy into psyching yourself out; it'll kill you in the starting gate. Filling your mind with thoughts about how poorly you're skiing, how tough the course is, how good the other racers are will only lead to poor performance. You want to be free of thought and full of excitement about the race so you'll be quick and skiing like you really want to ski."

I can remember reading an interview with Jean Claude Killy conducted some 10 years ago in which he mentioned a theme that is apropos to our discussion of psyche-o-drama and empty-ing the mind of thoughts. Probably many of you have had direct experience with this particular mind occupier. As he suggested in the interview, it's impossible to be a consistent winner in ski-ing when you're in love. How do you deal with such emotions? Constructively used, they can be a positive force in your racing.

Being nervous is another obstacle to overcome at the start of a race. I asked Christin about this, assuming she's had her fair share of nervous moments as a ski racer. "When I get nervous," she begins, "it's usually because I'm thinking about the results. 'I've got to do this,' I tell myself. 'I'm in good position and I can't screw up.' It's these negative aspects of nervousness that are disastrous to racers. You can't relax with all of this chatter going on inside your head: the have-tos, shoulds, what-ifs.

"What you want to do is take all of this energy and be in the moment. *Be the race* and say, 'Let's do this; this is going to be fun!' Then go out and do what you really know how to do."

The Difference Between Mistakes and Failures

Although chapter 10 explores the psychology of high perfor-mance skiing, special attention must be directed here to the criti-cal difference between *mistakes* and *failures* on the race course.

If you recognize mistakes you make on the course as due to your own stupidity, you're interjecting failure into your racing. It's a difficult enough activity without adding new obstacles. If, however, you view mistakes as correctable errors in technique or strategy you're injecting success into your racing.

Know how to identify the mistakes you make in a race. Some examples are that you: were late at the bottom of the course; didn't get any extension; didn't look ahead; skied too straight a line; hooked a tip; eased up at the finish; skied too much over your skis; let your arm get behind you; didn't anticipate the knoll; got too much air; or raced with a lazy mind (i.e., had no inten-sity). Any of these errors make your performance seem pretty grim; it is a wonderful skill, however, to be able to isolate the mistakes you make rather than seeing your race as a failure. Having the knowledge to identify correctable mistakes is great; if you can focus on what you did incorrectly, you can at least begin to think of strategies to correct the problems. This is much more constructive than getting down on yourself for making mistakes.

Unfortunately, this knowledge works better on paper where our mind can't censor what we perceive, or judge what we do. Too often the trap we spring on ourselves is self-criticism (e.g., "What a lousy skier") and name calling (e.g., "You jerk." "You fool."). The tendency for inexperienced recreational racers is to remember their mistakes and continue to put themselves down throughout the rest of the race; this leads to further mistakes. In this way, each racer experiences failure and builds emotional and physical obstacles to effective racing technique. The same is true for most competitive sports.

Seasoned racers make mistakes, too, but they adapt, adjust, and remain tough mentally; they ski the race course! Recall Steve Mahre's medal-winning run in the '84 Winter Olympics Men's Slalom. As Dirk saw it, Steve made as many as five mistakes in a row, including two huge ones in his second run, yet still finished the race and won the silver medal (Phil won the gold medal with a great second run).

George says flatly, "There's no question about it, you always make mistakes; of course not every time you ski, but as you progress in skiing you continue to make mistakes. If you didn't, you'd never get ahead. The key is to make the least amount of mistakes."

For the mistake of being late for a gate, you can make a corrective move (lateral step) to get you back on line. Similarly, you can learn the skills to make numerous adjustments to your mistakes as soon as they happen, but you must stay mentally resilient throughout the race to shed the mental interference and keep your mind alert to make adjustments. Sometimes, though, you find that you've had to make too many adjustments in a race, and this is reflected in your time. Sometimes you don't finish the race. In either of these cases, think of success in terms of brilliantly adjusting to your mistakes.

There's nothing wrong with admitting defeat when you blow out of the course, but not at the cost of your next race or your emotional well-being. Racers make mistakes. If you haven't figured out ways to adjust to these and would rather tough them out mentally, you're leaving room for failure. If, however, you're willing to use the *witness* in your racing and seek appropriate drills, exercises, and coaching from a race coach, ski school, or clinic, you're inviting in elements of success.

The Witness

The *witness* is a handy concept that concerns the process of enlightenment. Though never intended specifically for ski racing, the witness does have an application to this situation. Who's going to argue with a concept that provides both enlightenment and faster race times? Here's the idea: Imagine that a witness resides atop your shoulder. This is a wonderful creature because it is completely nonjudgmental and has a vested interest in nothing else but recording what's going on as you ski.

This is an ideal partner to have along when you're running practice gates or free-skiing. This is what the witness might record during a practice race: moving slowly at start, early line, round turns, hit ridge, late over the knoll, lateral step adjustment, skidded, late again, arms forward, extreme extension, big lateral step, throwing body downhill, charging hill, early line, fast finish.

Although there is certain valuation in an *early* line, *fast* finish, and *slow* start, these are not reflections of the value (i.e., whether it's good or bad) but the product of what you're doing. Valuing statements might be *terrific* line, *outstanding* finish, and *terrible* start. Valuing statements trigger your ego to respond with feeling; nonvaluing statements point out what you're doing. Valuing statements make you feel something, thus altering your concentration of the course; nonvaluing statements tell you how to ski better.

If you want to give the witness a try, do so while free-skiing. Take a run and have the witness speak aloud through you (i.e., say what the witness observes). Practice this over and over again, first at slow speeds and then at progressively faster speeds. Once the witness works for you in your free-skiing, take it into a practice course. Just try it out; don't make the witness a big production and don't make it a regular part of your racing. It'll create too much chatter in your head.

Keep in mind that in skiing, the witness is only a drill; it is designed to help you identify correctable mistakes by learning to readily recognize what you're doing and where you're doing it in the race course, without having to constantly evaluate yourself as a racer. Of course, the witness will also help you to recognize correct technique, but if you get carried away with the good stuff, you'll miss the errors.

Correctable mistakes can lead to either success or failure; it depends on how you react to them mentally and whether you have the skills to execute the corrections.

Common Problems and Corrective Drills

Chapter 8 is dedicated to the discussion of common problems in recreational skiing, along with a detailed presentation of drills and exercises designed to help correct these problems. Many of these drills will apply to your racing technique as well, and when reference is made to them, perform them as designed, with racing at the back of your mind.

It is essential to understand that while some of the drills are more or less isolated to one part of the body or one aspect of your skiing, the elimination of your difficulties is due to a combination of drills rather than a single drill or exercise.

As Chaz says, "Directing drills to one problem works for some people, but I've found the best way is to keep shaking up the drills and exercises. If it's an upper body problem, we work upper body and lower body, mixing them up. I've found that up to 50% of the time when I work the lower body (for an upper body problem) and get the lower body to function better, the upper body naturally does its job better."

The following problems and drills were identified by Mike, Chaz, Dirk, TJ, Fritz, Pete, and Jack. Reference to chapter 8 drills are made by noting the section in which these drills are found.

Braking With Skidding

Putting the brakes on is a common error among recreational racers. As Jack says, "They use their turn to slow up, instead of using the direction in which they're traveling after they've turned to control their speed." Their turns aren't rounded or smooth; a rounded turn would be easier to control at variable speeds. Too much uncontrolled speed in a very controlled space (e.g., the gates) leads to putting on the brakes in self defense. You should never ski a race course defensively! (See "Skidded turns," "Speed control," and "Edge control.")

In addition to *hot wedges* ("Edge control"), Jack suggests a more advanced drill, *javelin turns*, to simulate at a slow speed the pressure and angles generated in a high speed GS turn. Javelin turns are done on an intermediate slope by beginning in a slight wedge. Ski slowly across the slope and once you've picked up some momentum, lift your uphill ski off the snow and point it across your downhill ski as you're traversing the hill. This is a very aggressive pointing of your uphill ski. It should cross over the top of your downhill ski about a third of the way from the tip, creating approximately a 30 degree angle at the crossing of the skis. To effect this angle, your uphill ski boot should be just in front of your downhill boot and facing down the hill, knees slightly flexed, and hands and arms waist-high and pointing down the fall line. (You may want to drag the tail of your "javelined" ski to add stability and allow you to get the fullest range of pointing.) (See Figure 5.12.)

What you create with this drill is an alignment of your uphill ski with your center of mass as it faces down the fall line. By doing this, you exert pressures on your downhill hip and leg that keenly resemble the pressures you feel when moving over your downhill ski and dropping your hip into the hill while racing.

When you're ready to turn, move your javelined ski back just a bit and place it on the snow. Simultaneously lighten your downhill ski and you'll turn very smoothly on the old javelined ski; by being placed on the snow in a converged or stemmed position, the latter will immediately edge and become your new turning ski. As soon as you begin turning, javelin the new inside ski and

Figure 5.12 You may want to drag the tail of your javelined uphill ski to aid balance.

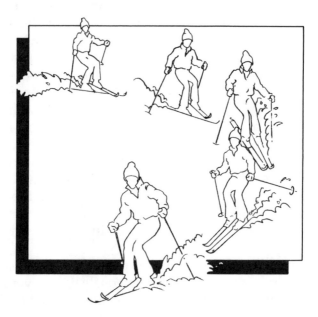

Figure 5.13 When you want to turn, step onto your javelined ski and steer it into and through the turn.

hold it until your next turn upon which it will become the new turning ski. Do this repeatedly down the mountain in rhythmic, linked, medium-radius turns. (See Figure 5.13).

Lack of Upper and Lower Body Separation

Chaz expresses concern about skiers' lack of aggressiveness, overrotation of the upper body, and failure to look ahead in the race course. This last difficulty can be addressed by learning to ski with your eyes ahead and off the snow: *target skiing* (''Tense and static skiing'').

An exercise he recommends for working on the alignment of the upper and lower body is to ski away from the sun on a gentle slope and look at your shadow in front of you. ''If you over-rotate in your skiing, you will find that as you watch your shadow one of your hands will disappear in each of the turns. What you want to do is keep your hands steady in that shadow, out beside the body'' (''Overrotation of upper body'').

Lack of Aggressiveness

Chaz offers an interesting perspective on aggressiveness. He's convinced that it is essential to racing, but concedes that in the absence of aggressiveness, an alternative would be to have superior skills that were reliable on the steepest of terrain. ''If you could ski the steepest terrain with confidence, even without aggressiveness, most courses wouldn't seem that threatening.'' In a roundabout way, aggressiveness is a racing skill, too. If you don't have it, you must rely on superior skills.

Lack of Pole Plant Rhythm

For slalom racing, Fritz emphasizes the importance of the single connected action of the skis rebounding, the pole being planted, and the shift to a new downhill ski; this complete action precedes each new gate of the course. It's a combination of quick moves, accompanied by the arm of the pole-touching hand being moved into the body immediately and rhythmically after each

Figure 5.14 Practice dynamic short-radius turns.

pole plant. This will help skiers avoid catching their arms on gates when running a tight slalom course.

A drill for working on the rhythm of planting the pole and then moving in the arm is to ski an intermediate or lower run making short-radius turns. Plant the pole with each turn and after touching the pole to the snow, bring your arm in to your waist. If you're correctly skiing a series of short-radius turns, by the time you bring one arm in, the other will be engaged in a pole plant. (See Figure 5.14.)

Lack of Knee and Foot Action in Slalom

Understandably, Fritz says, ''Giant slalom is much easier to learn for beginning racers than is slalom.'' One of the reasons is that the former allows more wide open turns and more time to react and respond to your mistakes. Slalom is much quicker. Whereas in the giant slalom you use hips, knees, and ankles, in the slalom you use primarily knees and ankles, having time only to react, not think!

Here are three drills to work on using the knees and ankles in your turning:

1. Hold your poles out in front of you and across your body. Make short-radius and short-swing turns by pressing down

Figure 5.15   Have fun working your skis.

and to each side with your knees only! Don't use your hips;
let your ankles flex forward to accommodate the action of
your knees. With each flexing of the ankles and action of
the knees, allow a slight rowing of your poles to the side
of the turn. (See Figure 5.15.)

2. Along with another person, take hold of one end each of
a 7- to 8-foot bamboo pole (or loop your poles together).
Designate one of you to call out the cadence and sync-ski
down an intermediate slope doing short-radius turns; the
emphasis should be on turning with your knees and
ankles. (See Figure 5.16.)

3. Create a funnel corridor, or use a slope that's appropriately designed. Ski down making short-radius turns at the
top moving toward more short-swing turns as you reach
the narrowest part of the funnel. Again, emphasize turning with the knees and ankles. (See Figure 5.17.)

Please note: In slalom, the knees and ankles initiate the turn
while the feet are actively steering the skis throughout the

Figure 5.16 Pairing up and turning can be challenging and satisfying.

turn. The angles created by the knees and ankles and the effect of these on the sidecut of a slalom ski, as well as its other properties of design, lead to dynamic turning (see Appendix).

Using the Downhill Ski Properly

Something of concern to giant slalom racers in particular is the instrumental role of the downhill ski. Too often, skiers don't trust the downhill ski enough to just stand on it and ride it through a turn. If they would, their racing would greatly improve.

To become more familiar with the downhill ski's function, try this drill from Pete that's done primarily on the uphill ski. Traverse across an intermediate slope standing only on your uphill ski. When you are ready to turn, lead your upper body into the turn, plant your pole, and feel the uphill ski roll onto its inside edge and become your new downhill ski. As soon as you turn across the fall line, move off the downhill ski and onto the uphill ski; repeat the drill. Continue for an entire run down the mountain.

Another of Pete's drills puts a heavy emphasis on your downhill ski. Go to an intermediate slope and make a series of long-

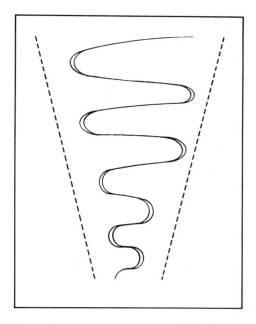

Figure 5.17 Start with a short-radius turn and progress to more of a short-swing turn.

radius turns top to bottom, stand only on your downhill ski at all times, and float the uphill ski off the snow. To add variety to both of these drills, do them in varied terrain including slush, bumps, steeper or gentler terrain, and even several inches of new powder. Ice is not recommended.

Other problems noted by my contributors:

1. *Static skiing*: Dirk, "Work your skis; move them around."
2. *Lack of independence of skis*: TJ, "Get your feet apart."
3. *Lack of precision*: TJ, "Go out and leave your signature in the snow; make arcs."
4. *Lazy free-skiing*: Chaz, "Too much free-skiing without a sense of discipline and aggressiveness to it leads to a lazy attitude and a skiing style that isn't primed to meet the precision demands of a race course."
5. *Bending over at the waist*: Dirk, "Too many people go to the race course and say, I'm going to race; I'm going to get low, and instead of skiing the course like they free-ski, they bend over at the waist and try to get low like

racers. They're not flexing and extending. They should ski tall; the flexion at the gates will start to come naturally.''

6. *Lack of good inside-outside edge balance*: Chaz, ''Not enough recreational racers feel ready to ski both edges when skiing on one ski. Being versatile is being able to stand on your right ski and turn right as well as left. You can get yourself out of any situation when you're able to ski both edges of both skis at any time.''

The following are additional drills and exercises offered by my contributors. Numbers 4 through 12 come specifically from Jack.

1. *Wedge hoppers*: (see chapter 8, Speed control) This develops precision edging and balance skills, particularly important for slalom.
2. *Sequential leg drill*: (see chapter 8, Erratic pole use and rhythm) This develops rhythmic pole planting for slalom, quickness from ski to ski, and independent leg action.
3. *Boot touch*: Touch your downhill boot with both hands at the time of maximum control and edging in the turn. This teaches you the kinesthetic feeling of getting over your turning ski in giant slalom, keeping your arms forward down the fall line, and dropping your inside hip into the hill.
4. *Hot wedges*: Use these to experiment with skiing on your heels to experience the sensation of your skis speeding up, not slowing down, during a carved turn.
5. *Accelerated turning*: Find an easy, unpopulated run and while turning try to accelerate as much as possible. You'll be skating off your outside ski right in the fall line (or perhaps a hair outside) to generate speed. Actively feather the edging pressure as you leave the fall line. Learn to glide out of the turn on a flat ski, edging briefly in the fall line.
6. *Ski the troughs*: Specifically, ski in the run-out of a mogul field, placing your skis against the sides of these and pushing off. Do it carefully and slowly; skating down the fall line can be dangerous.
7. *Master the step turn*: Take a diverging or lateral step with your uphill (inside) ski away from your turning ski and thereby establish your inside ski as the new turning ski. Learn to use it in all types of conditions and on all slopes,

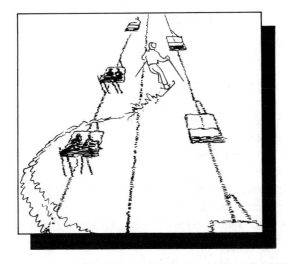

Figure 5.18 Slalom the shadows of the chairs above you.

so you won't ever have to think about it when the need to rely on it arises.

8. *Chairlift slalom*: This can only be done under chairlifts at certain times of the day when the sun is overhead. Ski beneath the chairlift, using the moving shadows of the chairs as slalom poles. This drill also gives great practice in rhythmic skiing. (See Figure 5.18.)

9. *Practice your start*: Do this on the side of a road or on a bump. First, though, practice your kick on the flats; once you possess the exact rhythm and timing, practice the start off the edge of a work road. Learn different ways to start.

10. *Shadow skiing*: Ski along the side of any course to which you have access safely, of course, and ski the course at the speed of the hill.

11. *Challenge skiing*: As you're skiing along, pick out spots, clumps of snow, or bumps that do not fall along the line of your skiing; go and turn around them. You'll be surprised at the extent of lateral movement you can achieve with this drill. It is a good confidence builder that sharpens quickness and versatility.

12. *Icy adventures*: Find short icy places off of which you can ski into the fall line. See if you can briefly grip the ice and then accelerate while maintaining control.

Summary

1. Properly running gates forces you to ski more precisely, use many skills, and employ your skiing senses and your kinesthetic memory; overall, it forces you to ski more reactionally.

2. In racing, fast doesn't always mean velocity. Fast is skiing smart: skiing the fastest line, using proper technique, making effective recoveries, concentrating on the course, and skiing with attitude.

3. In general, spend 60% of your skiing time free-skiing, 30% working on specific racing-related drills (practice courses included), and 10% actually racing.

4. In free-skiing you work on correcting your technical problems (while you're having fun playing with the mountain); when you're finally in the gates, you can ski more naturally. At the start of the season, free-ski 100% of the time (the first 10 to 20 days if you're a frequent skier).

5. Falling plays a beneficial role in learning to race because it helps you to appreciate what it's like to take yourself to the winning edge. Falling is not to be avoided if doing so causes you to ski more cautiously, more slowly, and less aggressively.

6. If you're afraid of speed and falling down, you're likely afraid to ski the fall line. You have to overcome your fear of speed and falling down to progress in ski racing.

7. The critical mind-set for the racer is one of remaining calm and staying focused on the important changes in the course's rhythm. To do this, you must ignore outside stimuli.

8. When you're first learning to ski, there's a lot of struggling and fighting to keep yourself together. As you become more comfortable and get more miles behind you, you realize you can work with the terrain and really play with the mountain. This same attitude can be carried into your racing.

9. A recreational skier who lacks conditioning and is skiing a hard, icy course will drift all over the course with wob-

bling legs and chattering skis. On rutted courses, this racer will lack the strength and stamina to meet the skill demands for actually using the ruts.

10. While you needn't be extensively fit when first learning to race, it helps; serious upper level skiers who want to rev up their racing profit greatly from being racing-fit. The best kind of training is that which you enjoy, of course, but for the highest return, make this training aerobic. This includes running, swimming, hiking, cycling, and aerobics classes: activities that make your heart and lungs work at a sustained level for at least 20 minutes.

11. The three Hs of advanced recreational (principally GS) racing: *hands* forward toward the next gate; *head* over your outside ski (when turning); *hip* (inside) into the hill (when turning).

12. The more you lift the uphill ski while turning, the more natural it is for your hip to fall into the hill and your downhill ski to hold its edge.

13. You've got to be able to move your skis around. Retracting, flexing, and extending your legs prevents you from skiing statically, especially in rutted and bumpy conditions.

14. Skiing the fastest line through a course, though not easily learned, is a skill that is highly efficient in getting faster race times. A fast line may seem slow and relaxed, and may be late (straight, turning at the gate) or early (more rounded, turning well before the gate).

15. A skill of great import to the recreational racer is being able to ski on one ski and turn it in either direction.

16. If you forget everything else while racing, at least remember to look ahead two gates ahead.

17. Slalom skiing requires great patience in its learning and pace in its racing. In slalom, start slowly and build up your rhythm; then build up speed. In GS, you need patience to ski an efficient line.

18. Without question, racing is competitive; everything that you think and feel may adversely or positively affect your performance. The elements of this fascinating psyche-o-drama emanate from within yourself as well as from others.

19. View mistakes as correctable errors in technique or strategy, regardless of how hard you've worked; if you

do so you're injecting success into your racing.
20. View mistakes as stupidity on your part and you're injecting failure into your racing.
21. Racers make mistakes. If you haven't figured out ways to adjust to these and would rather tough them out mentally, you're leaving room for failure.
22. Too often, the trap we spring on ourselves is self-criticism and name calling. A racer who brings failure into his or her racing builds emotional and physical obstacles to effective racing technique.

High Performance Tip #3

World Cup Racing

"It's so mentally challenging that you talk yourself into hating life," says Pete. "You wonder at times how long you can keep it up. It's grueling."

Indeed, the rigors of the day-to-day schedule with which World Cup racers must contend is both physically and mentally demanding. "It can get kind of lonely. The Europeans have family and friends to go home to after a race; we go to a crowded hotel room or van," says Mark. "You have to be able to rise above the demands of traveling and living on top of people, and not let these have an adverse effect on you. Sometimes you're with six to eight people you might not ordinarily hang out with. It's really an attitude adjustment of large proportions to race World Cup, especially as an American in Europe."

The Mahres (1985) say, "Ski racing for Americans in Europe is a test of mental toughness" (pp. 189-190). Yet, they note the heart of Christin's success in World Cup was not only that she was a fierce competitor and knew what was needed to win, but that she was outgoing and liked to have fun. "Christin was friendly. She never thought of herself as special, and she never insisted that people look up to her. It was this attitude that helped her succeed when she raced in Europe."

George is quick to say, "It's the racer who overcomes the stress of the World Cup schedule with determination and the desire to win who comes out on top. There are so many good racers and only a few who are great. The great ones are those with the greatest desire and who are motivated to win and ski consistently well.

"I think the reason one racer wins one day, and another the next day is due to fluctuations in desire and motivation. They're all in good shape, they're all strong, they're all fast, and most have the same qualities. The difference is a matter of desire.

"As far as technique, World Cup racers are highly individual. The basics are the same, but everybody skis a little bit differently depending on height, weight, natural skiing speed, body build, and reflexes. They ski to meet their personal needs, and it's their interpretation of skills that creates new ski racing technique. It's not we coaches who invent new technique, but racers. We watch them and learn by analyzing what they do. If we see a racer flying down the hill we say, 'My God, he is fast!' and we learn from aspects of his technique.

"A good coach has an eye to pinpoint things in the racer's skiing that contribute to his going fast. Most of the time, the racers themselves don't know what they're actually doing when they're creating new technique, they just know that they're going fast. The best on the World Cup have all the technique, power, strength, and attitude, and still ski by feel and instinct."

Summing it up, the Mahres (1985) write, "The racers who make it in the World Cup are the ones who can put aside the differences in culture, language, food, even the absence of simple things like a john in the room. They must be able to separate these things from their ski racing. They must be able to affirm to themselves 'The only reason I'm here is ski racing'" (pp. 189-190).

To *become* a World Cup ski racer is to continually work on sculpting and refining one's natural ability to ski fast and consistently well. Too much hot and cold and other racers will start breathing down your neck. The best must face what is sometimes tedious, often arduous dryland and on-the-snow training, coupled with the advice and critique of their coaches. This is a must to shape the kind of skier who can withstand the pressures of World Cup and be a member of the U.S. Ski Team. It takes skill, guts, determination, and heart—everyone accepts luck.

My work with the Ski Team Men's Slalom and Giant Slalom squad at their final pre-World Cup training camp at Copper Mountain (Winter 1986) helped me to appreciate the dymanics of training for World Cup and to sample the "soul" of these athletes: their drive to succeed, their team spirit, their lust for competition, and their love of life.

You have to wonder what motivates these young men and their coaches to train month after month for the opportunity to travel around the world, away from family and friends (many of these athletes and coaches are married) to be ski racers. Most have few or no sponsors yet work as hard or harder than other well-paid professional athletes. College degrees aren't unheard of, yet many forsake college to train to be racers—to be the best the U.S. has to offer.

Why would a coach with the breadth of experience of Jean-Pierre Chatellard ("JP" as he is affectionately called, who has coached the Australian, French, Spanish, and Swedish Olympic Teams) take on the challenge of a U.S. Ski Team that had recently lost Phil and Steve Mahre to retirement? Why would George Capaul devote a life to this sport, and to coaching all levels of racer—novice, recreational, amateur, professional, World Cup, and Olympic?

If one word applies to U.S. Ski Team coaches and athletes alike, it's *passion*; if one phrase applies, its *for the challenge*. In every sense of the word, but monetarily, these ski racers are professional athletes. These guys are for real; their coaches are gentlemen of sport. I am proud and honored to know them as athletes and men.

High Performance Tip #4

Principles of Recreational Slalom and Giant Slalom According to Fritz Vallant, Pete Patterson, George Capaul, and Chaz Kruck

Slalom is the quick race, giant slalom the fast race; your body moves quickly in slalom and travels at greater speeds in giant slalom. There's less time to correct mistakes in slalom and more time for recovery in giant slalom. Both, coincidently, require patience.

Principles of slalom:

1. Start off slow and build up speed as your rhythm develops.
2. The turning is done from the knees down with quick feet and flexible ankles.
3. Try to keep your upper body, hips, and hands moving forward toward the next gate at all times.
4. As you strive to move quickly from ski to ski, be patient and try to keep your upper body relaxed and square with the fall line.
5. Plant your poles immediately after passing each gate.
6. Plant your poles ahead of your center of mass by flipping your wrists *forward*, not to the sides.
7. The pole plant in slalom is a timing device that signifies the end of one turn and the initiation or beginning of a new turn. Properly timed, the pole plant helps to signal the release of pressure on your downhill ski so you can quickly get on your new turning ski.
8. The release of pressure on your downhill ski causes it to rebound, and thus you unweight as you transfer weight to your new turning ski—the former uphill ski.
9. Think "plant and up," right to left, left to right. When you plant your right pole (and your right ski *rebound unweights*) you extend up onto your left leg, which you've driven into the turn and toward the next gate. The extension and transfer of weight to the new turning ski is essential for bringing your hips around square to the next turn.

10. At the end of one turn (when you pole plant) there exists the state of counterrotation: Your legs are headed in the direction of the turn while your upper body is twisted or rotated away from the direction of the skis and toward the next gate. The amount of counterrotation will vary depending on the placement of the next gate. The pole plant serves to release the muscles that are holding your body in its counterrotated position.

11. When the body is released from its counterrotated position, it momentarily aligns itself square to the fall line before beginning to enter a counterrotated position for the next turn.

12. Sometimes, thinking left and right ski, rather than left and right turn, helps create a reactional attitude in slalom racing. Looking ahead in slalom helps you adapt rapidly to rhythm changes in the course.

13. In the flushes where the gates are set in a straight line, you must keep the hands forward and stay slightly forward on the balls of your feet so you can rely on very quick feet and knee movements to negotiate these gates.

Fritz and Chaz add when practicing slalom, try taking a free-ski run in between slalom runs to work on sharpening technique, and improving the rhythm of your short-radius turns on varied terrain, particularly with respect to changes in pitch, fall line, and snow texture.

Principles of giant slalom:

1. Ride your downhill ski for as long as possible and as soon as you get off it, move to your new turning ski quickly, without hesitation.

2. Drive your outside arm *out* and down the fall line to set up the pole-plant timing device to initiate the new turn.

3. Drive your inside arm through the gate to pass the gate without contacting it and to keep your body angulated in order to maintain an edge on your downhill ski.

4. Thrusting your hands forward and dropping your inside hip into the hill gradually toward the end of the turn creates a nice round GS turn, enabling you to carry speed turn to turn.

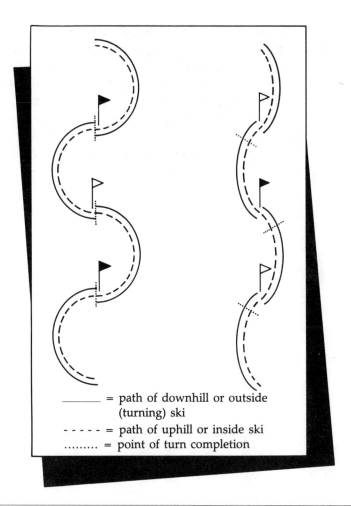

_____ = path of downhill or outside
(turning) ski
- - - - - = path of uphill or inside ski
.... = point of turn completion

Figure 5.19 On the left, a steep GS course; on the right, a flat GS course.

5. In most turny recreational courses, a higher, rounder turn is useful to stay on line for the next gate. To accomplish this, take a lateral step with your uphill ski just before getting off your downhill ski; that is, just after passing the gate.
6. Turny, recreational courses set on steeper terrain require a patiently executed and rounded turn with little scissor or lateral stepping of the uphill ski until the turn is completed.

7. Recreational courses set on flatter terrain will not be real turny, and to maintain speed, a scissor or lateral step with the uphill ski made early before the end of the turn is required. In effect, the scissor step actually completes the original turn. When this stepping is followed by a pole plant, the latter initiates *up-unweighting* into the next turn, thus releasing your muscles to make it easier for you to transfer weight to your new turning ski (the one you stepped).

Chapter 6

Special Situation Skiing

Difficult terrain can be tamed by discovering what it is about it you most fear.

One of the wonderful things about skiing is the variety of conditions and circumstances it offers. Few other sports offer such a range of challenges that may vary from minute to minute, hour to hour, day to day, slope to slope, or mood to mood. Versatility is no fool's goal in skiing; it's the spice of the sport. Come with us and ski a number of conditions, again, to broaden your versatility and sharpen your skills for high performance skiing. If you haven't given it much thought in the past, pay special attention to our discussion of a high performance way to approach your first day out this season; it comes just once a year!

A High Performance First Day of the Season

Situation: The first day of the season!

Conditions: The snow is just right and you and your equipment are ready to get started with the ski season.

Slope Traffic: A lot of first day skiers are out.

According to Mike, make this a high performance first day of the season! First, go to the very basics. Take an easy hill and go through *exercise lines*, a progression of exercises, that take you up a staircase to the level of skiing you had achieved by the end of the previous season. Rediscover what it feels like to be on the snow; find the center of your skis. Relax and don't muscle your skis around.

Instead of tipping your skis on edge right away, go out and do wedge turns for a half hour or so. Regrettably, a common fault of first day skiers is to be overanxious to get their skiing back to the level they left last season. On the first day out there's a greater risk of injury if you don't take it easy.

Do wedge turns; start out statically, then slowly add the active steering of your turning ski. Next, add movement by extending your legs to begin your turns and flexing your knees and ankles to complete your turns. Next add a more active transfer of your weight, foot to foot, leg to leg. Progress to an intentional lightening of one inside ski, then the other. Speed up and change the terrain until the lightened ski starts to match the other. At this point, you will begin to experience the inside or uphill ski becoming involved with steering.

Let the skis skid to make the turns very round and slow; it's almost like manipulating your skis to drag out these turns. You want to get a complete feel of the skis on the snow. These are patient turns, allowing you to gradually adjust to the conditions rather than rushing movement patterns to suit your fantasies of last season.

The ill-result of not slowly reacquainting yourself with skiing the first day out is that you miss the opportunity to make subtle corrections in your skiing NOW. The way you approach a wedge turn, extension and flexion, pole action, independent foot-leg action, and steering with your inside ski can be subtly corrected early in the season before last year's old habits reappear.

Time spent sharpening these skills by using very basic slow-speed exercise lines will automatically incorporate them into your skiing. Importantly, don't rush things; take some time to allow your natural movements to re-emerge. Don't start at the top on the first day. This is a process of going through your basic skills and recalling those higher performance skills that got you to where you left off last season.

Poor Lighting

Situation: Everything looks flat (i.e., the lighting is such that it's difficult to discern contours in the snow, angles, ridges, etc.). Everything looks the same and the light is institutionally drab.

Conditions: The snow is wonderful, if only you could see it! It's firmly packed (from machine-grooming), with a few bumps and ridges. You're faced with cold air, a slight breeze, and cloudy skies.

Slope Traffic: Sparse.

According to Mike, these may be frightening conditions, especially when the light changes rather suddenly. In poor lighting, you're denied the all important and customary visual inputs that help your body to make balancing adjustments while skiing in motion. To counteract this loss, it's critical to accentuate the inputs received through your feet, hands, and ears, for example. The first recommendation for skiing in poorly lit conditions is to reduce your speed. This doesn't mean your turns are shorter in radius; rather, ski medium-radius turns. Ski centered over your skis and taller so that you can make subtle adjustments to the terrain you can't see, which might include rolls, bumps, ridges, or characteristics in the slope that resemble both concave and convex formations of the snow.

Skiing centered over your skis, standing tall, and relaxing makes it easier to quickly adjust to varying conditions. By standing tall you establish the sufficient *range of motion* needed to make the subtle adjustments in your skiing. By skiing more slowly, you feel the direction and character of the slope. If you're skiing fast in this poor lighting, you may find a tendency to lean back or into the hill, which may throw you off balance when the terrain changes abruptly.

In addition to slowing down and staying tall (a) open your stance, which will give you a stabler base of support (balance); (b) ski within the range of trees or obstacles that provide a focal point. Use these shadowed areas near trees, large rocks, and other objects as visual aids to maintain balance, because with them you can *read* the terrain, how it slopes or falls away; and (c) look ahead, as this will establish a horizon and aid in balancing.

At the outset, when skiing in poorly lit conditions listen to what your skis tell you about the conditions via the tactile sensations transmitted through your feet to your brain as well as sounds transmitted through your ears. Listen, feel, sense, adapt, and be guided in poorly lit conditions. Remember, ski slowly, stand tall, and be in control. Trees and other obstacles will help you immensely.

Try a Pole-Sensing Exercise

Select a turn with which you feel comfortable; for example, a medium-radius turn. Open your stance and look for obstacles to establish your bearings. Lightly drag your poles and feel what they tell you about the snow, slope, and terrain. This will also help you to keep centered. As the pitch of the hill changes, the feel of your poles change accordingly; that is, if the hill slopes to the left, you'll feel your left pole dropping away from you. In this way, your poles serve as additional sensors to your feet.

The more information you can acquire about the particular skiing conditions, the more you will be able to ski them in a high performance mode.

Skiing Crud and Liking It

> *Situation:* You're mumbling to yourself, "So this is why it's called crud" as you struggle to turn out of this heavy and awkward snow.
>
> *Conditions:* Two days ago a foot and a half of snow fell, and by now it has settled over the mountain. On the groomed runs the snow is smooth and fast, but on a number of other runs, like the one you're on, there are 8 to 10 inches of cut-up snow, with mounds as deep as a foot. The snow gives, but it's demanding of you. The sun is out, lighting good, and there is moderate wind.
>
> *Slope Traffic:* Light.

According to Mike, skiing in the crud is another one of the more exciting challenges of skiing. To be truly versatile and high performance skiers we must learn to ski crud. Crud skiing is one of the least predictable conditions to ski; it can occur anytime during the season. To enjoy skiing crud and difficult snow, you must incorporate aggressiveness, a high degree of ski-snow sensitivity, a blocking pole plant, the active extension and retraction (pushing out and pulling in) of your legs, balance, and strong rotary and steering skills. Lacking all or any of these, crud may seem foreboding, but by approaching the condition with some preparation and the basic *guide and ride* technique, you can learn to make crud an enjoyable part of your skiing. But first, consider what not to do when skiing crud.

1. *Don't* try to ski crud on flat to moderate terrain—the lack of momentum you'll generate will lead to a lack of turning power.

2. *Don't* try to ski crud until you're psychologically ready to go for it—a tentative attitude leads to a lack of aggressiveness.
3. *Don't* try to aggressively ski crud until you're confident making parallel turns or up-stem type christie turns (i.e., skidded turns initiated by the brushing out of your outside or downhill ski) on groomed slopes.
4. *Don't* try to ski crud until you've developed a sense of pole use in your skiing.
5. *Don't* try to ski crud until you've gained some confidence in moguls and steeper terrain.
6. *Don't* ski crud in closed areas.

You might also want to avoid long-radius turns because they present too many chances for your skis to get into *railroad tracks* (the impressions made by other skiers). In a long-radius turn there's a much longer gliding phase that's accompanied by little steering. The risk in crud is getting caught in these tracks at the point in your long-radius turn where you're not steering. In medium-radius turns, you apply stronger rotary skills and steering and are more able to brush away the snow in these railroad tracks. Nevertheless, muscling your skis around with abrupt movements might just trip you up. If the slope is quite steep, don't hesitate to use the more aggressive, sometimes more abrupt, short-radius turn.

In most crud conditions, be more *compact* on your skis; in other words, become shorter. It is possible to become stronger in this position (Mike claims to be) and better able to deal with unexpected changes in the conditions and terrain. If you stand too tall, you are more vulnerable to being rocked backward or thrown off balance. In the lower position, you are stronger and have better control in putting pressure on the skis as needed because of the shorter angles that are created.

Guide and Ride

Foremost, use gravity. The steeper the terrain, the greater your momentum, and the easier it is to *guide* or steer your skis into each new turn. Knowing you have gravity on your side, makes it easier to maintain an aggressive, ''I can ski this,'' attitude.

Here's a game plan for beginning crud skiing.

1. Generally, ski with a friend just in case either of you need help in the event of an untimely tumble.
2. Sample the crud by standing, walking, hopping, and pushing your skis around in it.
3. Summarize the run you intend to take, and identify suitable exits you can make if the crud's too unfriendly.
4. Start into the terrain with an aggressive attitude, carrying good speed into your early turns. If the conditions call for it, you can decrease your speed. When you start off slowly, however, it's not easy to accelerate.
5. Try a few medium-radius turns to a planned exit, and see how the crud feels. As a beginner, you may need or want to rotate your whole body to get your skis into each new turn. Do this relative to the turn dynamics discussed later, and continue to practice it until you develop the confidence to keep it up for an entire run. In time, you'll begin to slow the rotary movements of your upper body while actively extending and retracting your legs as you leap out of one turn and into another. (In heavy crud, 90% of your turn is done during the leaping phase in which your legs are retracted and your feet are steered or *guided* in the direction of your new turn.)
6. Use your pole plant as an additional sensor for your feet and to momentarily block your upper body from moving down the hill while your legs are pulled out of the snow, *guided* into the new turn, and extended back into the snow. The extension and bending of your skis against the snow actually pushes the snow downhill, creating a platform against which you momentarily *ride* your skis and off of which your skis are deflected as you retract your legs and *guide* your skis into your new turn.
7. Go into crud knowing at first that the crud will probably get the better of you, but that after repeated exposure you'll have your day too. Try not to be discouraged by unexpected tumbles. If, as toddlers, we gave up after unexpected tumbles, we'd never have learned to walk. And let's face it: no walking, no running.
8. Ski crud like a kangaroo, using the strength of your legs

to bound in and out of the snow. If you can master difficult snow, your lightness and ski-snow sensitivity in powder and other snow conditions are bound to excel.

Heavier Crud

If you're a less aggressive skier, you might find simultaneous leg-foot rotation works well for you because you're moving the skis as a single force against stubborn snow. Aggressive skiers often use this approach in heavily chewed-up, deeper crud. Along with simultaneous leg-foot rotation, this kind of condition is best handled by skiing with a compact stance and by keeping your skis on top of the snow. To accomplish the former, use retraction (i.e., bringing your knees up toward your chest); to accomplish the latter, lighten the pressure of your skis on the snow by keeping your toes up off the snow. Surprisingly, the focus on keeping your toes off the snow will help your skis ride atop the snow. (See Figure 6.1.)

Figure 6.1 Keep your feet light, toes off the snow.

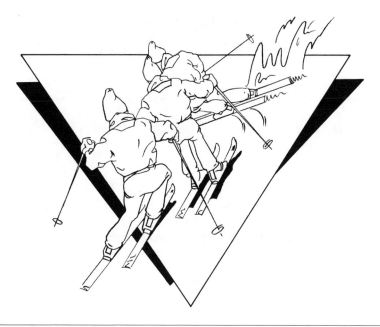

Figure 6.2 In heavier crud, independent legs can begin and simultaneous legs can finish your turns.

Be Versatile

As a few general rules for crud skiing, try to use a combination of independent and simultaneous foot-leg action and go into these conditions with an aggressive attitude. It's usually much easier to "roll back" an aggressive attitude to suit less demanding conditions than it is to muster an aggressive attitude in more difficult crud.

Use independent foot-leg action to guide or steer your skies into your turns, then engage simultaneous action to ride your skis through the belly and finish of your turns. The independent foot-leg action is highly instrumental in achieving proficiency and aggressiveness in the crud; the simultaneous foot-leg action helps to stablize the completion of your turns. (See Figure 6.2).

Want to learn to ski crud? Request a ski school lesson, private or group, that's oriented to these conditions. Don't hesitate to investigate this possibility; if enough students request such a class, one will likely be scheduled. Expect crud to be a bit of work at first but later you'll probably ski it for fun!

Spring Slush
or Soft Snow Skiing

Situation: Spring skiing in the late morning into the early afternoon; we're talking slush!

Conditions: Good snow coverage, no obstacles, and bright sunshine: mandatory spf-15 sunscreen weather.

Slope Traffic: Crowded.

According to Mike, spring skiing in the slush is another one of those interesting, often intimidating, conditions we need to add to our high performance versatility. Although soft spring snow that turns to wet, sticky slush is not always attractive to many hearty winter skiers, these conditions can be used to help strengthen your appropriate use of rotary skills, edge pressure, fore and aft leverage, and balance, as well as providing a marvelous opportunity to expose yourself to a variety of otherwise foreboding terrains.

More good news about spring's warm days and cold nights is the production of "corn snow" conditions—little ball-bearing or "kernals" of snow that develop from the overnight freezing and early morning thawing of surface snow. For high performance skiers, *corn snow* offers wonderful opportunities and adventures, especially those unique skiing conditions in wide open terrain and the exploration of hidden, inbounds, tree-lined corridors that receive early morning sun at just the right time. Foremost, think of this corn snow as an opportunity to be mentally aggressive yet physically subtle in your skiing. You go into the condition with a tough, "I'm going to get the most out of this condition," attitude, yet seek to ski lightly, even artistically— you and the skis and the snow are one in motion.

As the day goes on and more and more people ski the corn, the once-inviting snow changes to slush. The warmer the weather gets, the deeper and wetter the snow becomes. Still, few complain about the sunny days, short sleeve shirts, lightweight pants, and attractive tans. The problems arise when the natural dirt, pine tar, exhaust from grooming machines, dust, oil, and other manmade and natural debris build up on the bases of your skis and cause additional drag and poor ski and skier performance.

To prevent these conditions from ruining your spring skiing, you should take care of your skis and consider the following techniques and strategies. For example, (a) keep the bases of your skis as clean as possible; (b) avoid skiing across the fall line on any terrain where the slush is wet and deep—the added drag in the slush will quell your momentum, and in such snow you want to keep up the momentum; (c) keep your skis light on the snow; and (d) do not complete your turns as much as you would in firmer snow conditions. Too complete a turn will lead to additional drag and a loss of momentum.

Use the Conditions

Once you get on steeper, more demanding terrain, you may want to use the slowing effect of spring snow to control your speed. It's also advantageous to use the natural resistance in the snow and the shape of the terrain in which you're skiing to create turning adventures. Part of the art of skiing spring snow is using its characteristics to avail yourself of a variety of terrain challenges that you might have otherwise not skied had they arisen in more firm-packed conditions. Some of these challenges include steeper bump runs that encourge the development of your pole plants and areas in the trees alongside or in between marked runs. *Remember: Closed areas are off limits!*

Use Your Tracks

Spring conditions develop skier confidence when you take advantage of the many challenges you're afforded. Corn snow, for example, offers a great opportunity to review your skiing through an examination of your tracks. Go out and try a series of medium- and short-radius turns. Critique your tracks in the "corn." Are they symmetrical, rounded, S-shaped, Z-shaped? Next, take a close look at your tracks and see how you make your turns. Are you skidding early in the turn or late; are you riding predominantly one ski or two; are you carving through the snow; are you skiing a parallel or wedge-type turn?

Figure 6.3 Try floating or lightening your inside ski in slush.

Float (Lighten) Your Inside Ski

One of the tricks you might want to try in your spring skiing is *floating* or lightening your inside ski. Simply don't put much weight on your inside or uphill ski while turning. You should actually lighten it early in your turn, and leave it lightened as you steer it through the turn. Let your inside ski ride along the top of the snow while the outside or downhill ski is working or being guided or steered through the turn. Even if your outside ski is slowed by the slush, your inside ski will not be bogged down if it's kept *light* on the snow. Additionally, by keeping your inside ski *light*, it's ready to take over the responsibilities of the turning ski as soon as you transfer your weight from your outside ski to your inside ski. It's like walking or running down the slope through the slush and it helps to minimize the drag or friction that develops on the base of your skis. (See Figure 6.3.)

Follow the Sun

In the morning there is soft snow where the sun has been baking the slope. Ski here first and as the day progresses, follow the sun around the mountain, skiing the snow just softened; avoid staying in any one place after the snow is too slushy. On a really hot day, ski the first run once or twice. As soon as it softens, seek the shady areas that are just beginning to receive sun. The warmth of the day will have begun to soften the snow in these areas, and the direct sun will make the skiing great. Follow the sun, and you'll add two or three more hours of top spring skiing to your day.

Later in the afternoon, assuming you're well rested, you might want to revisit the slopes you skied earlier in the day. By then, the runs may have firmed up. If there's a large enough swing in daytime temperatures (there often is) you may find a little of that early morning corn on these late afternoon slopes. If you're interested and the corn isn't too chopped up, this can be enjoyable skiing.

As a Rule: Ski Early and Stop Early

In addition to the warm weather, glowing tan, possible first- and second-degree sunburns when sunblock isn't used, crudded ski bases, and the wise application of a strategy to skiing slush, there is another aspect of spring skiing that you must address: *fatigue*. Our advice: Ski early and stop early. If you plan to ski aggressively over varied terrain, you might want to start early in the day (taking rest breaks as needed and drinking plenty of fluids), ski through lunch, and then call it a day. You will enjoy your spring skiing experience much longer.

Ripply Terrain:
The Washboard Effect

Situation: Bumpity, bumpity, bump; the snow is rippled and hard, and you're skiing down the mountain on your way home.

Conditions: The snow is like a *washboard* or a roller coaster.

Slope Traffic: Mass exodus.

According to Mike, this *washboard effect* is a condition in which the snow becomes rippled and hard. It can occur in soft snow conditions, where continuous skier traffic has caused the snow to become "skied-out." The signs of this are ripples in the snow and characteristic rolling of the terrain. For various reasons, skiers get thrown off balance when skiing on these runs and their skis may skid and bounce, each time creating little bumps and ridges in the snow that lead to the *washboard effect*.

How do you handle these somewhat irritating conditions? First, lower your stance and try to be as loose as possible; open your stance as well. In some cases, use a very slight wedge to create more drag on the snow so you can check your speed. If the slope traffic is sparse, you can view these conditions as another opportunity for developing your skills. Ski in this condition repeatedly. The more familiar you are with these conditions, the more you will derive from them for increasing your versatility and improving your high performance skiing.

Learn how to walk or run through these ripples. Find an area where these ripples dominate. Begin from a standing wedge position, then move slowly through these ripples. Your task is to step over each ridge into its accompanying trough. Left foot, right foot; left foot, right foot; as if you were trying to walk downhill. As your pace quickens, imagine that you're running downhill.

The drill accents your independent leg movements and teaches you independent leg retraction for various terrain changes. As you encounter the same situation again, try to do this faster and more quickly. Stand on your skis very loosely and pedal your feet as you go.

Summary

1. Make your first day of the season a high performance day; go slow, be patient, and review the basics. Find out what it feels like to be on the snow and centered on your skis. Don't be in a hurry to get your skis on edge, or to pick up this season's skiing where you left off last season.

2. When you're unable to visualize changes in terrain: (a) slow down, (b) ski medium-radius turns, (c) ski more centered over your skis, and (d) ski taller.
3. Open your stance even more than you would normally; this will give you a more stable base of support.
4. At the outset, when skiing in poorly lit conditions, listen to what your skis are telling you about the conditions via the sensations transmitted through your feet to your brain, and those sounds transmitted through your ears.
5. Lightly dragging your poles will help keep you centered. As the pitch of the hill changes, the feel of your poles changes accordingly. In this way, your poles give you two additional sensors to your feet.
6. With crud skiing, ski with an aggressive attitude, though lightly on your skis; ski with a medium-radius turn because it's slow enough to check your speed and fast enough to allow you to glide across the top of the crud.
7. You must ski crud with more speed. Establish a platform and move from it smoothly. When you have finished one turn, move to your next turn immediately and smoothly. Muscling your skis around with abrupt movements is best reserved for steep, extraordinary crud.
8. Aggressiveness is not measured by how hard or fast you ski, but by how emotionally and physically primed you are to quickly respond to changing conditions.
9. Independent leg-foot action is highly instrumental for achieving proficiency in the crud, although heavier crud may require a combination of independent and simultaneous leg-foot action.
10. In skiing slush, be light on the snow and don't complete your turns as completely as you would in firm snow conditions.
11. In skiing slush, float your inside ski. It's not completely unweighted, rather lightly weighted so it's ready to be used for turning as soon as you get off the other ski.
12. In the spring, follow the sun around the mountain. Ski the snow that has just softened, but move on as the snow becomes too slushy.
13. In the spring, ski early and stop early; if you plan to ski all day, take plenty of rest breaks and drink plenty of fluids, preferably non-alcoholic.

14. If you encounter ripply, uneven conditions, lower your stance and be loose; you can use these conditions as another skills development opportunity. Learn how to walk and run through these conditions.

High Performance Tip #5

Blast Around in the Crud

Think of skiing like a rocket in the crud: Blast through the loose snow and fly over the heavier stuff. Be flexible, always keeping your hands and arms in front, and actively using your poles. When the snow gives freely, use independent leg action; if it's more resistant, use the power you can create with both skis rotating and steering together.

If you choose, get airborne in the heavier crud. There's less resistance in the air than in the snow, so use hopping where it works for you. In these cases, ski crud as if it were powder, only be more forceful and aggressive with your extension movements (such movements don't have to be muscled or abrupt). Stay centered over your skis, but always keep your upper body moving down the fall line ahead of you. Crud can be a blast when you ski it like a rocket!

Chapter 7

Everyday Warm-Up Drills and Exercises

Athletes in any sport who want to prevent injuries and enhance athletic performance use an individually designed warm-up progression.

First rule: Begin all warm-ups by filling the muscles with energy: oxygen-rich and nutritious blood. Accomplish this by performing activities that increase your heart rate, without excessively stressing or stretching your muscles and tendons before the blood has filled your muscles and joints.

This is a gradual process, taking perhaps 5 to 10 minutes to engorge your muscles and joints. There are safe shortcuts employed by highly trained and conditioned athletes who achieve sufficient engorgement and higher ranges of flexibility sooner because of their greater cardiac output. Even these athletes, however, use the principle of *gradually* working the torso and limbs.

Why Warm Up?

The intention of a planned warm-up program is threefold: (a) to decrease the risk of injury (ask several injury victims and you'll often find that warm-ups were never a part of their skiing day); (b) to keep your body flexible and ready to adapt to changes in snow conditions, terrain, or other demands you may place on yourself (prestretched muscles respond more quickly to demands than unstretched muscles); and (c) to promote your potential for skiing with the highest level of efficiency. Ask racers and competitive skiers if they warm up; most will admit that they ski better after a high-energy warm-up.

Warm muscles can be gradually stretched to greater ranges of motion than cold muscles, especially important for winter sports. The more flexible you become, the more this may help to minimize the injury you might sustain in a fall, because a flexible (warmed-up) body can better absorb the shock of falls, off-balance compressions, and awkward positions that are all potential aspects of aggressive skiing.

Unfortunately, flexibility is lost as we age, particularly in men, and this loss is seen in the late twenties and on. This is one of the reasons why young people can function on the slopes with little or no warm-up. They play more with the snow and ski less intensively and less aggressively. For over-30 skiers, daily stretching is crucial both before and after skiing.

Your body's reaction to changes in conditions or surprises in the snow (e.g., skiers darting out of trees, holes, rocks, cliffs, etc.) is tied to the quickness of response of not only your feet, legs, and skis but also your stabilizing upper body: hands, arms, shoulders, head/eyes. Your lower body in particular needs to be limber and quick to respond to signals from the brain. It must be ready to extend and retract; to change the pressure on the ankles, knees, or hips depending on the turn; to set an edge or get off of an edge; to ski onto an edge; to separate the skis and feet; to move the legs independently; to skate and step; and in general, to be very dynamic and versatile.

A series of planned warm-ups to use each time you go skiing will help to maintain your flexibility and versatility throughout the ski season.

Some Warm-Up Ideas

Many skiers I know like to engage in some kind of aerobic activity and at-home stretches before getting to the mountain. Admittedly, others I know dread such a thought. If you share my view, you know how the early morning warm-up acts like a prewarm-up for a more thorough warm-up on the mountain. If you don't do this prewarm-up, there are a host of activities to prepare your body for stretching once you get to the mountain.

Any of the following, done for 5 to 10 minutes prepares your body for preliminary stretches. Figures 7.1 through 7.5 illustrate several of these activities.

Activity	Where	High Fitness Level	Low Fitness Level
Without skis:			
1. Climbing stairs	Use those at the ski area or base lodge	Slowly to rapidly	Slowly
2. Running in place	Wherever it's comfortable	Moderately	Walking pace
With skis on the snow:			
3. Sidestepping	A flat area	Slowly to moderately	Slowly
4. Herringbone walk	An easy slope	Moderately to a short four- to eight-step sprint	Very slowly
5. Sidestepping	An easy slope: Step up and down	Moderately	Slowly
6. Ski skate	Flat open space	Moderately to quickly	Slowly to moderately
7. Ski skate	Down uncrowded bunny slopes or comfortable terrain	Moderately to quickly	Slowly to moderately
8. Baby rounders (making as many little turns as you can down the run)	Gentle slope	Slowly to moderately	Slowly to moderately

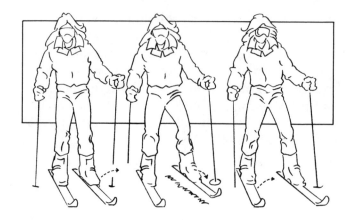

Figure 7.1 Sidestep on flat terrain.

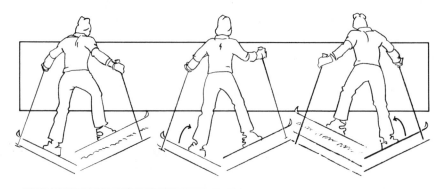

Figure 7.2 Herringbone walk up an easy slope.

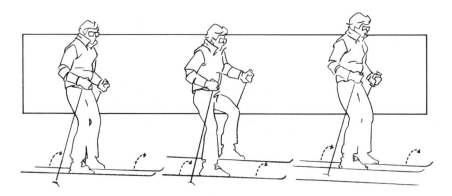

Figure 7.3 Sidestep up and down an easy slope.

Figure 7.4 Skate on flat terrain.

Figure 7.5 Skate down an easy slope.

Six Steps to An Effective Warm-Up

After a lifetime of athletics, I believe the warm-up is a major contributor to athletic performance. Consider the following in your skiing:

1. Do early morning sit-ups to warm the body. Strong and

Figure 7.6 Strengthen your abdominal muscles while protecting your back.

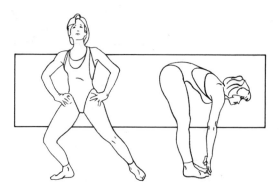

Figure 7.7 Stretch your groin and hamstring muscles.

toned abdominal muscles are one of the greatest allies to centered skiing and a problem-free back. (See Figure 7.6.)

2. Fill your muscles and joints with blood. Begin stretching after doing something that makes your heart beat faster and large muscles work harder, not excessively, for 5 to 10 minutes. Then stretch: a) the fronts and backs of the legs, b) the inner thighs and groin area, c) the lower back,

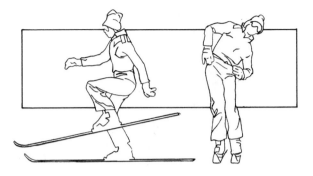

Figure 7.8 Stretch your waist and hip flexors.

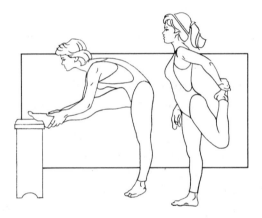

Figure 7.9 Stretch your quadricep and hamstring muscles.

d) the mid-section, waist area, and e) the shoulders and neck. In the process of stretching the inner thigh, groin, and legs, you will also exert proper stretch to the knees and ankles. (See Figures 7.7, 7.8, and 7.9.)

(*Please note*: If you do this stretching before getting to the mountain, you can abbreviate your on-the-mountain warm-up.)

3. Use your first chairlift ride to stretch! First work your shoulders by rolling them forward (imagine making small circles at your shoulder joints), then reverse direction and roll them back. Roll each way 5 to 10 times, repeating this sequence 3 times. Second, work the back neck muscles by leaning your head to the right over your right shoulder,

Figure 7.10 Loosen up your hips and waist for more dynamic turning.

then slowly roll your head forward in a semicircle until your chin is nearly resting on your chest. Continue rolling slowly until your head is over your left shoulder. Then roll your head back in the other direction, over your chest to your right shoulder. Repeat twice. Third, rework your shoulders by pressing them down into your upper arms and holding for a five-count. Lift them up toward your ears, holding for a five-count. Repeat three times.

If you have room, work your mid-section and lower body by twisting the latter (legs together) to the left, while you twist your upper body (at the mid-section) to the right. Hold for a 7 to 10 count and switch sides, upper body left, lower body right. Repeat as many times as you can, working on your upper and lower body separation: Twist to the extremes and hold a tight separation during the 7 to 10 count. You might even get the sensation of bringing your inside ski up slightly during the exercise to achieve even greater separation. Of course, be careful not to catch your skis on the lift towers. (See Figure 7.10.)

Work your thighs and knees by lifting your lower legs slowly, your legs out straight, tails of your skis perpendicular to the snow. Lift one leg at a time, or both legs together. Hold for 10 to 20 seconds each time, longer if you can. For safety reasons and effect, do the leg-lift movements slowly and avoid rocking the chair.

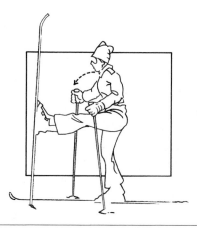

Figure 7.11 Stretch your hamstrings and calves.

Figure 7.12 A "World Cup" stretch for expressive skiing.

4. Casually ski two easy runs doing acquaintance drills, and follow these with some additional stretching. All you want to do with these runs is loosen up and integrate your flexibility stretches with your skiing body. Ski the first run very relaxed; the second a bit more aggressively. Do basic wedge turns for a hundred yards; stem (skidded) wedge turns for 50 yards; converging step turns without skidding; matched ski turns without skidding; a series of diverging turns; and some attempt to ski on a single ski, turning it in both directions.

Two helpful stretches to perform with skis on are (a) leaning down and touching or leaning as far as you can toward the tips of your skis and (b) standing tall, both poles steadying you, lifting one ski and placing its tail in the snow so it is tall in front of you; slowly lean into the raised knee and stretch the back of your leg. (See Figure 7.11.)

If you're feeling loose, warm, fit, flexible, and are ready for a more dynamic stretch, try my favorite: the *World Cup stretch*. (See Figure 7.12.) Straighten out your downhill leg and place your inside ski in an exaggerated diverging step, flat on the snow. The action of the World Cup stretch is to sit down on the inside ski as you turn your upper body to face over your downhill ski, which you have placed on an extreme inside edge. The stretch is completed by holding for a 10-count, allowing a bit of movement in your hips to push them more into the hill. Switch sides and repeat as often as you like for a few minutes. The fullest expression of the stretch is when you thrust your poles, hands, and arms forward over your downhill ski while pushing your hip into the hill.

5. Take a few minutes to think about how you want to ski this particular day: aggressively, casually, fast, quick, stylishly, efficiently.

6. You're ready to take a ''glory run!'' Ski the way your body feels like skiing and let your mind take a vacation. This run can set the stage for the rest of the day; why not give it your all? If skiing is sport to you, be an athlete and warm up to glory!

Summary

1. Regardless of warm-up, begin by filling the muscles with oxygen-rich and nutritious blood (giving the muscles energy). First, increase your heart rate; don't stretch before the blood has filled your muscles and joints. This is a gradual process, taking perhaps 5 to 10 minutes to sufficiently engorge your muscles and joints with blood.

2. Warm up to: decrease the risk of injury; keep your body flexible and ready to adapt to changes in snow conditions and terrain; and promote your potential for skiing with the highest level of efficiency.

3. Persons lose flexibility as they age (particularly men). Daily

flexibility stretches are crucial for over-30 skiers, both before and after skiing.

4. A flexible body helps to promote efficient skiing with less fatigue.

5. Six steps to an effective warm-up: (a) Perform abdominal exercises, (b) use activities to get your heart beating faster and muscles and tendons filled with blood, (c) use your first chairlift ride to limber up, (d) do acquaintance drills while skiing easy runs, and stretch with skis on, (e) think about how you want to ski this day, and (f) take a glory run!

High Performance Tip #6

Stretch Appropriately and Safely

A rule of thumb for many stretches is: The simpler they are to execute and the more familiar they are, the greater their benefit to you. You don't want to overstretch, but effectively stretch key areas of your musculature to achieve flexibility. Specifically, the targets of flexibility stretching are muscles and the tendons that attach the muscles to your bones.

Six caveats for all stretches:

1. Don't bounce into the stretch; gradually push into the stretch.
2. Don't forget to breathe while stretching, inhaling during the resting phase and exhaling during the work phase of the stretch/exercise.
3. Don't do exercises that require bending at the waist with your legs straight.
4. Don't do deep knee bends or full squats.
5. Don't use weights with stretching unless you've received proper instruction.
6. Don't use stretches unless they lengthen your muscles beyond their normal resting state while not forcing body parts beyond their normal range of motion.

Chapter 8

Corrective Drills and Exercises for Common Skiing Problems

> "What we have to learn to do, we learn by doing."
>
> **Aristotle**

One of the truly frustrating aspects of skiing is becoming stymied, and thereby inhibited, by our inability to do a number of things on skis. We wish we could carve a turn with minimal skidding; get by a certain knoll in a race course; feel relaxed after skiing moguls; execute a rhythmic pole touch for an entire mile-long run; stop on the dime; ski for long distances without becoming fatigued; and smoothly link turn after turn in a variety of conditions.

Discovering problems in our skiing is easier than accepting that these problems exist; unless we accept them, however, we may forever plant self-destructive bombs in our skiing. The answer is to recognize the problems and challenge yourself to do something about correcting them. Unfortunately, trial and error adjustments made to compensate for any number of our problems lead not to better skiing, but to better survival tactics on the slopes. The result is many hours of frustrating and fatiguing skiing, even though we're supposedly having fun.

In this chapter I've assembled the information gleaned from many on-snow and off-snow sessions with my experts, particularly Mike, John, and Brent for drills and exercises. We spent much of the time identifying problem areas common to the recreational skier on his or her way up the high performance ladder. With their assistance and my experimentation in a variety of conditions, I field-tested some 50 drills and exercises designed to be corrective for a host of conditions. Following each drill or exercise is a *kinesthetic hint*; that is, a reference to the sensations you ought to feel if you are properly executing the drill or exercise. These may be muscular, joint-related, or oriented to sense of perspective or general ski-snow awareness. All sections of this chapter were then reviewed for technical accuracy by Tony Roegiers, PSIA-certified instructor and ski school supervisor at Northstar-at-Tahoe.

Key Problem Areas

I asked George Capaul, assistant coach of the U.S. Ski Team (men's slalom and giant slalom), for his impressions of the average recreational skier. Although George is quick to applaud everyone's love for skiing, he is candid about what he sees on the slopes. "Most recreational skiers," he says, "have real technical problems and need a lot of work on basic fundamentals." His fundamentals include being balanced on your skis forward, sideways, longitudinally, and to the rear; being able to respond to all conditions with a proper pole plant, upright stance on skis, and even weight distribution along the entire length of the outside ski while turning; skiing square to the fall line; and keeping your head up and looking ahead or what George calls *high beam* skiing.

It's not until you master these basics, George says, that you're ready to deal with technique.

"A problem modern recreational skiers have is that due to all the grooming, it's easy to go fast, and many equate going fast with intermediate skiing. Unfortunately, when the fundamentals are lacking, going fast is not intermediate skiing. Still, these skiers go out on groomed trails and say, 'Yeah, I can handle this,' but were these skiers skiing at a time when trails were skier-packed, rough and mogully, they might be very beginning skiers. In a way, the groomed trails have hurt ski schools because before, skiers needed instruction to get down steep hills; today, they feel they can handle anything . . . that's groomed. Ski schools teach basic fundamentals, and lessons are an essential part of high performance skiing.''

The key problem areas common among the ranks of recreational skiers are addressed in this chapter. These include over-rotating or twisting the upper body while turning; lack of carving (excessive skidding while turning); lack of rhythmic pole use; overall lack of extension/movement in skiing; lack of edge control; lack of speed control (unfinished turns); lack of variety in turning skills and choice of turn radii; and tense and static skiing.

Each problem area is discussed briefly, followed by an explanation of applicable drills and exercises. As you might imagine, a number of drills and exercises are useful for more than a single problem, and reference is made to this when applicable. Sometimes these multipurpose drills and exercises are presented with adaptations according to the particular problem. Similarly, some drills and exercises are designed to accomplish much more than has been indicated in this chapter; these are presented only for their specific application to the problem under discussion.

A Perspective On Drills and Exercises

Think of the drills as narrowly focused opportunities to learn by doing. Don't regard them as a critique of your skiing. They are sensory as well as mechanical experiences. Think of the exercises as broadly focused opportunities to draw your skills together while concentrating on the task of the exercise.

When doing either drills or exercises, proceed with an eye toward allowing change to creep into your skiing: It will! Execute them with precision; the purpose of the drills and exercises is not to make you change but to expose your body to a host of biomechanical movements that, once incorporated, allows your body to make natural adjustments and adaptations to find the perfect rhythm for your style of skiing.

Admittedly, some drills and exercises will seem complicated and impossible, whereas some may strike you as infantile to your level of skiing. These are not reasons to avoid them. In fact, the more effort you have to put into doing a drill as prescribed, the greater the technical benefit to your skiing. This continues up to the point at which you can perform the drills effortlessly as a means of warming up before more aggressive skiing.

You may be thinking about the embarrassment you'll experience while falling all over the mountain trying to do a basic or advanced drill and about how silly you'll look performing drills on beginner slopes when you consider yourself an advanced skier. These egoistic thoughts get in the way of high performance skiing. The drills are necessary for you to become a better skier.

A five-year member of the U.S. Ski Team, Mark Tache encourages drills and instruction that require you to focus on the fundamentals of different aspects of skiing. Without drilling and training, Mark says, "A lot of would-be performance skiers will spend a lot of skiing time practicing bad habits over and over again. Without direction, they'll tend to stay at the same level in their skiing. Some choose to get to a point where they're comfortable on their skis, bad habits and all, and these skiers will likely never be motivated to ski better. It takes an annual commitment to getting better to really improve. That's what is so unique about this sport: You never reach a point where you say, 'I know how to ski.' It's always a challenge; you're always learning."

Pete Patterson, another former U.S. Ski Team member and medalist in the downhill, highlights the importance of practicing the basics to develop high performance skills. "Learning to ski by picking up the ability to negotiate different terrain in a year's time shows a skier is working real hard on his or her skiing. But, even though this skier appears to be rapidly progressing, you can see the real inexperience in the more subtle aspects of their skiing. It takes years of experience to be able to ski efficiently."

Commenting on the plight of many weekend-only skiers, Pete adds, "Unfortunately, they don't have the opportunity to ski as much as they might like, and they may find it difficult to get to the level at which they feel good. They must be patient, though, because there's just no other way to develop high performance skills without practice and time.

"What you've got to realize is you always need practice, coaching, or instruction. The best skiers in the world go out, work with a coach, and discover things about their skiing that they're not doing as well as they were a couple of weeks earlier. The coach lets them know; it's really a never-ending process even at the World Cup level. You can always use, and probably forever need, the fine tuning of a coach, instructor, whomever."

Five Easy Rules for Drills and Exercises

1. Understand what the drill or exercise is designed to accomplish.
2. Be aware of which condition is most appropriate to the drill or exercise, for example, groomed slope, slight bumps, firm snow, soft snow, bumpy, or steep. Also, know the slope rating for the intended drill or exercise: beginning, intermediate, advanced, and expert.
3. Know how to perform the drill. If it's performed incorrectly it may enhance errors. Further, you won't get that kinesthetic appreciation of what you've accomplished: a ski feeling that can accelerate a refinement in your skiing when you use it to guide your increasingly more subtle and proper adjustments for skiing in the high performance mode.

   If you know what it feels like to "hold an edge" or "angulate your hip" into the turn, you can use this *kinesthetic knowledge* to prompt you to replicate this *feeling* at certain times during your skiing when you must subtly adjust to get more hip into the hill, more completely finish a turn in the bumps or steeps, or ride your turning ski a little longer in the recreational race course.
4. Commit yourself to a block of skiing time and, unless you're already familiar with the drill or exercise, do it

several times to work out the bugs before using an entire run for it. You will find some drills immediately frustrating, especially single ski skiing and turning, hopping drills, and a number of angulation drills; this is to be expected. These cases will require more than a few attempts to perfect. If so, try them again each time out, until you learn them!

5. Don't take the easy way out by avoiding difficult or embarrassing drills that cause you to fall down. By doing so, you're likely to ignore an aspect of your skiing that's undeveloped. Achieving this development through more difficult drills will boost your confidence and enhance your skills acquisition.

If you have the opportunity to rehearse any drills at home by thinking through their mechanics and/or physically arranging yourself (without skis) in the positions called for by the drills, do it!

Getting Started With Drills and Exercises

In the drills-exercise format of the following section as well as for the remainder of the chapter, there is reference to *conditions* and *slope rating*. Unless otherwise noted, conditions are smooth, groomed, firm snow; slope rating is intermediate to advanced. These are referred to as *standard* in the text. The environment created by these conditions and slope rating is ideal for learning to do drills. As a rule, when you are able to perform drills efficiently, take them to more challenging terrain and variable conditions.

Reference is made to assuming the *drills position* when performing the drills. Always assume the drills position when doing drills, unless otherwise noted. The position: skis parallel, hip-width apart; knees slightly bent (flexed); upper body relaxed, head up, chest tall; hands and arms forward about waist high, poles extended out behind you on or off the snow, and back straight (unless you have a lumbar spine problem). (See Figure 8.1.)

Figure 8.1 Begin drills with hips and upper body centered over your skis, ankles and knees slightly flexed, upper back gently rounded, arms in an open balanced position, head up and looking straight ahead.

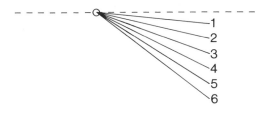

Figure 8.2 The higher the FLEP number, the greater your gliding speed.

Reference is made to *fall line exercise position* (FLEP) numbers one to six. Refer to the diagram in Figure 8.2 and acquaint yourself with these positions according to their specific use for each drill.

The following terms appear throughout the drills and exercises. To *flex* is to press down and forward. To *flex the legs* is to press the ankles and knees forward. To *rotate* is to twist. To *counterrotate* is to move your lower body (legs, boots, and skis) one way, while twisting your upper body (arms, shoulders, head, chest, and upper abdomen) the other, at least as far as facing down the fall line; the place about which all the counterrotating takes place is your waist (upper hips and lower abdomen). To *touch a pole* is to tap it in the snow. To *plant a pole* is to decisively push the tip into the snow.

To *traverse* is to go across the fall line in the #1 position; a *slight traverse* is to go across the fall line in the #2 position; a *slight traverse to pick up speed* is to go across the fall line in the #3 position.

A *comfortable turn rhythm and slope* is something you define for yourself, but it implies that you feel absolutely no intimidation from the kinds of turns you must do or from the slope upon which you're going to perform the drill or exercise.

To *steer* your skis is to use all of the turning moves you make, including gross or subtle foot/boot and lower leg/knee movements and the rotation of your femur (thigh bone) in its hip socket, to guide your skis in either the predetermined direction or in the direction they naturally seek because of the angles you've created with your ankles, knees, hips, and shoulders. *Angles* are created when you collapse any of the foregoing body parts into your center of mass and thus break the vertical axis of your body. Your *center of mass* is the abdominal region around your navel, between and above your hips, as differentiated from the *center of gravity*, which can be outside of mass.

Weight transfer is moving the weight of your body from one ski to the other. Usually, this transfer occurs from your downhill (outside, working, or turning) ski to your uphill (inside, resting, or inrigger) ski in preparation for your next turn. The weight transfer occurs after the turn has begun, however, with the White Pass turn popularized by the Mahres and with a converging step turn. As soon as the transfer takes place, the skis switch roles.

Your skis are referred to in many ways: Basically, the ski that's doing most of the edging, has the most pressure applied to it, and is closest to the bottom of the hill is *downhill, outside, working,* and *turning*. The ski that's doing the least amount of edging, has very little pressure applied to it (although it's actively turning), and is closest to the top of the hill is *uphill, inside, resting,* and an *inrigger*.

Problem:
Lack of Speed Control

This may not only be the most common problem among skiers but also one of the most dangerous. Add *uncontrolled* speed to your skiing and you increase the risk of serious injury. Add *controlled* speed to your skiing and you increase the potential for safer risk taking.

Consider the following drills and exercises to learn to subtly control your speed while skiing all out or as slow as you like; think of acquiring speed control to add versatility to your skiing without having to rely on dramatic braking measures and skidding to slow you down. In fact, learning to slow down in stride is also a wonderful way to learn how to accelerate at will.

Speed control can be achieved by learning to finish your turns and to use platforms and preturns in your skiing. When you learn to finish your turns, you learn how to carve the inside edge of your turning ski as well, and stop the excessive skidding of both the turning and the inside skis.

Drill:
Steering Up to a Preturn Platform

Purpose: To control speed by the momentary steering of your skis away from the fall line to effect a smooth decrease in speed, which allows you to set up for your next turn with a rhythmic dip up and into the hill. This is especially useful for setting up your first turn in the steeps when you've had to traverse to the place where you're going to drop in and ski the steeps with commitment. The degree to which your edges are engaged while steering up and away from the fall line determines the rate of deceleration of your skis and the distance they travel up the slope. This movement is actually a preturn in which you steer your skis up the slope an instant before turning them down the slope. The distance you travel in the preturn varies, but is measured in feet, not yards.

Conditions: Standard; once you've got this down, take it to the steeps, bumps, and skiable ice.

Slope Rating: Standard; truly advanced skiers should take this to an expert slope.

Performing the Drill. Begin in drills position, FLEP #2. Keep a definite pressure on the inside edge of your downhill

Figure 8.3 Steer your feet/boots/skis up the hill to a stop.

ski while lightly maintaining contact with the snow on your inside ski. Midway through your traverse (you're not moving that fast), begin to steer your feet and lower legs/knees up. As you do so, allow your upper body to stay square with its original direction. Follow your skis until you stop just to get the feeling of steering up. Turn around and repeat in the other direction. The inside edge of your downhill ski will naturally increase its angle of edging as you steer your legs away from the fall line. Repeat side to side until you can control the steering up motion of your skis. (See Figure 8.3.)

Next, do the same procedure at FLEP #3 or #4, only shorten the distance traveled across the slope and, instead of stopping when your skis turn up the hill, use their movement to initiate your next turn down the hill. It's easy, but you've got to trust yourself. As your skis start up the hill, you touch your pole and throw or lean your body down the hill in the direction of your pole touch. Concentrate on only this and you will begin to get the feel of steering up to a preturn. To smooth it out requires a number of subtle skills, not the least of which is active inside-ski steering. Do the drill and learn to steer up; the other pieces to the puzzle will emerge in other drills.

Kinesthetic Hint. During the steering-up phase, you should feel your lower body pulling away from your stable upper body. As you refine the preturn, you'll use a corresponding dip up with your upper body to propel you into your turn. Muscularly, you'll feel the most pressure in the middle of the front of your downhill quadricep (thigh); with corresponding knee angulation, the pressure is felt more to the outside of the thigh. For a change of pace, hold your thigh with your hand as you do the exercise to feel the pressure while gradually steering up. The thigh feeling is more intense and short-lived when steering into and out of the preturn.

Drill: Diverging Turns

Purpose: To control speed by getting you to ski away from the fall line, yet allowing you to fluidly link turn after turn by making subtle adjustments in your speed. This is more dynamic than steering up because, in part, you're transferring your weight early to your new turning ski. The quicker you get your weight to your new turning ski, the sooner you can turn; the sooner you can turn, the more quickly you can establish speed control.

Conditions: Standard.

Slope Rating: Standard.

Performing the Drill. In drills position ski across the slope in FLEP #3, but instead of steering up at the end of your traverse, push (don't step or lift) your uphill ski/boot, lower leg/knee up the hill away from the fall line and in the direction of your outside ski. As you diverge your inside ski away from your outside ski, let your body follow the direction and pull of your inside ski. As soon as you put your weight on this diverging ski, your outside ski, which is madly edging in response to the diverged ski, will correspondingly lighten and be easier to steer up the hill, in part because it is attached to the body and in part because the momentum of your turn is away from the downhill

Figure 8.4 Diverge your inside ski up the hill.

ski. Do this until you stop. Practice to both sides until it feels comfortable. (See Figure 8.4.)

Next, to make this drill more dynamic, instead of stopping after you've diverged your inside ski, use the same movement as the last drill to turn down the fall line. Unlike steering up to a preturn in which both skis are steered up, with diverging turns you are relying on one ski to make a quick and subtle diverging move to check your speed. So long as you have not yet transferred weight, this maneuver will make your turning ski carve in the snow and move in the direction of the diverged ski. When the diverged ski is stepped into its position at high speeds it becomes a very dynamic form of skiing, used routinely in racing and at times in bumps.

Kinesthetic Hint. Muscularly, you'll feel pressure in the lower thigh and on the inside of the knee of the diverging leg. The outside of the thigh and knee of your downhill leg will feel increasing amounts of pressure as your downhill ski edges in response to the divergence of your other ski.

Drill: Wedge Hoppers

> *Purpose:* To establish quick on and off edge-speed control for skiing very steep and bumpy terrain.
>
> *Conditions:* Standard.
>
> *Slope Rating:* Standard.

Performing the Drill. Hold yourself in a comfortable wedge at the start of your run, FLEP #6. Keep your upper body upright and flex your knees and ankles, favoring one side by making it your downhill ski and putting most of your weight on it. Spring off this ski (assume it's your right ski), extend up, and hop to the left ski, making it the downhill ski. Each time you spring to a new ski that ski is always wedged toward you. Hop back and forth, ski to ski, maintaining the wedge. Try to land softly, keeping your center of mass facing downhill while your lower body hops side to side. Incorporate a natural pole plant rhythm, planting your poles out in front of you toward the tip portion, not the sides of your skis. (See Figures 8.5a and 8.5b.)

Figure 8.5 Do wedge hoppers, from ski to ski, with pole planted for stabilization and pushing off.

Kinesthetic Hint. A tremendous feeling of frustration is usual for not being able to do it right away or even after a while. The trick is in the positioning of the lower body and the non-working ski, the amount of edge angle on the working ski, and the relationship of the ski to the fall line. The nonworking side of your body should feel like it's coiling or crunching in on the working ski. You should experience a feeling of control and heavy breathing!

Drill: Discovering Platforms

Purpose: To control speed at a specific point in time or specific spot on the slope; to learn to establish the positioning on your skis for initiating a preturn; and to gradually or abruptly check your speed just before you reach the point of turn initiation at which you know you've started to physically influence the turning of your skis in the other direction. According to Brent Boblitt, "Platforms allow you to slow down or speed up in accord with the rhythm of your skiing and direction of your descent. If you're able to make a good platform, you can utilize an effective pole plant. With a proper platform, you're stable and you can make offensive and defensive moves. Offensively, you use the rebound set up by the platform to project yourself down the hill with more speed and authority (slalom). Defensively, you use the platform to check your speed by absorbing the rebound with your body and using only a minimum amount of rebound to help redirect your skis down the fall line (hockey stops, steeps)."

Boblitt notes three conditions necessary for a good platform:

1. You must have your skis away from your body, so you can put your skis on angle and apply pressure to them to produce rebound.
2. As you come around the turn, you want to be more on the tails of your skis, because the point of maxi-

mum hold is generally a couple of inches behind the center of the ski beneath your heel. This allows you to have your knees in front to absorb the rebound or redirect it into the next turn.

3. You need to plant your pole at the proper place and time to increase your base of support and stabilize your upper body. Offensively, you find the pole plant more during extension; defensively, it occurs more during flexion.

Conditions: Standard.

Slope Rating: Standard; the steeper the better as you become more comfortable with platforms.

Performing the Drill. You've got to be creative. First, put your skis in a platform by standing on the side of a hill in parallel position, perpendicular to the fall line; hold yourself there. Now, bounce up and down until your skis come off of the snow, ready to land again in another platform to keep you from sliding away. Be more aggressive: Hop high, land on your skis, and plant your downhill pole on the downhill side of your boot, forming a platform with your skis and pole. Ski around the mountain and whenever you get a chance form check platforms and propulsion platforms. Have fun with them; they add versatility to your skiing and help you in the steeps. Using a gentle slope, try to hop up and turn your skis 180 degrees, ending up with a platform in which your former uphill ski becomes your new downhill ski.

Kinesthetic Hint. When you hit a check platform with pole plant, you feel the pressure on the balls of your feet (i.e., pressure forward). If you feel the pressure of your lower legs against the fronts of your boot, it may mean that you're too far forward. You may feel pressure on your downhill knee and your uphill thigh as well. Your uphill ski is slightly ahead of your downhill ski. In a very exaggerated check platform on steep terrain, your downhill hip is pinched and your uphill is stretched. As Tony notes, ''The proper place to feel the pinch is the iliac crest at the top of the pelvis.'' (See Figure 8.6.)

Figure 8.6 Work on check platforms on a variety of slopes.

In a propulsion platform, your heels set quickly and you experience a brief but distinctive flex at your knees and a quick propulsion/extension out of this flex as you project yourself into the next turn. There's a very definite feeling of floating or weightlessness at this moment of propulsion.

Exercises

The following exercises are designed for standard conditions and all slope ratings. Although the first exercise lends itself to bump skiing and powder, it's very important to have your speed control skills in check before taking off on someone's heels in the bumps or on fast icy terrain. Generally, it's not a good idea to follow skiers into very big bumps, on steeps, and in powder. Following a skier in spring slush and crud can be a good learning experience, but be sure to leave plenty of room between you and the skier in front of you so you can react to unexpected turns or falls.

These exercises help you not only to use more speed control tactics in your skiing but also to be more reactional in your skiing, to look ahead, to anticipate, to experiment with different rhythms, to add timing to your skiing, and in general, to be more versatile.

Follow Someone's Tracks. Ski right behind another skier. This adds discipline to your skiing and forces you to make subtle speed control adaptations to keep you from crashing into the skier you're following. If you're crowding the skier ahead of you, it's not because you're a great or superior skier, but because you haven't refined your speed control skills.

Ski a "Figure-Eight" With the Skier in Front of You. Create the same shape of turns as this skier in such a way that when your tracks cross his or hers, they form a figure eight.

Problem:
Lack of Carving
and Excessive Skidding

Although most skiers who lack speed control end up skidding excessively at the end of their turns, not all skiers who skid excessively lack speed control. These skiers are skidding their tails not to brake but to steer their skis: It's easier for them to turn a flat ski rather than an edged ski. The first group of skidders usually rides medium-length and long skis on more advanced terrain; the latter group of "skidders" usually rides shorter skis.

Whatever the length of ski, Tony notes, "Any radius of turn of under approximately 90 feet will have some displacement of the ski (exceptions: skiing in crud and Mark Girardelli)." This is true for even the mythical perfectly carved turn. Indeed, there are times when we intentionally skid our skis, as in *short-swing* turns, to make a descent while sideslipping, to maneuver through tight areas, to react to unexpected obstacles (accompanied by quick foot movements), to perform *stem christies* in the crud, bumps, or slushy conditions, and to stabilize oneself in the bumps. (See High Performance Tip #7: Short-Swing Turns.)

I don't want you to throw skidding out the window; I do want to provide you with a series of drills designed to help you finish your turns and learn the skills that will give you the choice of whether, when, and just how much you want to skid your skis.

Drill: Wedge Progression
(With Ankle and Knee Angulation)

Purpose: To develop finished turns through the use of subtle and more obvious angles.

Conditions: Standard.

Slope Rating: Standard.

Performing the Drill. Begin in a comfortable wedge with the insides of your boots at about shoulder's width, the tips of your skis approximately four to six inches apart, assuming FLEP #2. Traverse the hill at all times maintaining the wedge with the rest of your body in drills position. As you pick up speed, allow only the downhill ankle to tip into the hill toward your uphill ski. This is a very slight tipping: Your knee should barely move at this stage of the drill. (See Figure 8.7.)

You'll notice that your downhill ski will begin to edge more decisively; this is due to the angulation of your ankle. Now it's time to add knee angulation by gradually tipping your knee into the hill after you've tipped your ankle. As you do, you'll feel the downhill ski solidly edging and carving through the snow.

Figure 8.7 It takes discipline to hold a wedge while traversing.

The greater the pressure created by your angles and the more you tip ankle and knee into the hill (at least in this drill), the more your skis will turn up the hill to their eventual stop.

As soon as you become acquainted with this drill move to FLEP #3 or #4. Remember, the most difficult part of this drill may be in maintaining a wedge throughout the carving of your downhill ski (you must do this to better isolate the subtle control you can exert on your skis through the use of these two angles). Go across the hill and angulate until you come to a stop: Continue this all the way down the run. Give yourself plenty of room.

Next phase in the progression: Pick a comfortable line down the mountain. Maintaining the wedge and drills position, practice the same ankle and knee-ankle pressure, but instead of coming to an uphill stop, transfer your weight to your uphill ski at the instant your skis feel they're beginning to slow down (i.e., when they begin turning up the hill). As you move your weight to your wedged or stemmed uphill ski, it becomes your new turning ski. Therefore, if you want to turn easily without resistance, you simply have to lighten that old downhill ski, but still keep it wedged.

Assuming you've held the wedge position with both skis, as soon as you transfer your weight to that uphill ski (new turning ski), it will turn. In its wedged position, the ski is technically *converged* in the direction of your next turn; as soon as it feels the pressure of your weight and the force of your momentum, its ski mechanics will project it down the fall line. (See Figure 8.8.)

Repeat this over and over again, each time exploring the use of your ankle and knee in creating angles. If you begin to skid through your turn, first apply a little ankle angulation, then knee angulation and see if this helps to lessen the skidding. Again, in this progression maintain a wedge at all times. As a rule, persistent skidding suggests that you're abandoning your edges too soon or not using them with much conviction. Use this drill for learning how to patiently ride your edged downhill ski all the way through a turn until you've transferred your weight to the other ski. (See High Performance Tip #8: Converging Turns.)

Kinesthetic Hint.   When angulating the ankle, you only feel pressure against the inside of your downhill boot. When adding the knee, you feel the added pressures on the inside of the down-

Figure 8.8 Transfer weight from ski to ski to effect turning when in the fall line.

hill knee as well as the inside portion of your lower thigh (the gracilis and sartorius muscles as well as the inner portion of the quadricep). Isolate the pressures and relax the rest of the body to realize the precise value of this drill. Tony adds, "When I combine steering and knee angulation, and the resistance to the resultant pressures increases, I feel the muscles on the outside of my quads near the knee."

Drill: Foot Pedals

Purpose: To develop the balanced and independent use of your legs in order to use each ski more effectively relative to terrain changes, the action of the other ski, and changes in conditions.

Conditions: Standard.

Slope Rating: Standard.

Performing the Drill. Ski parallel across the hill at FLEP #2 to #4. Actively pick up one foot/ski and set it down; pick up the other foot/ski and set it down; continue across the hill, turn, and continue back the other way. Do this as rapidly as you can as if you were pedaling a bicycle. At all times keep your hands in drills position.

Kinesthetic Hint. You experience a feeling of momentary weightlessness when each ski is lifted off the snow, especially when the downhill ski is elevated. To stay in balance, you must keep the upper body quiet and relaxed and let your legs do the work from a stable pelvis.

Drill: Ankle Flex
(With Active Foot Steering)

Purpose: To finish your turns by the use of subtle ankle angulation and active foot steering throughout the complete arc of your turns.

Conditions: Standard.

Slope Rating: Standard.

Performing the Drill. At first, use FLEP #2 or #3 and drills position to get accustomed to the mechanics of this drill. As you cross the hill, tip your ankle into the hill, then relax it; tip-relax; tip-relax, all the way across the hill. (Recall in an earlier drill that when you tipped your ankle into the hill you were in a wedge and were supposed to hold the angulation constant.) See how much control you can have on the movement of your skis with these subtle tips into the hill. You'll find that there is quite a bit.

Now, make this more challenging by *steering* your feet up the hill when you're ready to end your traverse. Coordinate your

Figure 8.9 Turn or steer your downhill boot up the hill as you guide your uphill ankle up the hill.

ankle tipping with your foot steering by turning your downhill foot/boot up the hill at the same time you tip your ankle. Simultaneously lighten your uphill ski and steer it up. (Lighten doesn't mean lift; rather, it means leaving your uphill ski in contact with the snow, but exerting no pressure on it to drive it through the snow, or push it against the snow.)

Ignore any awkwardness you may feel at first and, when you're ready to turn, concentrate on transferring your weight to your uphill ski as soon as you start to steer up. If you direct your upper body and center of mass down the fall line as soon as you've transferred the weight, you'll add rhythm and the sensation of smoothness to your turns with less skidding. You don't necessarily need a huge angulating movement to control a skid; ski with edge control by learning to use your ankles more subtly. (See Figure 8.9.)

Kinesthetic Hint. You feel distinct pressure against the inside of your downhill boot with twinges of pressure radiating up to the inside of your knee. After doing this consistently across the slope, your downhill leg feels wobbly on both sides of your knee. Your uphill leg is very quietly steered, feeling little or no pressure.

Drill: Diverging Step Turns

Purpose: To use your uphill ski to prevent your downhill ski from skidding by learning to pressure and steer your skis to a more aggressive edge while not losing the ability to hold the downhill ski. By steering the inside ski away from the working ski, you help to tip the working ski to an edge by simultaneously increasing knee and ankle angulation. By stepping the diverging uphill ski away without this angulation, you are moving your mass away from the working edge and decreasing its effectiveness.

Tony explains, "A key thing in skiing and the purpose of knee and ankle angulation is to maintain the edge angle of the ski while keeping the mass close enough to the ski to give it bite [edging]. This is why banking and hip angulation at the platform stage of a turn is ineffective." Ankle and knee angulation, along with a diverging step, creates a carving effect.

Conditions: Standard.

Slope Rating: Standard.

Performing the Drill. Refer back to the discussion of diverging turns in the section on lack of speed control; instead of pushing the diverging ski away from the downhill ski, step it away by lifting its tip slightly off the snow and stepping it into a diverged position.

In this version of the diverging turn, you make your step very soon after crossing the fall line and thereby cut way down on your traverse across the hill. You get into the rhythm of diverging, getting tall (extending), and turning rather than the previous drill's rhythm of diverging, getting tall, turning, and gliding. In this way, you can learn to more quickly round your turns and shorten their radius. (See Figure 8.10.)

Kinesthetic Hint. If you exaggerate the drill (in this case a good idea), you may experience a pronounced pinching in the downhill hip/waist area similar to the feeling of an extreme side bend.

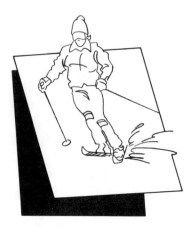

Figure 8.10 A diverging inside ski will increase the carving of your turning ski.

High Performance Tip #7

John Hoffman: Short-Swing Turn

Short-swing turns have definite platforms at their start and finish, but very little pressure in the middle. In fact, it's one abrupt platform to another, turn to turn. There's a lot of quick swiveling; in a sense, the middle of the turn occurs off the snow.

People often think of a short-swing turn as a short distance turn; however, when I perform a short-swing turn at a high speed, making one very quick edge set to the next edge set, I travel perhaps 20 feet between turns. At a very slow speed, I can do the same move and travel only four feet. Besides the mechanics of the short-swing turn its distinguishing characteristic is not in the distance traveled but in the signature it leaves on the hill.

When you look at a series of short-swing turns etched in the snow, you clearly see where the edge set occurred to begin a turn, as well as where the edge set ended and initiated the next turn. These two edge sets look like railroad tracks set across the fall line at the particular angle you skied. Between the tracks the snow has been brushed away, creating a windshield-wiper effect; the snow always brushed off to the side of the fall line.

In sum, the short-swing turn has extreme pressure at the edge set in the beginning of the turn, no pressure in the middle (the windshield wiping phase), and extreme pressure at the finish (the new beginning). Understand that the short-swing turn is nothing more than a very dynamic short-radius turn and one that's an essential part of high performance skiing.

High Performance Tip #8

John Hoffman: Converging Turns

Unfortunately, converging turns are associated with snow plows and stem christies, things that people generally want to out grow. The stem christie is quite valuable; on a very steep hill, it is sometimes your most effective turn. I like to use the stem christie on the race course at times when I want to hang on to the speed of my outside ski, yet still be set up for the next turn. What I do is keep my weight on the outside ski coming out of the turn and allow my center of mass to fall down the hill. Just as I'm about to catch the outside edge of my outside ski, I step onto the converged (or stemmed) inside ski, making it the new turning ski, and I ride it through the next gate.

A converged ski shoots you directly down the slope to where you want it to go and at a quicker pace. You are taking a force that is aimed in one direction and decelerating it very quickly; this creates forces, mass, and acceleration (M-A). Mass is constant; yet whenever you put a ski across a resultant force line, you create resistance. If you can deal with the result of that resistance, you will execute dynamically balanced turning; if you can't, you're going to crash.

We are, however, at the mercy of gravity as we go down the hill. In a turn, I cannot accelerate when I'm turning, I can just decelerate less (you accelerate when you turn into the fall line).

One of the differences between a skilled skier and one who is less skilled is that the former decelerates less than the latter when turning. Done correctly, a converging turn can give you a measure of acceleration at the very beginning of a turn. Sometimes you want this in your skiing, whether it be in a race course, mogul field, or free-skiing, the latter of which requires you to make dramatic changes of direction to avoid obstacles or other skiers.

High Performance Tip #9

John Hoffman: The Round-Finished Turn

The whole trick to a rounded turn is to allow your center of mass to get down the hill before your skis so that the skis will follow you, rather than the opposite. As your skis follow you, they will form the letter *s* in the snow. Generally, skiers who keep their center of mass up the hill from their skis tend to make a very quick, choppy initiation of the turn; they ski straight ahead for a while and then make a rather abrupt, sloppy finish to the turn because they are not steering the skis to finish the turn. These skiers are being steered by their skis. You want to lead the action rather than follow it and let your skis catch up with your body.

Problem: Lack of Edge Control

Though it's possible to ski without using your edges, going straight down a hill can be very boring. Most recreational skiing consciously uses the inside edge of the downhill ski and the outside edge of the uphill ski, even though in actuality both edges of both skis work in subtle ways as you work your way down a slope. High performance skiing consciously incorporates both edges of both skis whenever they're needed. So, when we refer to *edge control* we refer to the ability to use both edges of both skis whenever the conditions and situation call for it. The following drills are designed to help you explore the possibilities of edge control from many different perspectives.

Drill: Sideslipping (Different Variations)

Purpose: To increase your sensitivity (e.g., balance and pressure) of your edges relative to the movements of your feet/boots, with respect to the influence of your angles, your position on your skis (forward or back), and the position of your skis relative to the fall line.

Conditions: All kinds.

Slope Rating: Intermediate through expert.

Performing the Drill. In each of the following sideslipping drills, you're most often riding *flat skis*; that is, skis that are not gripping an edge and that glide or drift down the slope over the snow, sometimes brushing away the snow. Sideslipping is slipping in balance sideways. It is guided by the influence you give the skis with the weight of your body and by the subtle manipulation of the edges with your feet. As a rule, sideslip in the drills position but with your skis a little bit closer together and your center of mass and upper body facing down the fall line.

Stand at a 90 degree angle to the fall line, edges set, with your uphill ski slightly ahead of your downhill ski. Tip both of your boots down the fall line, just enough to allow the edges of your skis to release. If you keep your legs together, you allow your downhill ski to slip completely free of any edge pressure, using a subtle feathering or edging of the outside edge of your uphill ski to give you stability and control your speed.

On steeper terrain use the subtle edging and feathering of the uphill edges of both skis to control speed. Sideslipping is an excellent drill to do on very steep terrain or ice where it really tests your edge control skills.

To sideslip straight down the fall line, keep your weight centered right over your boots. If you want to move forward while sideslipping, anticipate the change by directing your weight slightly ahead with a forward flex on your boots, initiated with a slight flexing in the ankles. If you want to move back while sideslipping, direct your weight slightly behind with a comparable flex in your heels.

These subtle weight transfers in anticipation of the directional change, along with slight knee flexions and ankle movements that change edge pressure, influence the appropriate directional shifts of the tails and tips of your skis. Don't think too much about executing subtle ankle movements; instead, constantly keep your downhill ski running free or sideways. Learning the subtle control of your edges comes with practice of sideslipping in varied conditions.

Play with the following variations of sideslipping, realizing that you'll likely have a strong side and weak side for slipping. Work on both.

Basic Sideslip. Sideslip straight down the fall line; on an angle down the fall line with the tips of your skis leading the way; and on an angle down the fall line with your tails leading the way. (See Figure 8.11.)

Repetitive Sideslip to Hockey Stop. Sideslip to a point where you make a hockey stop: Simultaneously set the uphill

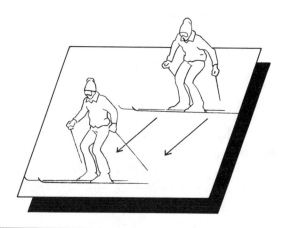

Figure 8.11 A basic sideslip.

Figure 8.12 Sideslip to a hockey stop.

edges of both skis by flexing at the knees and tipping your boots into the hill. To complete the hockey stop, flex and tip simultaneously, planting your pole down the hill from your boots to square your upper body down the fall line for balance; angle your knees into the hill to keep your skis from slipping. The platform developed by this hockey stop drill resembles the kind of platform you would use to ski the steeps.

Continue the drill by standing tall, releasing your edges, and sideslipping to another hockey stop. Repeat in a straight line all the way down the hill, switching sides and experimenting with different speeds. If you want to vary this, make half-hockey stops by flexing and tipping to a stop without using the pole plant, though still facing your upper body down the hill. (See Figure 8.12.)

Expect to feel pressure against the inside ankle, outside knee, and outer portion of the thigh of your downhill leg; also expect to feel pressure against the outside ankle and hip of your uphill leg.

Falling Leaf.   Sideslip like a leaf falling from a tree; first, slip the tips forward and then slightly uphill so that the skis almost stop; second, slip the tails back down the hill and then slightly uphill so that the skis almost stop. Continue down the hill, alternating the sideslip of the tips and tails. You can accomplish this by incorporating the directional changes of the preceding

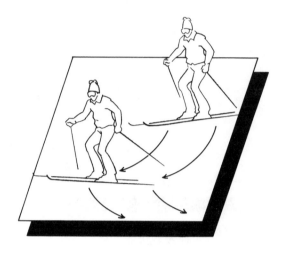

Figure 8.13 Falling leaf exercise.

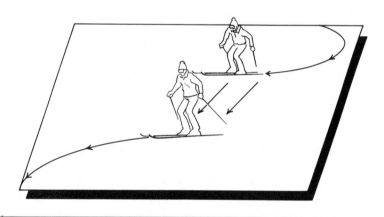

Figure 8.14 Turn, traverse, and sideslip.

drill and by keeping your upper body relaxed rather than moving it to try to move your skis. The movements are very subtle. *Continue to allow your downhill ski to run free by not pressuring its edges during these adjustments*; feather the uphill ski by subtly applying on-and-off edge pressure to control direction and speed. (See Figure 8.13.)

Directed Sideslip. Pick a target down the hill and sideslip to it; make this a moving target and sideslip to follow it.

Turn-Traverse Sideslip: Traverse-Turn Sideslip. Make a comfortable turn at slow speed, traverse for 20 to 30 feet, then let your skis sideslip down the fall line for another 20 to 30 feet. Traverse diagonally across the hill, turn, and at the end of your turn let your skis sideslip. You can do this by skidding, but concentrate on sideslipping. (See Figure 8.14.)

Pole Push Sideslip.   Assume a sideslip position, flexed low so that you can place your poles to your sides and in the snow up the hill behind you; your center of mass is facing directly down the fall line. Release your edges and, pushing off with your poles, propel your slippage down the hill. Push easy and push hard; work with staying in balance over your skis. Employ your subtle foot action to keep you going straight and skiing a flat ski.

Sideslip Sprint.   Just for fun and to get loose, sideslip as fast as you can down a slope. You experience being in balance and relaxed with effortless motion as if your boots were hooked with hinges to your lower legs; your upper body stays quiet while the hinges allow for subtle foot movements. You have to concentrate to feel your knees moving.

Drill: Single Ski Traverse

Purpose: To develop balance and pressure-edge control.
Conditions: Standard.
Slope Rating: Standard.

Performing the Drill.   In drills position, stand only on your *downhill ski* and traverse the hill at FLEP #1 or #2. Lift your uphill ski completely off the snow. Repeat in the other direction; go back and forth several times. Next, ski across the hill, each way, standing on only your *uphill ski*, holding your downhill ski completely off the snow.

Kinesthetic Hint.   When skiing on your downhill ski, you feel pressure in your downhill knee and quadricep muscle; when skiing on your uphill ski, you feel a balancing tension in the inside of the uphill knee and inner thigh (gracilis and sartorius muscles, as well as the lower quadricep). Overall, you experience a feeling of balance in your hips. During the most awkward part of the drill, skiing only on the uphill ski, counterbalance with the downhill ski by holding it off of the snow, slightly converged toward the uphill ski.

Drill: Hot Wedges

Purpose: To develop greater responsiveness to dynamic edge pressure, which is especially important in steep terrain and greater quickness with on-and-off pressure, which is especially important in icy conditions.

Conditions: Standard and varied.

Slope Rating: Advanced and expert.

Performing the Drill. From a wedge position, use exaggerated ankle and knee angulation to tip your skis on edge, *one at a time*, making quick dynamic turns straight down the fall line. Hold your angles long and hard for deep carving; hold them briefly for quick on-and-off edge sets. When skiing longer edged turns, let the inside wedged ski float in a slight wedge to avoid resistance. When skiing quick on-and-off edge sets, keep the non-turning ski in contact with the snow in its wedged and ready position.

To make your wedges "hotter," add aggressive extension and flexion movements of your legs and an active pole touch rhythm. Vary the angles as much as possible and be very active with this wedge. Next, take it into moguls.

Kinesthetic Hint. You feel persistent pressure on the insides of your knees and lower thighs when holding the hot wedge. Repeated on-and-off wedges produce a lot of pressure on the insides of the ankles; if you don't feel it, you're not edging enough. In either case, you breathe a lot when performing hot wedges, yet your upper body is very quiet.

Drill: Chase Skating

Purpose: According to Brent: To develop more mobility in your skiing, flexibility in your moves, and better independent leg control, weight transfer, and edge control!

Conditions: Standard.

Slope Rating: Standard.

Performing the Drill. This drill requires a lead skater and a chaser, but is predominantly for the *chaser*. The lead skater takes off across the fall line at FLEP #2 or #3. Skating at all times, even when turning, the chaser takes off after the lead skater and tries to catch him or her by using the same tracks as the lead skater. If you pick a skater who's a little faster than you, this is an excellent drill. If you're faster, give the lead skater a head start before you take off in pursuit.

Kinesthetic Hint. There's a very active pushing off of your downhill ski with each skating step. As you push off, simultaneously extend your uphill arm up and forward (elbow bent about 20 degrees) and thrust the elbow of your downhill arm in to your waist (elbow bent at 45 degrees). *Very active* are the key words in this drill!

Drill: Long-Leg, Short-Leg

Purpose: To acquire versatility on skis and learn both how and when to use your edges; specifically, transferring your weight with subtlety when turning, riding a flat ski, getting your hip into the hill, and facing your center of mass down the fall line and your upper body over your turning ski.

Conditions: Standard.

Slope Rating: Standard; can be done on expert slopes.

Figure 8.15 Work from ski to ski and flatten your uphill ski.

Performing the Drill. Assuming a wedge, ski across the slope at FLEP #2 to get used to the drill. Your task is to really ride the inside edge of your downhill ski, which is extended as far as possible away from your body. To make it straight and more on edge tip your upper body out over the downhill ski. When you do this, extend your short leg somewhat to stay in balance. Your wedged or converged inside ski should ride flat on the snow with your knee up under your chest, your boot under your hip. (See Figure 8.15.)

As you do this, allow the inside ski to be very light, in contact with the snow, but exerting little or no force. Just ride the downhill ski until you're ready to turn and use the finish of the carving/turning to initiate your transfer of weight to the weightless inside ski. At this point of weight transfer, simply extend this new turning ski (your long leg) while retracting the other ski as it becomes your new inside ski (your short leg). Repeat this all the way down the hill, getting the maximum extension out of your long legs and the maximum quiet and flat-riding out of your short legs.

Kinesthetic Hint. If you feel a pressure in the downhill hip when you're doing this drill, you're performing at a basic level. If you feel a definite pinch with the pressure in the waist and hip area, you're getting more extension out of your long leg and working at an advanced level; as a result, you're getting more of your hip into the hill: the giant slalom racer's goal. In either case, your inside leg feels like it's doing very little; it's as if you had to lift your inside knee up to shorten the leg and get it out of the way in order to fully extend your long leg.

Drill: High Speed Stem Christies

Purpose: To develop a sense of sequential leg rotation or, more simply, the use of both of your legs independently to effect a more dynamic turn. In that christies were designed to include some skidding, the edging of the downhill ski is gradual; but in this drill, the gradual edging is more like quickly graduated skidding, which allows your lightened inside ski to smoothly match the downhill ski. In a way, when the drill works you are matching the inside ski with the stepped ski at approximately the same time the latter stops skidding.

Conditions: Standard; can be variable.

Slope Rating: Advanced and expert.

Performing the Drill. First, you must think of the words dynamic and refinement. At slower speeds, this drill is used to teach skiers to match their skis while turning. We're going to rev it up for the advanced skier's acquisition of more refined edging skills. Start in drills position, FLEP #4. Ski comfortably but a bit more aggressively down the hill. When you're ready to turn, actively step your uphill ski out and down the hill ahead of your present downhill ski, pointing the tip of your ski in the direction you want to go. As soon as this stepped ski makes contact with the snow, it will be flat and skid, becoming your new turning ski. Stand tall for a moment and then flex at the ankles to make the edges of your ski seek to stop skidding as you move your new inside ski to a parallel position. If you do this at a high speed and in control, you'll learn a great deal about the tiny movements your edges make with the help of your feet—to

Figure 8.16 Be lively, and match your skis in the fall line.

propel you down the mountain. At first, be very obvious with this drill and use a lot of exaggerated movement; even make it playful! Step side to side all the way down the run. (See Figure 8.16.)

Kinesthetic Hint. You should feel yourself becoming very extended and tall when making the step, until the ski begins to skid. When you begin to skid you sense a momentary loss of speed, which is not regained until you match the other ski with your flexing movement.

Drill: Swiveling (Parts One and Two)

Purpose: To develop greater edge sensitivity and control as well as balance and confidence.

Conditions: Standard.

Slope Rating: Beginner and low intermediate (can be taken to all levels after drill is perfected).

Performing the Drill. Part One: Just as in the dance, the twist, you swivel both skis together with little edge pressure or angles. Move to a run where there is plenty of room and swivel away. Move the two relatively flat skis in unison to the beat of your twisting at the waist. This involves counterrotation: While the upper body twists right the skis twist left; upper body left, skis right. If you need to add directional force to the drill to avoid obstacles, feather the inside edge of your downhill ski as you swivel.

Part Two: Swivel as above, but this time travel across the fall line while swiveling. Gradually bend your upper body at the waist into the hill while swiveling, moving from a slight to an exaggerated bend. Your skis will react by edging with each bend of your upper body because you've created angles. Many high performance skiers consider the relationship between the hips and edges one of the most important in skiing. If you add ankle flex with this bending you can exert even more directional control over your swiveling. Again, it's all a matter of edge control and subtle angles.

Kinesthetic Hint. In part one you sense that you are twisting madly, yet if your skis are not flat, you'll catch an outside edge and fall. While keeping your skis flat, you feel the focus in your feet. In part two, while executing the exercise across the fall line, the movement of your hips is abrupt and forceful; the sensation of your skis edging is quick and definite.

Problem:
Overrotation of Upper Body

Problems arise when you use the weight and force of your upper body to make your lower body turn the skis. The obvious problems are skidding turns, edging without precision, falling back on your skis, skiing out of balance, becoming fatigued easily, and looking and feeling as awkward as a child taking his or her first steps.

These problems won't necessarily disappear if you stop overrotating your upper body. This is because controlling your upper body is only one aspect of the remedy. Fortunately, overrotation has such a major impact on your skiing that learning to control it will take you a long way in overcoming these problems.

Imagine trying to walk if you were always throwing your body forward when you stepped forward. Your body's natural reaction would be to coil back to restore balance. The same forces operate in skiing. Your arms complicate matters: When you overrotate your upper body by swinging your arms around like helicopter blades, one arm ends up down the fall line (which is okay) and the other arm ends up pointing up the hill behind you (which is not okay). Quickly, you adapt by swinging back the other way and, subsequently, throw yourself out of balance. Back and forth down the mountain, you ski out of balance, out of control, out of sync, falling back, falling forward, skidding, slipping, losing direction, and following your skis.

This description of the consequences of overrotation should make it clear that skiing in the high performance mode involves getting the most out of the rotational balance between upper and lower body. To quote Dr. George Twardokens (1986):

> The standard source of turning force in advanced skiing is rotation of the lower limbs turning against a relatively stable upper body. The mass of the upper body is composed of the head, chest, upper extremities and the ski poles. The lower body mass includes lower limbs, skis, boots and bind-

Figure 8.17 Keep your tips on the snow during pole feelers.

ings. The pelvic region sometimes rotates together with the lower limbs, and at other times it provides resistance for the lower limbs together with the upper body. (p. 291)

In the most basic language, overrotating your upper body excludes the opportunity to make precise turns; that is, turns that are free of the problems noted earlier, and turns that do not lead to muscular fatigue. Try the following drills and exercises to work on stabilizing your upper body relative to lower body rotation.

Drill: Pole Feeler; Poles in Front (Short-Radius Turns)

Purpose: To develop a quiet, stable upper body that is square with the fall line and not used as a force to make your skis change directions.

Conditions: Standard; mild bumpy terrain with good snow.

Slope Rating: Standard.

Performing the Drill.   For the *pole feeler*, find a comfortable turn rhythm and slope. Instead of using your poles to initiate turns, grip your handles as if they were swords. Extend your arms and poles to your sides forming a human cross; then assume a lower than normal skiing stance, allowing the tips of your poles to touch the snow. Your ski poles are now your antennae. Ski down the run, using your lower body to make the turns, at all times keeping your poles to your sides and in contact with the snow. If your poles come off the snow, or drift in front of or behind you, *stop*. Begin again in the starting position, and resume the drill, skiing the entire run doing pole feelers. (See Figure 8.17.)

If you have problems with this drill, you may be guilty of some or all of the following: twisting too much at the waist/upper body; dragging your arms behind you while turning; not moving your knees; not working your skis independently; and not using subtle foot/boot pressure, steering, or banking.

Poles in front is performed like pole feelers except that you stand taller and grip your pole one fourth of the way up from the tips and extend the handles out in front of you, shoulder high, and off the snow. At all times, keep your poles pointed down the fall line and create a corridor between your poles within which you perform short-radius turns.

If, for both drills, you're having trouble keeping your poles stable, either in front of you or to your sides, you are probably depending on the overrotation of your upper body to help turn your skis. For this reason, and for the sake of discipline, it's best to make only short-radius turns while doing these drills. They're wonderful for learning to keep your upper body facing squarely down the fall line; your lower body can then move independently to turn your skis against your stable upper body.

Kinesthetic Hint. Your overall sensation is that your upper body quietly hangs out over an active pair of legs that do all of the work. You may notice fatigue in your upper arms near the shoulder joint and the sides of your hips, particularly where the large bone of your thigh (femur) inserts into the hip socket.

Expect to experience some muscular and joint discomfort during drills of this nature; the fatigue arises from the static nature of the positioning of the body, notably your arms, shoulders, and hips. Although working to a point of fatigue is a basic training principle in athletics, in this case, working beyond fatigue to the *pain zone* (no pain, no gain) is not considered a sound training principle and instead is a precursor to injury.

Drill:
Hoppers to Turns on the Snow

Purpose: An advanced drill to develop an acute sense of facing your center of mass down the fall line while your feet and legs are moving dynamically from side to side, ultimately half-turning in counterrotation to your upper body.

Conditions: Standard; mildly bumpy terrain.

Slope Rating: Intermediate to expert.

Performing the Drill. Begin like wedge hoppers in the section on lack of speed control; instead of keeping your skis wedged, allow them to move together toward a parallel position after 5 to 10 hoppers per foot. Once the skis are together, continue the momentum of the drill with short, quick, on-edge, off-edge directional changes. These directional changes are not complete turns; this is a drill! They are half-turns made with a hopping motion, designed to help you become accustomed to quick counter movements of your lower body versus a stable upper body. Do as many half-turns as you can. Stop. Begin again, and add a pole plant rhythm that's natural for you.

Kinesthetic Hint. If you're having a lot of trouble with overrotating your upper body, this drill's too advanced to do correctly. Build your counterrotational skills first. (See kinesthetic hint for wedge hoppers.)

Drill: Active Inside Ski Steering

Purpose: To develop a familiarity with the sensation of your lower body rotating away from your upper body and into the turn while your upper body remains relatively still except for the slight activity required to keep it facing down the fall line.

Conditions: Standard at first; then all kinds of conditions.

Slope Rating: Intermediate to expert (can be done on beginner slope).

Performing the Drill. Ski as usual, linking turns, and just after you've transferred your weight to your new turning ski, steer your new inside ski in the direction of your new turn. Do this steering by lightening your inside ski and moving your inside knee and lower leg away from your upper body and the turning ski. Instead of thinking of matching the turning ski, allow the turning ski to follow the directional lead of your inside ski. Just keep your center of mass down the fall line and this maneuver will add magic to your turning. Do this for an entire run; there's much in this drill to incorporate into your everyday skiing! (See Figure 8.18.)

Figure 8.18 Follow the lead of your inside ski.

Kinesthetic Hint. The most pronounced feeling is that you're leading the action with your inside leg; also, your turns feel smoother and somewhat effortless.

Drill: Push the Uphill Ski Forward

Purpose: Unlike inside ski steering, you want to experience the rotation of your lower body away from your stable upper body to initiate an early transfer of your weight to your new turning ski. This is accomplished by unlocking your uphill or inside hip by pushing your uphill ski forward a few inches. In a normal stance where you're traversing parallel across the fall line, your hips become fixed to maintain balance and the separation of your legs during motion.

You don't want to move both legs at the same time to effect a turn and you do want to separate your upper and lower body. Therefore, you have to unlock the hip, which releases the leg that will be pushed or steered to become the new turning ski. As soon as your hip is unlocked, you can allow your skis to move away from you as you (a) more easily move your hips into proper alignment down the fall line, (b) discover how easy it is to fall into your next turn, and (c) realize that it's easier to match your skis during the active steering part of the turn.

Conditions: Standard.

Slope Rating: Standard.

Performing the Drill. Ski as usual; when you've finished your turn or traverse and are ready to begin your next turn, first push (slide) your uphill ski forward (3 to 6 feet) with your foot and leg, and the slight projection forward of your uphill hip. Understand, this is not a diverging move, converging move, step, or stem; rather, it is the pushing of a relatively flat ski, as you might when sliding through a lift line. (See Figure 8.19.)

When you make this push, you must transfer your weight to the ski that's been steered or advanced. Move with it as you flow into your next turn. Rely on your basic turning skills and continue steering the uphill ski through every turn for the rest of the run. What you should notice is that there is a twisting of your upper body in relation to your downhill leg as soon as you push your uphill ski; if you face yourself down the fall line by turning your upper body in that direction, you influence your

Figure 8.19 Unlock your hips by pushing or steering your uphill ski forward.

new turning ski to roll onto its inside edge and turn you effortlessly. This breaks up the static nature of many recreational turns.

Kinesthetic Hint.   You may feel your knees touching as the inside ski pushes ahead; at this point you feel the pressure of the uphill leg's calf resting in front of your downhill leg's knee, or approximating this positioning if your skis are further apart. This will vary according to the terrain.

Exercise

Here is an exercise that is recommended for skiers who overrotate their upper bodies to effect the turning of their skis.

Long-Radius Turns.   Use these turns to grow accustomed to subtly relaxing your upper body's inclination to overrotate to turn your skis. Long-radius turns allow you to more slowly turn your skis across the fall line, giving you longer and wider arcs you can use to get accustomed to riding your skis through rather than jerking them around turns. Another benefit of using the long-radius turn here is that you can get accustomed to looking ahead to your next turn and getting your weight into that turn early.

Problem:
Erratic Pole Use and Rhythm

There are a lot of reasons to use poles in skiing. Mike notes seven:

1. To propel ourselves by pushing off with them
2. To help us to get up after we fall
3. To help us clean snow off of our boots and skis
4. To add points of balance for emergencies
5. As sensors to give us feedback regarding our balance and equilibrium
6. To provide body stabilization; that is, through blocking and pole planting in difficult conditions, we stabilize our upper body while we modify the angles and edges on our skis to get us into the next turn

7. To provide a timing rhythm; that is, as we touch our poles in comfortable conditions we establish a cadence for linked rhythmic turns

The following drills, along with an exercise, are designed to add turning power to your use of poles.

Drill: Pole Touch Rhythm Five-Part Progression

Purpose: To develop conscious movement and rhythm in your skiing that leads to natural extension and relaxation by releasing the muscles' often static flexion. The important lower body muscles used in dynamic skiing include: quadriceps, rectus femoris, gracilis, sartorius, hamstrings, gluteus maximus, gluteus medius, gastrocnemius, and soleus. This drill also teaches you to integrate early weight transfer and more dynamic turning into your skiing.

Conditions: Standard.

Slope Rating: Standard.

Performing the Drill. Part one: assume the drills position, FLEP #2 or #3. As you ski across the hill or down a fairly flat hill, swing your poles out one at a time, moving only your wrists as you extend your poles. This helps you to have a more controlled pole touch and gives you a proper perspective of where your pole should end up once it's past your body and then returned to your body after a pole touch. When you swing your poles forward, just flip your wrist and relax your little finger to affect an effective pole touch feeling. During this drill, you are not to let the poles touch the snow. Make a couple of traverses or straight runs on flat terrain swinging your poles as above. (See Figure 8.20.)

Part two: following the part one instructions, add an up-and-down movement by extending and flexing your legs while traversing at FLEP #2 or #3. At this stage in the progression, learn

Figure 8.20 Swing your poles without touching the snow.

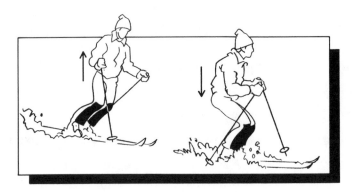

Figure 8.21 Add flexion and extension in your legs to accompany your pole swing.

to couple your up-and-down movements with the rhythmic swinging of your poles. Again, don't let your poles touch the snow. Do a couple of traverses using motion and pole swings. (See Figure 8.21.)

Part three: continue with parts one and two, adding a simultaneous turning of your skis to the right and left. In a sense, you're swiveling them with very little edging, although the swiveling is controlled to correspond to the movement of your poles. For example, when your skis are swiveled to the left, your right pole swings forward. Again, do not touch the snow with

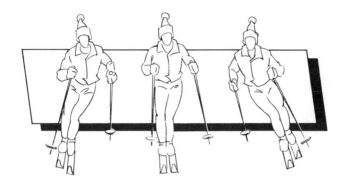

Figure 8.22 Experiment with swiveling on one ski and with both skis.

Figure 8.23 Get your skis turning to the rhythm of your pole touch.

your poles. Do this for a couple of traverses. (See Figure 8.22.)

Part four: continuing the former three parts, let your poles touch the snow as they naturally come into play. Use your pole touch rhythm no matter what; keep it up and let your skis begin turning by applying edging pressure appropriate to your rhythm. (See Figure 8.23.)

Part five: graduate from the turns above to decisive, short-swing turns accompanied by a rhythmic pole plant. Now, start down a run and go through the five parts of this progression in succession without breaking in between. (See Figure 8.24.)

Figure 8.24 Actively turn your skis in sync with your pole plant.

Kinesthetic Hint.   When swinging the poles you feel them floating up and back with most of the effort focused in your wrists. When flexing, the forward pressure is focused in the balls of your feet. When flexing accompanies the touching of poles, this boot pressure is foot to foot in sync with your pole rhythm: right pole touch, left boot pressure; left pole touch, right boot pressure. It's subtle; feeling it adds sensitivity to your skiing.

Drill: Sequential Leg Drill

Purpose: To increase efficacy of timing the use of your poles and the setting of your edges to effect quickness in your skiing.

Conditions: Standard.

Slope Rating: Standard.

Performing the Drill.   Start in a comfortable wedge, facing directly down the fall line. As you ski, hold the wedge and begin to use your pole touch rhythm, not touching the snow. Add the extension and flexion of your legs, still holding the wedge. Next,

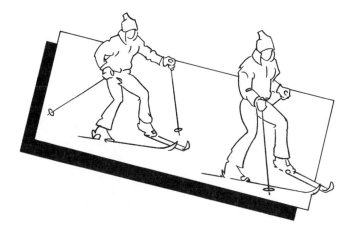

Figure 8.25 Ski in a wedge, swing your poles, but don't touch your poles to the snow.

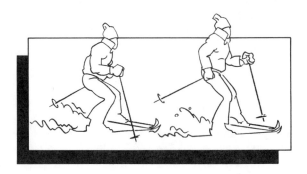

Figure 8.26 A good way to practice a more dynamic pole touch rhythm: up and touch; up and touch.

add foot turning (like hot wedges), putting most of your weight on one ski at a time while keeping the other one wedged on the snow. In effect, you're bounding quickly from ski to ski while traveling at a good pace and holding a wedge. It's an exciting, dynamic movement that makes you a believer in the utility of the basic wedge. (See Figures 8.25 through 8.27.)

Kinesthetic Hint. When you start turning from foot to foot, the sensation is like making half-short-swing turns to each side: skid, edge, rebound to the right; skid, edge, rebound to the left. The more you increase the edge angle, the more you rebound. Your body can only take so much of this, and as you pick up

Figure 8.27 Pressure one ski, then the other.

speed, the skier in your muscles and bones wants to progress to short-swing turns; this is exactly what you do. The predominant feeling is that there's no time to think about anything but moving as quickly as you can and breathing!

Drill:
Open the Door With a Pole Touch

Purpose: To help you free up the movement of your upper body relative to your pole use; to get you to move more directly into your next turn by going through the door you've opened with your pole touch.

Conditions: Standard.

Slope Rating: Standard.

Performing the Drill. Find a comfortable slope and turn rhythm and concentrate on medium-radius turns. Upon the completion of one turn begin to face your upper body and your downhill pole down the hill in anticipation of your next turn. Touch your pole early and as you do, extend your legs and reach down the hill away from the skis and imagine that you've opened a door through which you'll direct your upper body. Don't think about your lower body and skis; they'll follow your lead! This

Figure 8.28 Get your upper body down the mountain and into your next turn early.

is an exaggerated movement that helps you to develop a greater sensitivity for using your pole touch to manipulate your turns and get you to commit to your turns earlier. It's great for bumps, slalom, powder, and the steeps. (See Figure 8.28.)

Kinesthetic Hint. When you reach your pole out early, you feel a distinct stretching of your pectoral muscles between your shoulders and your breast.

Exercise

Sync Skiing. Team up with another skier (or skiers) and let that person set the rhythm for your skiing. Ski in any condition you choose, but place yourselves as close as is comfortable, and follow your partner's lead. Push off, and when the leader turns, you turn. If you wish to truly accomplish synchronized skiing, you and your partner have to touch your poles simultaneously and ski to the same rhythm. This is not always as easy as it seems, because we have our own particular rhythms, and our bodies remember them well. Still, this is a terrific exercise for adding discipline to your skiing.

Problem:
Lack of Extension/Movement

A common complaint among infrequent recreational skiers is excessive fatigue, principally in the front of the thighs, but also in the lower back and the back of the calves. Researchers have discovered that there are many different types of fatigue. As a rule, the muscular demands for different sports predict the kind of fatigue that can be expected after performing the requisite movements of the sport. Whether aspects of the sport are repeatedly performed correctly or incorrectly, it is common to experience some fatigue.

The good news about fatigue for the recreational skier is that it's self-protective to a great extent. At the cellular level, the body shuts down to protect itself from overuse and damage; in a way, chemical messengers and specific cells stop cooperating and prohibit muscular contraction. Injury often results from a powerfully competitive mind and its brain chemicals along with adrenalin cooperatively circumventing the body's efforts to shut down to protect itself.

In skiing, as in all sports, we practice muscle/energy-conservation and capitalize on any and all uses of momentum, gravity, physical forces, laws of motion, the design of our equipment, and any other resources to which we have access. We can accomplish conservation by respecting the complementary work of muscles and muscle systems—especially those that affect the actions of our knees, ankles, feet, hips, and legs—and by making movement an essential component of our skiing. Not only do we need to ski with flexible muscles conditioned to accomplish the work they're requested to perform, we must also learn to use momentum to maximize other skiing resources. The design of our skis, for example, with their broad tip, narrow waist under boot, and wider tail, foster curved, arc-shaped turns when we apply the appropriate amounts of foot and leg steering, pressuring, and edging to our skis.

Using extension and flexion in our skiing is the best way to integrate the above themes. One of the main reasons recreational skiers experience excessive fatigue is that they ski flexed (knees and ankles bent in such a way that muscles, not the skeletal structure, must hold the body in position) too much of the time. In this position, recreational skiers rarely relax their muscles by using the momentum generated as they ski to help direct their skis down the hill. Nor do they relax extending their legs to create brief moments of skeletal bracing (recall the discussion of skeletal bracing in chapter 1) and to assist in the initiation of new turns. In addition to a lack of movement (i.e., extension and flexion), there are several technical aspects that lead to fatigue in recreational skiers. These include leaning back, following rather than leading their skis, skiing terrain that overtaxes their skills, poor upper-lower body separation, overrotation of shoulders, arms, or hips, for example, and generally, tense and static skiing.

Many persons think that *extension* means upward movement and that all you need to do is raise your arms, shoulders, and chest high and stand tall. This, however, is not at all the case. Although standing tall is advised, the image of an extended upper body is not an accurate interpretation of extension; rather, a skier who extends correctly does so through the lengthening of his or her legs as in standing up from a squatted position, whether this extension be vertical, lateral, or projected down the hill into the new turn.

If you watch World Cup racers, you'll notice little movement upwards and a lot of extension laterally (i.e., the racers are moving their legs out and away from their bodies). The more dynamic your skiing becomes, the more lateral extension you achieve. For many recreational skiers, movement up (i.e., standing tall to initiate their turns) would be a wonderful beginning to adding extension and relaxation to their skiing.

When you add extension to your skiing, you momentarily come to a point of balance over both skis. Extension allows you to move your skis on and off their edges, making them flat (no edging) during an important phase of your turns when you want your skis to pivot easily in the direction of your new turn. Good extension also assists the transfer of your weight from your old turning ski to your new turning ski through an easier, more fluid movement of your center of mass across the path of your skis. This introduces your body early into your new turn (i.e., if your skis are traveling to the right, you must allow your upper body to cross over the line that your skis have traveled, and project down or extend into the fall-line to the left). Extending your legs also gives your contracted muscles a chance to relax, preventing fatigue caused by persistent contraction or flexion. Use the moment of extension (i.e., muscle relaxation with the aid of skeletal bracing) to boost your turning power by letting it provide a moment for your lower body to untwist into the new turn if your upper body had been held in a countered or anticipated position in preparation for this turn.

Because the abdominal muscles tie the ribs and pelvis together as well as providing stability to the lower back, it is important to keep these muscles taut, especially when you are in the countered or anticipated position. Without keeping the abdominal muscles taut, the lower back is vulnerable to aches, pains, spasms, and poor performance. When referring to the countered or anticipated position in skiing, we are speaking of lower back strength as well as flexibility (i.e., strong, toned abdominal muscles).

In high performance skiing, think of the upper and lower body as connected and as two complementary units. In other words, when you twist your upper torso at the waist, you exert deliberate tension on your hips. If you immediately give in to this tension, your lower body will twist in the same direction as your upper body. This practice may lead to jerky, imprecise skiing if you abruptly swing your body around to make your lower body turn. If, however at the end of each turn you hold your upper and lower body in a twisted relationship, with your upper body pointed down the hill, this twisted relationship becomes turning power when you extend to initiate your new turn.

If your skis don't extend away from your upper body, you often rely on excessive muscular effort, swiveling, and skidding to turn your skis. Turn after turn in this muscular fashion wears you out and leads to those ubiquitous burning thighs, aching legs, sore hips, and throbbing lower-back pain.

The easiest way most recreational skiers learn extension and movement in their skiing is to think of standing tall or moving up and down: up to begin a turn, down to control and finish a turn. This is a proper first progression. As noted earlier, the high performance skier approaches this more extremely. For this skier, up is often extending the upper and lower body into the turn and down the fall line or extending the legs out laterally, side to side, while keeping the upper body stable. Although the upper body may appear low, the high performance skier doesn't tire as easily using this kind of lateral extension.

Whatever your level of performance, you'll want to ensure extension in your skiing. Yet, for all I have written, the truth of the matter is that each of us has a perfect way to get extension in our skiing and a perfect muscular sense about what's best for us in terms of performance and efficiency. The earlier comments in this section will help you appreciate the need to discover these important features of extension in your skiing; the following drills, added to those in the previous section, will give you an opportunity to explore extension.

Drill: Starting Block Turns

Purpose: To experience extension off your uphill ski; more dramatic movement into your next turn; and independent leg action and weight transfer.

Conditions: Standard.

Slope Rating: Standard.

Performing the Drill. Find a comfortable slope and turn rhythm and concentrate on medium-radius turns. As you finish your turns, note the distinction between the uphill and downhill legs, placing special emphasis on pushing off down the fall line with your uphill leg like a sprinter exploding out of the starting blocks. After you explode down the fall line, work to smooth

Figure 8.29 Push off your uphill leg and down the fall line.

out the abrupt pressure on your new turning ski, which is created by pushing off your uphill ski; relax and allow yourself to float with the movement and ride your momentarily flattened skis, and use your new inside ski to steer you to a controlled edging of your new turning ski. As you become comfortable with this drill, take it to steeper terrain and shorter-radius turns. (See Figure 8.29.)

Kinesthetic Hint. You feel a lot of pressure on the ball of your uphill foot, the front, lower part of your uphill leg and against the top of your boot. Coupled with this is the distinct sensation in the uphill knee as you release this pressure and explode. It feels something like skating down the hill.

Drill: Start Turns Off the Top Step

Purpose: To experience extension from your downhill ski to your uphill ski; more dynamic movement to prepare your body to extend down the fall line and get you into your next turn; and weight transfer.

Conditions: Standard.

Slope Rating: Standard.

Performing the Drill. Find a comfortable slope and turn rhythm and concentrate on medium-radius turns. As you finish one turn and prepare for the next, think of your downhill ski as being on the bottom step and your uphill ski as being one step higher. As you begin your next turn by touching your pole and transferring your weight, make yourself extend off the higher step and stand tall: Your legs will be very extended, your upper body proudly upright, and your head looking down the fall line. Exaggerate your extension and this will make it easier for you to cross over the path of your skis and fall into your turn. Smooth out the abruptness of this drill by using inside ski steering and riding out your momentarily flattened skis. (See Figure 8.30.)

Kinesthetic Hint. When you stand tall there's a distinct pressure in the hip socket of your uphill leg. As you cross over

Figure 8.30 Extend off the top foot and down the fall line.

or project your upper body down the fall line, there's a free-falling sensation that encourages you to throw your upper body down the fall line (actually you're extending your legs). Try to extend as far as possible; you won't fall, and your boots and skis will bring you back to earth.

Drill: Launch Yourself Into Turns; Pole Touch Launch Into Turns

> **Purpose:** To encourage exaggerated extension into your turns and exaggerated response to weight transfer and the touching of your poles.
>
> **Conditions:** Standard.
>
> **Slope Rating:** Standard.

Performing the Drill. Find a comfortable slope and turn rhythm and concentrate on medium-radius turns. At the finish of one turn, project your uphill hip, shoulder, and arm down the fall line and into your next turn, then make a pole touch. Do this by thinking of launching yourself in the direction of the turn. Think less of the position of your skis, pushing off, and stepping up; seriously attempt to launch your upper body down the hill. Become very aggressive and animated with this drill.

To add a slight variation, focus on the touching of your pole as the supercharger to your launch. In the steeps, you haven't

Figure 8.31 Launch your upper body down the hill.

the time to do anything but continue to turn from these pole plants. This is a great drill for sharpening that skill. Concentrating on the projection of your uphill hip, shoulder, and arm down the fall line and into your next turn will add a new thrill and dimension to your skiing; one you can count on in the steeps, which is the next place you'll want to take this drill. (See Figure 8.31.)

Kinesthetic Hint. This feels like starting block turns amplified many times over; if there were no boots on your feet, you'd sail 5 to 10 yards down the hill with each launch. Also, you'll notice a distinct stretching of your uphill hip and of your rectus abdominus muscle (the abdominal muscle that runs down the middle of your abdomen from your rib cage to your pelvis) when you launch. It's a great feeling!

Problem:
Lack of Variety in Your Turns

It's elementary: The more versatile your turning ability, the more dynamic your skiing, and the greater your potential for successfully skiing more challenging terrain. Try the following drills and exercises to encourage you to add variety in your turning.

Drill: Single Ski Skiing

Purpose: To develop balance, agility, greater sensitivity to edge control, and foot steering; turning is edge control and foot steering! (Note: Many high performance skiers struggle with this drill due to the difficulty in learning to use both the inside and outside edges of both skis. To be sure, it's a high performance balancing drill advised for racers, bump skiers, and others who want to add versatility to their skiing.)

Conditions: Standard.

Slope Rating: Beginning to advanced.

Performing the Drill. You begin by building up momentum; then lift one ski off the snow and turn the opposite ski to the right and then left. If this ski is your right ski, your left turn will be easy (because you're used to turning on the inside edge); it's the right turn that will be tough. If you overturn the familiar way, turning on the outside edge is all the more difficult. To turn

Figure 8.32 Turning on the outside edge of your single ski takes balance and commitment to getting your hip into the turn.

a single ski to the side of its outside edge, fully extend the lower body and then slightly retract the single ski that remains on the snow. Then, with your foot, steer the ski in the desired direction. Simultaneously, steer the ski that's off the snow into the turn, and throw your outside hip over the outside edge of the turning ski. Add to this, rhythmic pole use to give you tempo and balance, and to keep you from overturning.

To continue the drill, ski on one ski for 5 to 10 turns; then stop. Ski on the other ski for 5 to 10 turns; then stop. Next, ski a few turns on one ski and, without stopping, ski a few turns on the other ski. Do this repeatedly. (See Figure 8.32.)

Kinesthetic Hint. Your most predominant sensation is one of falling over the outside edge of the ski that you're turning to its outside.

Drill: Discover the Extremes of Your Turning Ski

Purpose: To develop greater sensitivity to the most balanced position on your skis during turning and greater control of your turning ski.

Conditions: Standard.

Slope Rating: Standard.

Performing the Drill. Find a comfortable slope and turn rhythm and concentrate on medium-radius turns. You'll be experimenting with three different pressures while turning: to the tips of your skis, to the middle, and to the tails. First, plan a series of five turns in which you'll direct extreme pressure to the tips of your skis in all phases of the turn, beginning to end. Stop and evaluate how this feels. Do the same for mid-ski and tail pressures.

After you've evaluated all three, return to the pressure that felt best to you; ski a run very aggressively trying to maintain that feeling of pressure. If maintaining it was easy, it is likely that this pressure area is an important aspect of your skiing. It is hoped that the middle pressure felt most natural to you, but in actuality we use all three pressure areas depending on slope, conditions, and where you are in the turn.

Kinesthetic Hint. With tip pressure, you feel as if you were going to fall over the tips of your skis; there is lots of pressure on your toes, the pads of your feet, and your lower leg from the flex against your boot. With tail pressure, you feel tightness in your thighs, which begins very subtly and then becomes pronounced; there is the sensation of being led through your turns and of being late. The pressure is against the backs of your boots. You experience spurts of speed and are generally stressful when turns are constantly emphasizing the tails of the skis. With middle pressure, you feel as if your whole foot were flat in the boot and in contact with your ski; you feel very relaxed.

Exercises

The following exercises put you in situations where you must adjust your skiing to different turn radii and conditions.

Sync Skiing. As discussed in "Erratic pole use and rhythm."

Figure Eighting. As discussed in "Lack of speed control."

Follow Someone's Tracks. Select a partner and follow in that skier's tracks. Be adventurous and force yourself to ski the same line at the same speed as the leader.

Vary Your Turn Radii. Start down a long run and commit yourself to skiing 5 long-, 3 medium-, 6 short-, 2 long-, 2 medium-, and 10 short-radius turns; then 10 short-swing turns; and finish with 3 medium- and 4 long-radius turns. The object is to vary your turns, nonstop, on any hill, but an upper-level slope is preferable. Assigning a specific number of repetitions to each turn commits you to a measure of discipline.

Problem:
Tense and Static Skiing

In the broadest sense, tense and static skiing is both the cause and the result of the majority of problems discussed in this chapter. When it's the cause, it usually pertains to inexperienced skiers who are avid about their sport, yet muscularly tense and emotionally tentative in their approach to skiing anything but the surest of conditions.

Being tense and tentative, these skiers are unable either to move freely or to make the emotional commitment to ski a run with any particular attitude (e.g., "I'll ski this aggressively; I'll ski this like a butterfly; I'll bash those bumps; I'll fly; I'll ski loose"; etc.). Lacking relaxed muscles and emotional commitment, these skiers have difficulty experimenting with their skiing, and subsequently, difficulty acquiring the skills that would liberate them from static skiing.

When tense and static skiing is the result of problems, it usually pertains to more experienced skiers who are also avid about their sport, yet remain muscularly awkward and emotionally stubborn in their approach to skiing everything they have the guts to try. Not lacking in attitude, these skiers have an ambitious approach to skiing, yet lack the skills to stay with it once fatigue and awkwardness set in.

Their lack of edge control, extension, pole use and rhythm, upper-lower body separation, and speed control all cause the skiers' muscles to become increasingly tense. Instead of interpreting this situation as time to take a break or to investigate their technical shortcomings, they remain emotionally stubborn and continue skiing under physical and mental fatigue. The result: tense and static skiing.

Drill: Turning Ski Pole Drag

Purpose: To place your upper body down the hill over your turning ski throughout the duration of your turn. Leaning into the hill while turning is a prominent sign of tense and static skiing.

Conditions: Standard.

Slope Rating: Standard.

Figure 8.33 Drag the tip of your downhill pole to establish balance.

Performing the Drill. Find a comfortable slope and turn rhythm and concentrate on short- to medium-radius turns. As you turn to the left, allow the tip of your right (downhill) pole to drag on the snow while holding your left (uphill) pole parallel to the slope. Reverse this when turning to the right. Ski down the hill making a series of short- to medium-radius turns, continuously using this pole drag/pole parallel action. Keep your pole in constant contact with the snow throughout the turn, you'll be able to control the movement of your body away from leaning into the hill. (See Figure 8.33.)

Kinesthetic Hint. Ironically, what's involved is a static feeling; however, the drill forces tense skiers to do something they don't do normally, which contributes to their problems. It gives you the sensation of always having to look down the fall line with your upper body over your downhill ski. In a muscular sense, this drill is felt intensely in your downhill leg during each traverse.

Drill: Inside-Outside Single Ski Traverse

Perform as described in "Lack of edge control."

Drill: Sequential Leg Drill

Perform as described in "Erratic pole use and rhythm."

Exercises

Perform the following in a variety of conditions, and where applicable, behind skiers with a broad range of abilities.

Follow Someone's Tracks.   Follow the description in "Lack of speed control." It's valuable for advanced skiers to occasionally follow the tracks of less advanced skiers; this adds discipline to their skiing. This is accomplished by following the tracks exactly and employing precise skiing skills in negotiating rhythms to which you're likely unaccustomed.

Sync Skiing.   Perform as described in "Erratic pole use and rhythm."

Target Skiing.   Using whatever slope is comfortable, concentrate on making short- to medium-radius turns (short-radius are preferable); fix your eyes on a target somewhere down the slope (e.g., a tree, trail sign, knoll, another skier, a bump, etc.). Ideally, select as the target someone who's standing at the bottom of the run waiting for you to ski down. The essential to the drill: Pay attention to the target at all times; don't pay attention to your skiing!

Kinesthetic hint.   There is a strong sensation of not knowing what's going on with your skis and poles. Your dominant kinesthetic feeling is that your hips are moving along with your legs. Moreover, you can see the tips of your skis with your low peripheral vision; that is, at the bottom of your field of vision you're aware that your skis are moving back and forth, although you never really focus on them.

Cadence Skiing.   Find that comfortable slope and pair up with another skier. To his or her commands, spoken or mechanical (poles tapping), make turns or other prescribed movements as the two of you ski down the run with you in front! Ideally, the signals should be rhythmic and include changing rhythms. This helps you to remain flexible, alert, and quick rather than tense and static. If the exercise produces the latter in you, go to an easier slope and experiment with more predictable rhythms until the exercise feels like it's working for you.

Use a Bump to Loosen You Up. Find a bump or two that you can comfortably ski up to at a controlled speed (preferably slow); then ski right over the top of it. When you get to the bump, let your legs retract and your knees come toward your chest. Go over the top of the bump, keeping your head and chest upright, arms held in drills position, and legs folded up into your torso. As you come to the down side of the bump, keep your upper body still and push your legs into the trough. Stop! This is not bump skiing; this is only an exercise to get you used to less tense and static skiing.

Summary

1. Although it's unwise to view one problem area in your skiing as isolated from others, you may find commonly occurring problems very troublesome. Addressing these by using the appropriate sections in this chapter helps you by working on drills and exercises that touch heavily on your main problem while simultaneously touching on aspects of lesser problems.

2. As you perform drills and exercises to correct one problem, you may notice that another problem becomes more obvious. Good! Now, work on this problem. The drills and exercises really ask you to simultaneously address many aspects of your skiing. Their crossover effect is tremendous.

3. Have fun with the drills and exercises. They're meant to add to your skiing pleasure and variety, not to detract from it. Enjoy the difficulty and accomplishment in drills alone. This says something positive about you and your skiing!

4. Dwell on problems in your skiing only while you are working on them in drills and exercises. Otherwise, free-ski and smile a lot. Laugh, joke, have fun, and remain relaxed!

High Performance Tip #10

John Hoffman: On Balance

Exercises are fun, even though they're often more difficult to do than the maneuver they're designed to improve. Anyone can have fun with exercises, especially good skiers. Try something different: a get-you-out-of-balance fore-aft exercise. Begin by skiing down the hill and leaning as far forward as you can for the entire run. Next run, lean back as far as you can. Let's call your furthest forward position *5 forward* and your furthest back position *5 back*.

See if you can find 4 forward and 4 back and progressively work to a point where you're playing with 1 forward and 1 back. Pair up with someone and put yourselves in different positions fore and aft. Let each other know your numerical positions as well as the ones to which you are moving. Make a game of it. Recognize that the 1 position is going to lead to 2 unless you put the skids on and start moving the other direction.

The key here is to know when you're progressing away from zero. This is the ideal for each person: neutral or zero balance. The five positions forward and backward are the easiest to identify; the other positions come with experimentation. Focus your attention on moving from higher to lower numbers in your skiing until you find your zero balance.

Sticking with this theme of fore and aft balance, let's say that you recognize you're in 4 forward. Okay, what do you do to get to 3 forward? Drop your rear slightly, stand more on your heels, or move your feet slightly ahead. Now at 3 forward you realize that you're still too far forward. Adjust backward. Now you feel that you're standing on your heels and that your toenails are pressed against the tops of your boots. This is a tipoff that you've overadjusted to the rear. Try to find that zero position by bringing your skis back under you or flexing your ankles forward.

High Performance Tip #11

The Inside Ski

We often think too much about the outside ski, especially with respect to turning, edge control, and carved turns. Although it is the quintessential ski to racing, the outside ski alone is neither the sole secret to great turning nor to expert, recreational, nonracing skiing. In fact, a microscopic look at the turning skis reveals that both skis steer through the turn, albeit each in a distinct relationship to the snow and power in the turn. Racers ride the downhill (outside or turning) ski from gate to gate (an exception being the White Pass turn, which is made on the inside ski) because it's efficient, smooth, quick, and precise; and because they must if they want to stay in control at high speeds, and to contain the momentum of their bodies flying down the mountain.

In the breadth of recreational skiing, however, sole reliance on the outside ski leads to a lazy attitude about the inside ski. By never really working to make the inside ski an active part of their skiing, some skiers approach their turns by lifting the inside ski off the snow and cramming the edge of their downhill ski into the snow to effect a turn. This may work for a while (forget what it looks like), but as soon as fatigue sets in, it's not unusual to see inside ski lifters tripping over their inactive inside skis. As Mike puts it, "The sooner skiers discover the impact of the inside ski, the more prepared they will be for changes in snow conditions, moguls, unexpected surprises, and terrain changes."

The use of the inside ski in high performance skiing is not a hardcore technique or mechanical manipulation; it's subtle and artistic. As you learn to use the inside ski by trying the various drills in this chapter, you come to understand the functions of the inside ski with respect to steering and leading the action through turns. Once incorporated in your mind/muscles/joints, you neither need nor want to consciously think much about the inside ski while you're skiing.

Of course, the development of this understanding of the inside ski takes plenty of time on skis; the use of mental reminders to steer or lead with the inside ski can be helpful both during drills and exercises that utilize the inside ski and while free-skiing for fun and precision on comfortable terrain. In the high performance mode, however, you've got to think less and feel more by using the sensors in your feet, hands, eyes, knees, ankles, hips, arms, shoulders, skin, and ears. These sensors support what you know about your inside ski: that it is the ski that leads into the turn.

Think about it: The inside ski not only goes into the turn first, it is the last to come out of the turn. In many ways you can consider your inside ski a fail-safe mechanism for all of your skiing. Foremost, you must be aware of the position of your inside ski and how to use it to your best advantage. Rely on it! Concentrate on the drills that have you work your inside ski and you'll notice leaps in your skiing performance.

Chapter 9

How to Use a Ski School Class to Rev Up Your Skiing

Attainable, yet remotely distant goals in life inspire commitment in persons, and promote self-mastery and accomplishment. All realistic and self-defined skiing goals are worth the effort.

I'm an upper level skier; why should I consider taking a ski school class?

Let me first clear up a common misconception: Ski school classes are not just for beginners; they exist for all levels of skiers. In fact, your presence in an upper level ski school class is more a statement of your skiing ability and willingness to learn than your inability and timidity. Admittedly, many skiers in beginning and lower level classes are lacking in skills, scared of aspects of the sport, and insecure on skis; but once you've made a commitment to take a ski school class, there's a great deal to be gained, particularly if you are an upper level skier.

Ski school instructors take classes (clinics) from other more skilled and trained instructors (clinicians); World Cup racers have coaches; Olympic skiers have coaches; coaches have clinics. Skiing is a sport of continual learning. The best skiers in the world learned the basics before becoming high performance skiers, and the coaches of the best in the world strongly advocate using ski school classes to advance your skiing. As George puts it, "You can't get anywhere without the basics. You need fundamental skills from which to develop upper level skills if you ever want to get into the big league."

What should I expect of a ski school class?

Of course, this will vary among ski schools and instructors; but I like to think that ski school class should offer an expert arrangement of three keys to rev up your skiing: recognition, exposure, and guidance.

Recognition. You learn about how you ski: correctly or incorrectly; efficiently or inefficiently.

Exposure. You are given the opportunity to experience a variety of drills and exercises that can, if performed properly, acquaint your body with the biomechanical feeling of skiing more efficiently and, depending on instructor, what it feels like to ski inefficiently (see High Performance Tip #13 on extremes in learning ski technique). In the fullest sense, you are exposed to the fundamentals of skiing through a progression of exercises and drills that help you to continually expand on your foundation of skiing skills. When you are well grounded in the basics, new movements you learn in more advanced ski lessons can lead to dramatic leaps in your skiing.

Guidance. You are helped to explore a variety of adaptations in your skiing through the words and comments of the instructor, your exposure to the many movements you are asked to perform, and your interaction with others in the class. By accepting guidance and enjoying the spirit of learning, you are free to discover the style of skiing that is best suited to your fullest enjoyment of the sport. A discovery that leads you to conclude that an open-ended no-style perspective to your skiing is most advantageous, because it allows you to constantly evolve and change.

How do I select the correct class?

Be honest in assessing your skill level and talk candidly with ski school personnel to determine which class is right for you. Even after choosing a class, once it has begun your instructor or a ski school supervisor may reassess your skiing and suggest you be placed in another class to give you a better and more appropriate learning experience. If it's a lower class, you may find yourself battling with your ego for self-respect; best to defer to your best interests and admit your skiing lacks some of the basics, which the trained eye of the instructor identified when he or she watched you ski. It is odd that these deficiencies may exist even though we may not recognize or feel them in our skiing.

If you have trouble with one level of skills (e.g., making parallel turns on smooth terrain), don't try to get into a higher level class (e.g., parallel turns in all terrain) for the challenge of it, even if your friend or spouse does. Why? Because you'll have the tendency to rely on slope survival tactics instead of skiing skills when exposed to upper level challenges and drills. The search for a challenge is the wrong reason to take a ski school class.

Can I take a private lesson?

Yes; you may also request a particular instructor, usually in hourly increments, on the hour. If you are serious about taking a private lesson, the courteous and smart thing to do is book the instructor a day or two in advance to make sure his or her schedule is clear. Many agree that private lessons are best used to satisfy an individual's or family's specific ski performance needs, and are suited to the shy skier who is uncomfortable in groups. In my opinion private lessons are not appropriate for learning the fundamentals; group lessons are far more economical and ultimately support psychological comfort with the emotional ups and downs of skiing while on the slopes.

How do you choose an instructor for a private lesson? You are your most important resource. If you've had an exceptional class with an instructor whom you perceive to have appealing teaching qualities, then a private lesson from this instructor might prove to be an incredible experience. Tips from friends or other instructors can be helpful in selecting an instructor for a private lesson, or you can seek out instructors you've read about in a magazine or book, seen on television, or heard about via the skiers' chatter in the lodge or chalet. Above all, follow your instincts. You can also present your particular skill problem to a ski school supervisor, and he or she will help select an instructor who's right for you from those available.

How do I get the most out of a ski school class?

First, go into the class (clinic or race camp) with the attitude that you're supplementing your skiing by giving yourself opportunities to refine your skills through recognition, exposure, and guidance. If it's early in the season, you may want to use the class to get reacquainted with your skis and the basics of your level of skiing. If you're adventurous, consider taking classes to study the condition of the day.

For example, you're deficient in powder skills, and it's a day with new-fallen snow. Most of the upper level classes will concern powder or at least deal with powder skills. This is a perfect day to take a lesson to work on your powder skills. The same concept holds true for other conditions.

The important message is to make ski school classes work for you. Use them to complement your efforts to solve the recognized problems in your skiing; be open to those other problems in your skiing that are revealed to you by an astute instructor or merciless video. Videos are sometimes ruthless intrusions into our fantasy world about how we see ourselves skiing. If you can overcome the tendency to remember how awful you look and concentrate on the areas of skill improvement, videos are an excellent tool to help you achieve greater performance in your skiing. If, however, you weaken for a moment, videos can devastate even the sturdiest of egos and give you the wrong mental images with which to go skiing.

How do I get the most out of my ski school dollar?

Keep these eight points in mind during class.

First, be an open vessel; that is, assume no skill level, no bias, and no prejudice and listen to everything the instructor and other students say. Allow all that you hear to fill your conscious mind.

Second, don't go into the class assuming you're the best or worst skier in the class; your ego will interfere with learning.

Third, don't assume that the obvious is really that obvious; don't hesitate to ask questions and seek clarification of drills and exercises.

Fourth, don't assume that everything the instructor says is scripture.

Fifth, have a physical attitude about the class; that is, try the exercises and drills demonstrated by the instructor, performing them as perfectly as you can. As a rule, most skiing skills are best learned by exaggerated movements that, when done collectively, produce a skill. Exercises and drills are often designed to provide numerous repetitions of these exaggerated movements until the correct movements become second nature and the skill is firmly established in your skiing.

Sixth, *expect some exercises and drills to feel awkward* and make you look like a less-than-advanced skier. Other drills will boost your and others' opinions of your skiing. Accept that a great deal of these drills will seem difficult to do at first and feel quite awkward. Your reward will come in a "perfect" effort to properly perform these exercises and drills, and your success in performing them will come with continued effort—not avoidance.

On the one hand, one of the biggest complaints of disgruntled ski school students is that they feel they don't learn enough from classes. On the other hand, one of the biggest complaints I hear from ski school instructors is that too many students don't make a serious effort to do the exercises and drills. Interesting. Understand that most of the exercises and drills given to you in ski school have undergone a great deal of experimentation on the slopes. Also, they have been designed to follow a certain progression, taking you from familiar to unfamiliar movements that accompany your acquisition of a new skill. Avoiding these because they appear difficult or embarrassing to do is a waste of your ski school dollar as well as precious skiing time.

Seventh, know the mind-set that must accompany the physical attitude; that is, for the effect and benefit of the exercises, avoid the tendency to make your exercises or drills exhibitions of your wonderful skiing skills for instructor and students alike. Such ego involvement obfuscates the value of these exercises.

Eighth, think of yourself as a perfect learner: a perfect student of skiing. Listen attentively and try to understand what is being said. Ask questions when you don't understand what's been said or when you're confused about a kinesthetic feeling you experience in relation to an exercise or drill. Pay attention to why something is happening to your skis, what is going on in your body when this is happening, what happens if the same action is repeated, and what it feels like to perform a task awkwardly and then more fluidly. Pay attention to how you can take something out of the class (a drill, exercise, perspective) and use it for practice in your everyday skiing.

Let's assume that you learned a number of helpful drills separating your upper and lower body while skiing. Which drill should you take from the class? All of them? The easiest? The most difficult? You can't realistically take all of the drills, so take the one(s) that will help you the most: those that are the most difficult. The difficulty of a drill often reveals a significant problem you're having with particular aspects of your skiing.

When you take a difficult drill from class, perform it on a gentle slope until you can do it well. Then graduate the slope and conditions in which you practice the drill. Always work to vary and upgrade the terrain in which you practice your drills as long as you can perform them as intended. Similarly, drills that were easy in class can be done on increasingly more difficult terrain. In all, the commitment to taking drills from classes and practicing them on your own is the single most important aftereffect from ski school class that ensures improvement in your skiing.

Should I talk to the instructor?

Yes! Talk to your instructor and discuss your skiing, but don't nag about it. Be sensitive; sometimes instructors need the time to reflect on the different skills of class members and plan appropriate drills and exercises. Don't monopolize the instructor's time when there are other students who might want to ride with him or her, but do assume you deserve your fair share of chairlift time.

Express your concerns and allow the instructor to think about them and respond in the most efficient way. He or she may address your concern privately, or may reason that your concerns are similar to those of others in the class, and pay special attention to these concerns in the exercises and drills presented to the class. While it's unrealistic to assume that all of your concerns must be attended to by the instructor, many instructors welcome your input, and use it to shape the overall structure of the class.

What do I do if I am unhappy with an instructor?

I have some fairly strong opinions about this. Wait until the end of class and ask to speak alone with the instructor or in the presence of his or her supervisor. Let him or her know exactly why you're unhappy. Think through your unhappiness before speaking with your instructor; you may not be sure just what it is that's upset you. There are several possibilities. You may have had a misunderstanding that one or both of you blew out of proportion or your chemistries may have collided. Perhaps one of you was in a bad mood (brought on by personal problems that had nothing at all to do with skiing). Maybe the snow conditions or the choice of slopes disturbed you; others in the class could have been the reason as well. Finally, perhaps you didn't think that you got enough attention or your money's worth. If this last one is true, your anger may be better directed at the person who placed you in the class.

Whatever the cause of your unhappiness, expressing it helps both you and the instructor. Many of the above problems can be discussed and put in perspective; however, if the instructor was anything less than professional, you deserve an apology. If you express your unhappiness in the spirit of fair play and understanding, you're bound to achieve a more satisfactory resolution.

Why do some people leave ski school class being disappointed?

Regrettably, one problem with large or inappropriately chosen ski school classes is that some advanced and upper level recreational skiers risk frustration; they are disappointed with themselves and the instructor because they go into classes expecting quantum leaps in aspects of their skiing with which they've been having trouble; for example, mogul skiing. Their problem is sometimes one of degree: They don't fully appreciate that skiing skills develop over time (i.e., weeks, months, years). Furthermore, in order to ski moguls efficiently and without excessive fatigue, for example, you need a host of skiing skills and skill development. (See chapter 3.)

Lessons in the bumps only begin to help you learn to understand how to ski them. It's the practice outside of class that provides you with the opportunity to experiment with bump-skiing strategies at your own pace and in a variety of bump-like terrain. A two- to three-hour class isn't enough to teach you all there is to know about skiing moguls. If, however, you go into the class with the idea of picking up exercises, drills, and strategies that you can practice and perfect during your free-skiing time, the lesson can be a boon to your bump skiing.

Another conflict for some upper level skiers is boredom. Ski school class seems redundant, as if nothing new were being said and you'd heard it all before. Class may even seem to be below your level of skiing. Have you ever been sucked into this head trip?

Every time you perform something with discipline on skis, you learn. Pros go out and ski disciplined turns; racers and instructors take part in countless clinics where they perform wedge turns, skidded turns, carved turns, and so on. The sometimes bitter truth is that regardless of your skiing ability, a return to the basics is something that leads to more refinement in your higher level skills.

How are ski instructors trained?

Ski instructors are trained to teach you to ski, and teach you to ski better (more efficiently). Different countries have different methodologies. While there are many methods of learning to ski, high performance skiing in any language translates into efficiency on skis, and using instructors is one way of achieving this goal.

Instructors are trained by experts in their ranks who offer them a host of clinics and training programs, with both technical and written exams to test their skiing knowledge. What you perceive as uncomfortable, awkward turns they may perceive as late turn initiation and overrotation of your upper body. What you call thigh burners they may call sitting on the backs of your skis, skiing in the back seat, or not getting extension in your turns. They are schooled to look at your skiing through their subjectively objective eyes, using their observations to choose exercises and drills to help improve your skiing.

Perhaps the greatest value of ski instructors is that they can observe how you ski and give you immediate feedback. Thus, even as you must be an open vessel to get all you can out of ski instruction, you stand to get the most by approaching ski school as one tool of many to help you achieve the level of skiing performance you desire.

Christin makes the point, ''Some skiers are really good at picking up proper images from expert skiers, and by watching they get instruction. But it's a much slower process. It's much faster to have someone show you what to do while telling you what's right and what's wrong about how you're doing it. But, you have to want to learn.''

Adding to this, George is quick to explain, ''Kids more easily pick up new skills through observing others doing them, properly or not. Their muscles are very keen at learning new movements. Adults, however, are more limited in making the adjustment from observing skills to incorporating these in their muscular movements. When attempting to mimic movements they observe, adults tend to be rigid, and unable to ski loose. To learn new skills, you've got to ski loose. This is where a well-run ski school class can help a great deal by introducing movements bit by bit through drills and exercises.''

Go for it: Be bold; ask questions; try it all; listen; experiment; practice; take risks; be vulnerable. You may excite yourself and your instructor to new highs.

Summary

1. Ski school classes exist for all levels of skiers.
2. From ski school class, you can expect to: (a) learn about *how you ski*; (b) be exposed to a number of drills and exercises to acquaint your body with what it feels like to ski more efficiently, and (c) explore adaptations in your skiing to make it more efficient. Of course, the degree of these will vary among ski schools and will be conditional based on your level of skiing; the closer to beginner you are, the least amount of *how* you ski, and more about getting the *feel* of skiing. More advanced skiers can anticipate higher degrees of how they ski, and adaptations (guidance) in their skiing.
3. Best not to ski over your head or take an upper level class for a challenge when you haven't yet sufficiently developed the appropriate skills.
4. Consider taking a ski school class to study the condition of the day. If you're deficient in powder, take a class after

a new-fallen snow. No doubt you'll be in the powder if it's an upper level class.

5. Indeed, talk to instructors about your learning needs; just don't monopolize their time if others need to talk to them.

6. Eight points to getting the most out of a ski school class: (a) Be open; (b) don't go into class assuming any skill level; (c) don't hesitate to ask questions when anything's unclear; (d) don't assume all an instructor says is scripture; (e) try to do the exercises and drills as demonstrated by the instructor; (f) accept that a good many drills may feel awkward or even impossible to do at first; (g) don't use your drills and exercises as a stage upon which to perform for others in the class (including the instructor); (h) think of yourself as a perfect student of skiing by listening, asking questions, paying attention to your skiing, and trying to take something out of the class.

7. If a ski school class seems too boring or redundant, use it as a time to refine your basic skills, as the best skiers in the world do, and you'll be glad you went to class.

8. A private lesson can be a wonderful boost to your skiing if you want special attention paid to your style of skiing and problem areas, and when your head might profit from the upbeat attitude of an instructor you know or have heard about from others.

High Performance Tip #12

John Hoffman: Extremes in Your Skiing

We spend so much of our time trying to do things correctly, I think many times it's more valuable to recognize the feeling of doing things incorrectly. Unless we're aware of what it's like to not do it properly, we will not change.

Try getting really low and standing really tall on your skis; ski different kinds of terrain in these positions. Start with comfortable terrain and exaggerated low and tall positions, and progress to more challenging terrain.

I learned something very interesting in the Army. The shipping officers had been putting "This Side Up" stickers on boxes. Unfortunately, one had to see "This Side Up" on the boxes to know they were correctly placed. Someone got the idea of putting "Turn Box Over" on the bottom of boxes instead of "This Side Up" on the top. When you saw "Turn Box Over," it meant, turn it over to make it correct. In other words, when it wasn't wrong, it was right.

I think we often teach skiing the "This Side Up" way: only the correct way. The "Turn Box Over" method allows us to know when we're incorrect in a positive way: We can learn to do something about it instead of going along and skiing out of control. If we know what it's like to "Turn Box Over," we are covered on both sides: We know both the correct and the incorrect ways to ski.

You need to experiment with all kinds of extremes to get the feel for this. Someone says, "Hey, you're sitting back." Because you've gotten so used to it, you don't know any different. Try moving forward. Maybe that's not good either. Go back again, but not as much. See what that's like. Too far back doesn't feel good, so you keep trying a variety of positions. Keep experimenting with these extremes to find a point of balance.

Play around with your turns and skiing low and skiing tall. On some turns, start low and finish tall; on others, start tall and finish low. Also, try starting tall, getting low, and finishing tall; or starting low, getting tall, and finishing low. Find where it's most advantageous to be low or to be tall.

Through all of this, you are learning how to ski, rather than trying to remember how to ski. Sometimes you just hear the words. "Get tall; down-up, sink-rise." It's difficult to memorize how to ski; instead, feel it. Feel what it is like to move better, or to move worse. Know the extremes. The purpose of exploring them is for you to change the feel of your skiing and ultimately, the level of your performance.

Chapter 10

Psychology of High Performance Skiing

"It's not just a question of getting rid of butterflies. It's a question of getting them to fly in formation."
Jack Donohue

The only constant you can count on in life is change; the constant in skiing is motion; your mind holds the key to your acceptance of each.

I can't tell you how many times I've referred to Donohue's quote with my students and myself (most commonly in the race course), but I can tell you it works! And it works for one simple reason: You're the one who's flying point in the formation. Getting the butterflies to fly in formation is entirely a mental directive you give yourself to take those gurgling, churning emotions and sensations you feel in your gut, and use them to invigorate your body's muscles and limbs. You get the butterflies in formation for basically two reasons: to achieve maximum performance and to enjoy flying.

In practical terms, you convert those starting gate jitters into a more forceful start and better overall race; convert that "gulp" feeling on top of a cornice to three "prime time" turns; and use those skiers on the lift above you as an audience of admirers, rather than an assembly of critics. Importantly, however, you can't use any kind of mind game to convince your butterflies to fly in a formation that you haven't the technical skills to create.

Mental Imagery

For the past couple of decades, athletic communities have been buzzing with the concept of mental imagery: using your mind to create pictures of you performing a sport or activity in a very specific way, while kinesthetically and otherwise feeling what it is like to be performing it. The skiing community jumped on the bandwagon in due course, and the slopes became filled with the advice and insight to visualize this or that with the expressed purpose of improving your skiing.

The problem I have with this is not in the practice of using the mind to create pictures. Nor is my concern centered on the use of the mind to create pictures to aid performance in any sport. Rather, the problems I have with mental imagery for recreational skiers are the following: (a) the mental imagery as a mythical reliance on the ability of a person to accurately create pictures of persons they've never watched, met, or talked with, and to use these as images and models to visualize themselves performing skiing feats they have neither the sense of, nor the skills for; (b) the misleading implication that one's mind can learn the skill for one's body; and (c) the suggestion that if one watches and studies, then visualizes *skier A* long enough, he or she will be able to ski like skier A.

In the first case, it doesn't work to create the image of a top flight racer as your model when you can't yet ride a single ski through turns. Second, your mind doesn't know how to move, even though it directs each movement through neural pathways; much of what your mind knows about movement has been learned from your body's adaptations to sport skills; it's really a two-way street. And third, watching Steve or Phil Mahre for

100 hours in slow motion will do little to make up for the 20 years of skiing they've got on you.

I cry foul to the suggestion that this use of the mind be used by recreational skiers who, I think, would rather have fun with their skiing. In all candor, it seems silly to burden the mind of a fun seeker by asking it to imagine the unlikely, or the impossible, when we have so many other handy uses for our minds in the quest for high performance. Join my revolt to keep mental imagery explorative, flowery, surrealistic (expecially with respect to following the lead of your dreams), playful, and fun. At those times when you want to become more serious, as high performance may demand, you can more effectively rely on mental directives (see below) that are appropriate to your actual skills and potential leaps in performance.

By working with what you've acquired skillwise, creating mental pictures of yourself skiing helps your body to refine and rehearse a variety of movements that will naturally lead to incremental improvements in your skiing. In plain language, your mental commitment to the act of skiing will help sharpen you body's commitment.

Although some will disagree with my stance, I believe that unless you're able to spend a good deal of time skiing, using your mind to ski when off the mountain may be just as bad as practicing bad habits while skiing. There's really no sense in confusing your body with complex mental images when it can't experience them until next week or next month. In working with athletes, it's only a few exceptional learners who can carry accurate mental images week after week without distortion. Most athletes, and recreational skiers, need to immediately apply what's in their minds to the actions of their bodies to create effective mind-aided learning. If they don't, their mental images grow increasingly flawed and inaccurate. I've found the use of mental directives far more realistic for all types of skiers: recreational, amateur, and professional.

Mental Directives

A *mental directive* is actually an order you issue from within your self to the rest of your body to perform! There's nothing fancy about it. It's simply a command to get out there and do it, which is loaded with as much power as you're willing to give it. There's no magic formula to follow, no rehearsal, no modeling, and no special mental and physical preparation. All that's required is sincerity in your commitment to your sport, honesty in your evaluation of your skills and potential, and the courage to allow your body to go for it.

The best use of mental directives is to set the mood for the task at hand. Let's suppose you're standing on a cornice and figuring out your first three turns. Your visualization might be to see your first three turns. This is fine for a first-time jumper, but you're a veteran. Knowing you can make those turns, your mental directive might be: Ski this loose; ski this tight; ski 10 turns; don't stop and never look back; get the heck off this cornice now! (And off you go.)

Suppose you're in powder. Try these engaging mental directives: Ski with dynamic legs; ski loose with a noodle-like upper body; fall and float, fall and float, fall and float all the way to the bottom. What an imaginative way to explore your skiing and learn to play with the conditions; the more you ski, the more you know what you're capable of, and the closer you get to understanding just what potential leaps in performance or accomplishments are within your reach this time out, this week, and this season.

When it comes to leaps in performance, your insight and judgment weigh heavily in your use of mental directives. Most of the time, leaps in performance come only after repeated exposure to a variety of drills and exercises, or a lot of time in the same condition. You're the best judge of when you're close to this breakthrough; when the time draws near, your best mental directive is to stay with the condition. Order yourself to ski it out! Something will happen to your skiing, possibly something very exciting. Ironically, the most difficult thing to accept with a leap in performance is believing that it is actually for real, and not just a fluke of the day.

Be assertive: Believe in yourself and use mental directives!

Go Ego Skiing

This is one of the nicest things you can do for yourself when you want to feel good about your skiing. Ego skiing is your ego trip on skis on which you go out and ski a run or condition in which you feel particularly ''hot.''

As a rule, high performance skiers use ego skiing to validate their accomplishments on skis. They shred a race course, blast through the bumps, fly through the powder, attack the steeps, play with the fluff, dominate the crud, and skate down the ice; do you see all the mental directives? A bit of daily ego skiing keeps the blahs away and infuses your skiing with liberating energy. Ego skiing is a fine way to celebrate your passion for skiing.

Learn From Mistakes

Each time you make a mistake, an error in judgment, or an error in the execution of a skill, you have the opportunity to learn from it. This premise is liberating because it encourages you to reject other more disturbing premises: that you're a fool for making a mistake; that you're not really a very good skier; or that you'll never get the hang of it. This is not very positive, yet very common. Who needs it? Don't continue to ski after falling or screwing up; not until you take a look at your mistake in the context of what it can teach you about your skiing.

It's difficult for me to imagine a process of learning that does not include making mistakes, and using these as stepping stones to greater knowledge. Looking for mistakes in your skiing, however, can be counterproductive because it focuses you on failure rather than success. Don't go on a head-hunting expedition for mistakes in your skiing; simply recognize those mistakes that are obvious in the kinesthetic feel of your skiing. Overall, skiing should be a relaxed experience. Tension in your body, sore arms and legs, an aching back, sore knees, and the like suggest something's awry. Body signals speak boldly! Listen. Deny the pain and you deny the problem.

Think Aggressiveness

Many recreational skiers try to escape snow conditions when they really ought to be aggressive in their skiing. Other skiers who are no more aggressive, just more adventurous, may attempt to ski the condition anyway. Unfortunately, instead of skiing it, they survive it cautiously and proclaim to friends and the world that they had a great run. Regrettably, they learn little by this practice except that they can survive increasingly more difficult terrain. Instead of being victorious in their aggressiveness, they are victims of their lack of it.

Use the mental directive to ski aggressively and go out in search of terrain on which you can experiment: Look for crud or heavy powder; ski a difficult, rutted race course; ski spring bumps. Liberate yourself from the word *impossible* by incorporating aggressiveness-on-demand into your skiing.

Think Light

A contradiction to the above? Not at all; lightness is the complement to aggressiveness. You need both to counter your avoidance of difficult situations. While you control the snow and conditions with aggressiveness, you flow with the snow and conditions when skiing lightly. Don't try to make your skis conform to the design of the turn you have in mind; no matter what, let your skis conform to the terrain.

When skiing lightly you become liberated from the ill-perceived feeling that you have to dominate the snow when skiing in the high performance mode. There are many approaches to skiing different conditions, and you might want to ski lightly in the crud by lightening your inside ski and steering it through your turns, or lightening your inside ski to match a brushing, turning ski. Similarly, you might want to ski lightly in slush bumps by floating your inside ski through the troughs.

Thinking light adds subtlety to your skiing and it, too, can be practiced. Be light on your skis, but not light as a feather; rather, light as if you were softly touching or massaging the snow with your skis.

Think Quick, Think Slow

Here's where these lack of skills catches up with you, because if you haven't the ability to quickly move your arms, feet/skis, knees, ankles, and hips, then *thinking quick* will be of little value to you. Lacking skills, you are the observer in those situations where the high performance skier would use quickness to negotiate the condition.

The purpose of quickness training is to acquaint your skiing body with what it feels like to respond to immediate cues. It's a lot like a "generic rehearsal"; that is, you practice general moves quickly to get used to moving on demand.

The complement to quickness is *slowness*, however, and the analogy doesn't work quite the same. You don't rely on skiing slowly to liberate you from difficult situations, but you use slowness in your skiing to heighten your awareness of subtle aspects of your skiing technique. By adding slowness to your everyday skiing, you can more easily focus on your movements. You can learn to ski your skis to an edge, rather than cramming your skis on edge. You can experiment with subtle moves that get you on and off your edges, and you can vary the rhythm in your turns with slow rather than exaggerated movements in your hip and knee.

The biggest mental block you have to overcome to use slowness in your skiing is to realize its value. Good skiers ski slowly some of the time. Skiers who ski only fast may be using speed to cover their mistakes. The idea that the only good skiing is fast skiing is true for downhillers and speed skiers. Put your skiing in slow motion on occasion and see what you can learn about yourself.

Think Progression

In a very real sense, you can view all movements in skiing as steps in a progression, and all progressions in skiing as steps to your desired goals. A macroprogression is actually the product of a whole series of microprogressions. For example, each turn is actually a combination of movements that begin with preparation movements and end (at least figuratively) with completion movements leading to new preparation movements, gliding, or stopping. (See the next section, Think Fluid.)

The liberating quality of thinking progression is in knowing that, whatever we do with our skis, in whatever condition, and however great it is, is not completion, but another step along the way to finishing an even greater progression. This attitude not only helps you to focus on your goals but also keeps your skills acquisition in perspective to increasingly higher levels of performance.

Think Fluid

When I think of fluidity, one man comes to mind: Ta-yeh Wu, my former Tai Chi Master. Tai Chi is based on the principle of the interaction of *yin* and *yang*, the opposing forces of nature and humankind. According to Ta-yeh, ''The interaction of these forces produces continuous change: negative and positive, quiescence and movement, lightness and firmness, softness and hardness, yielding and advance, passive and active, closed and open, slowness and swiftness.''

In the practice of Tai Chi, students learn to move their bodies according to ancient forms or postures. Some think of it as dance; others approach Tai Chi far more philosophically. The exercise begins with movement, and until the exercise is complete, movement never ceases! In the long form of the Yang School (my practice), the complete exercise may take up to 45 minutes, yet it is not fatiguing. Rather, it is both invigorating and relaxing.

If you look at Tai Chi's basic tenets of self-defense, and apply them to skiing, you come up with an invigorating and relaxing picture of skiing. Never use force against force (don't muscle around your skis). Neutralize the force of your opponent (the snow conditions). If an opponent does not move, you do not move (don't ski the terrain the way you want it to be, ski it as it is). If an opponent makes the slightest move, you move sooner (anticipate, be early, look ahead). Melt your opponent's force and make use of his force to unbalance him (retract and extend in the bumps, ski the ruts, be light in the powder, ski like a cat in the soft, loose, crusty stuff).

Both skiing and Tai Chi embrace *perpetual motion* as central to their proper performance, and both embrace the concept of forms. In Tai Chi, we move from one form (specific posture and positioning of your extremities in relation to your *tantien* or lower abdomen/center of mass) to another without a break in the flow. In high performance skiing, we move one form or position relative to our center of mass, to another, without a break in the flow.

Liberate yourself from static skiing, in which there seems to be a distinct beginning and an end to every move. Keep up the perpetual motion and when you finally do stop, it'll be to take a few well-earned, deep breaths. When you fully embrace the role of the mind and body working together in the milieu of life (e.g., relations with other persons, social pressures, deeply intrapersonal emotions, changes in the physical environment, etc.) as well as on the slopes, you'll find that the calm, liberated, and inquisitive mind enjoys the role of encouragement, support, direction, and perspective as well as the fun of fantasyland and the privacy of thought.

Summary

1. You get the butterflies to fly in formation for two reasons: to achieve maximum performance, and to enjoy flying.
2. You can't use any kind of mind game to convince your butterflies to fly in a formation that you haven't the technical skills to create.
3. Mental imagery may present conflicts when it's (a) used to create images of your skiing that you haven't the technical skills to ski; (b) implied that your mind can learn the skill for your body; and (c) suggested that if you watch and study a skier long enough, you'll be able to ski like that person.
4. Mental imagery may serve you best when it's used to create pictures reflective of your actual skills, or those but a step away, and in this way, help your body to refine and rehearse a variety of movements that will naturally lead to incremental improvements in your skiing.
5. The use of mental directives is an effective way to use your mind to help your skiing. They are orders you issue from within yourself to the rest of your body to perform. They often set the mood for the technical or skiing tasks at hand.
6. You're the best judge of when you're close to a breakthrough in your performance. When this time draws near, your best mental directive is to stay with the condition. Order yourself to ski it out.
7. Go ego skiing; it's a fine way to celebrate your passion for the sport.
8. Each time you make a mistake, an error in judgment, or

an error in the execution of a skill, you have the opportunity to learn from it.

9. Body signals speak boldly! Listen. Deny the pain and you deny the problem.

10. Liberate yourself from avoiding difficult situations by incorporating aggressiveness-on-demand into your skiing.

11. Be light on your skis, but not light as a feather; rather, light as if you were softly touching or massaging the snow with your skis.

12. Quickness, as in being able to quickly move your skis, can help liberate you from a number of potential disasters when on the race course, in moguls, in the trees, or when confronting obstacles.

13. Slowness, as in attempting to ski technically sound while moving at a slow speed, allows you to more easily focus on your movements. Put your skiing in slow motion at times, and see what you discover.

14. If you look at Tai Chi's basic tenets of self-defense, and apply them to skiing, you come up with an invigorating and relaxing picture of skiing.

High Performance Tip #13

Try Setting Goals

Mental directives and the perpetual motion of Tai Chi will alienate some skiers. These concepts aren't right for all athletes, most notably those who respond better to a more concrete approach to improved performance like *setting goals*. You can use goals to sharpen your focus on what you seek to achieve, isolating it from a universe of possibilities, and what you need to do to achieve this. Goals like, ''I want to become a better, more efficient skier'' are far too general, and subsequently, difficult to bring into focus. A more appropriate goal helps you to focus on specific activities: ''I want to carve my turns instead of skidding them.''

The beauty of goals is that they help you pursue athletic excellence in your own way and at your own pace. I like to think of goals as *paper coaches* available to you on call, 24 hours a day, which you can use to measure whether the strategies you've been using to achieve your goals (e.g., skiing drills, exercises, free-skiing time, etc.) are working, or whether these need to be modified to move you closer to your goals.

For example, it has just snowed and there are 8 to 10 inches of new powder out there waiting for you. You've been floundering in powder lately and decide to set three goals for yourself.

1. Ski with a very loose body (which implies an active pole touching rhythm).
2. Constantly throw your body down the fall line (which implies that your center of mass is relatively square with the fall line).
3. Don't think about turning (which implies you've already got the skills necessary to turn, but your thinking mind has been in the way of turning in powder).

Go ahead, try them out. There's no commitment beyond a single run, a few runs, half a day, or a day of skiing. These goals are good excuses to try something diffferent and, perhaps, to greatly improve your skiing by discovering new dimensions to your ability.

Consider the following five points when contemplating the practice of setting goals for yourself:

1. The process itself can be self-defeating if your goals are not realistic for your present life-style or skiing ability.
2. Goals are opportunities to explore more of your skiing ability.
3. Goals allow you to dream about what level you want to be skiing and to set your sights high.
4. Goals can liberate you as a skier if you can truly divorce yourself, physically and emotionally, from your slope survival strategy.
5. Goals are most beneficial when used in a variety of conditions.

Let your goals give you a sense of what you hope to achieve in your body once you've accomplished them.

High Performance Tip #14

Skiing in Wu Wei

In Tai Chi there is a concept, *wu wei*, that proposes we *do by not doing*. In skiing, it is thinking by not thinking. In *wu wei* you ski without putting any thought into the actual doing of the skiing. It makes the action effortless; the skiing relaxing.

Wu wei is the harmony of the movement of intellect, spirit, and body. Applied to skiing, you want to understand concepts, perspectives, and head sets, so you can interpret them for your body during drills and exercises, a time when it's fitting to think about and analyze what you're doing on skis.

The point at which you have drilled your body sufficiently so it no longer needs reminders to ski like you want it to is when you've achieved some blend of intellect and skill. These are those moments of breakthrough, those leaps in performance; these are moments when you are skiing in *wu wei*.

Yes, they are fleeting; such harmony is an uncommon event unless you can liberate yourself from your mind. The irony? It's your mind that must agree to let go at times. It's your serve; how convincing can you be?

High Performance Tip #15

When an Okay Day Becomes a Bad One

So, things didn't go as well as you would have liked. You took a class and it was a bummer; you had a terrible time in the race course; you fell under the chairlift; you crashed your skis in the moguls and got hit with your pole as it rebounded into your chest. This is a good time to start thinking about changing your strategy. Apparently, you can't quite ski this one off your mind, so it's time to *stop skiing*.

I can't read your mind or analyze your skiing from here, but it seems to me that you may be practicing a lot of bad habits; this won't get you anywhere but frustrated with yourself. Many times, I adhere to my perspective of making a bad day better by attacking the conditions, but it may not work for you; it doesn't always work for me. As Robin says, "It's time to get out of there. Go take a rest; take a break; come back later and ski something on which you can reestablish your rhythm."

Another tactic is to go back to skiing fundamentals: the basic wedge and wedge turns to reestablish confidence in your skiing. Think slow; look and listen to your skiing. Find a run on which you can do a bit of ego skiing. Completing a run, top to bottom, of perfect wedge turns can also be ego skiing.

Importantly, seek the sensation of being centered on your skis, in control, and not fighting them to move with mental admonitions. Don't ever trust your mind when it's in a scolding, accusatory mode; you're not friends at this time. Remember, your mind serves you best when it is supportive and validating of your accomplishments; it punishes you most when you lack confidence.

As George observes, "We, the U.S. Ski Team, are fast. We have good athletes, and we can ski, but we sometimes lack the confidence of many Europeans. There's no reason we shouldn't be as tough mentally. An edge like this can mean an easy second (tenths or hundredths of a second) in a race. Why give anyone such an advantage?"

Chapter 11

Training for Glory

The high performance skier's five best friends— other than his or her equipment, nice snow and challenging conditions— are conditioning, strength, flexibility, food-liquid, and rest.

I'll get right to it: If you want to be a high performance skier you've got to get tough with yourself. You have to realize that skiing pretty is not what high performance skiing is all about. Rather, high performance skiing is skiing efficiently from the run's beginning to the chairlift, and right onto the chair when there is no line.

In the days of leather boots and less flexible wooden skis, it took muscle to move the skis to create turns. Skiing was a sport of strength. Most turns looked quite acrobatic due to this equipment. With the refinement of equipment, however, skiers were given greater lateral support and easier flex in the ski. The side-cuts changed; the weight changed; lengths changed; attitudes changed; slope conditions changed; in general, everything changed except the memories.

When I was 11 years old, my father bought me a pair of wooden skis and ski poles. I think he picked them up at a garage sale. The bindings were ineffective in that I had no ski boots, but I was going to a Boy Scouts' snow camp and he wanted me to have some skis to take along. A lucky kid, I loved my father (and still do), and he always supported my athletic interests, albeit this ski adventure was a bit off-key.

While my friends watched and laughed (skis were alien to them), I climbed these little hills, tied the bindings onto my snow boots with twine, and shushed down on the verge of madness until I slowed down enough to stop, and then bailed out to the side to stop, skis going every which way with my legs attached.

A fascinating introduction to alpine skiing. After repeated hikes up the hills, a few close calls, and utter frustration with my lack of mobility, I hung up the skis for the rest of camp and went tobogganing. Back at home, I cut up the skis and used them as cross-supports for a coaster wagon I had built out of scrap lumber. Growing up where I did and with the friends I had, there was little incentive to learn to ski. In my neighborhood, we played football and baseball, rode skateboards and bikes, ran fast, took long hikes, and built coaster wagons.

George's story is quite different. In his home town of Chur, in southeast Switzerland, all the boys grew up learning to ski and playing soccer. The better you skied, the more respected you were among your friends. In his home town there were no lifts, just this one hill on which he and his friends trained by hiking up, skiing it, and hiking down. "We got maybe five runs a day when we had to hike it all the time. When I was about 15, we built a rope tow by hauling up an engine, pulleys, and the equipment needed in the summer. After that, our winters were spent skiing one run after another. It got down to this: If we wanted to ski, we had to plan on two hours of hiking up; five hours of skiing; and a two-hour hike down."

Today, few of the above antics are likely. Ski areas abound, and new methodologies for teaching people to ski have developed over the years. Although many people have learned to ski in less time, getting them there faster also meant that they more quickly hit a plateau in their skiing. Why a plateau? Why did they improve to a certain level, and then seem to level off or progress very slowly? Mike says simply, "They don't have the physical conditioning to give them the endurance to continue to learn to be technically sound, and without the commitment to fitness and training, they lack the psychological strength to seek those higher goals."

Given this introduction to what we must consider in becoming high performance skiers, the remainder of this chapter will take a candid and quick look at the *why* and *how* of conditioning, strength, flexibility, nutritional needs, and rest for the recreational skier who wants to rev up these aspects of his or her skiing. The nice bonus to a serious training program for skiing is that it not only makes your winter more enjoyable, it offers you a higher quality of life.

Training Seasons

Getting in shape for skiing is a year-long process of varied activities and personal achievement, based not on what you must do, but on what you choose to do. Here's how I break down the year-round program. During the *off-season*, engage in a variety of sports and recreational activities that provide you with pleasurable fitness, mental intensity, skills application, and overall agility. For us, summer is water skiing and tennis season, and filled with running, hiking, cycling, swimming, and aerobics.

Next comes the *preseason*, that four to six weeks before actually skiing in earnest; an *early season*, those first two or three weeks of the season when you're getting your skiing legs and reacquainting your body to the movements of skiing, continually building to that time when you feel the fire's burning efficiently; the *skiing season*, when skiing is your sport and the other stuff just feeds it; and finally, a *postseason*, those several weeks in which you graduate your body to new sports interests or stay active for summer racing camp.

Importantly, whatever your time frame for these seasons, you want to be sure to maintain overall, year-round conditioning and flexibility; that which you lose by inactivity must be regained by diligent work. With respect to certain more specific needs, the preseason means *key body area flexibility*, overall body endurance strengthening, and the end of specifically targeted off-season strength training; the early season means increased flexibility and refined endurance (with weights), and speed or quickness work with conditioning; the skiing season means continued flexibility and maintenance with respect to strength and endurance with weights, and conditioning activities that complement your level and amount of skiing; postseason requires a renewed interest in weight training and an appropriate shift in flexibility and conditioning strategies; and off-season means plenty of strength training and conditioning activities.

Keep in mind that as you pursue these conditioning activities, you are your coach! It's you who must make the choices and, at times, the sacrifices to become stronger or get fit. This isn't always as fun as I suggest it to be at least at first. The skiers who take my preseason 8-week ski conditioning class know it very well! Nevertheless, even the most arduous of work and effort can be mentally overcome with an attitude of performance and self-achievement. This attitude is the mind-set of the high performance skier who's *going for glory*!

For a moment, consider what George has his skiers do in the off-season. "The season is over around the 15th of April, and we take off about two weeks. Beginning in May, we start training, and it's extremely hard training. First, we do a lot of aerobic training: running, biking, swimming, hard hiking. As well, we begin weight training and encourage participation in all the sports the skiers can do: golfing, racquetball, tennis, soccer, you name it. We do this all summer. By September, we definitely run shorter distances: miles, half-miles, quarter-miles. Essentially, we do stadium track work, interval training. It's very tiring, but good for the development of strength and speed.

"As the season progresses, we continue weight training (pretty much all year round), and add more circuit training. We use a variety of exercises that are a minute or two long, moving from one exercise to the next. Our weight training consists of basically one set of 12 exercises, 2 to 3 times a week: 5 for the legs, 6 for the upper body, and 1 for the abdominals. In each exercise we do repetitions until exhaustion.

"With the legs we try 12 to 13 reps with the 13th being total failure (exhaustion). With the upper body we try 9 to 10 reps with the 10th being total failure. Something we're working on right now is building our hamstring strength. I'd like to see it increase by at least 20%. For recreational racers, I think it's very important to keep up with a physical training program, but not one as vigorous as ours."

Conditioning

Physical conditioning is so important because the majority of recreational skiers don't ski enough days to ski themselves into shape. Because you exert a tremendous amount of muscular energy while skiing, conditioning (as in cardiovascular conditioning) allows you to get more oxygen to your muscles while exerting less effort. The more you ski, the more exposed you are to potential fatigue from exertion as well as weather and snow conditions; fatigue leads to injury. Physical conditioning allows you to ski for a longer time without resting so that you can progress more quickly in your acquisition of high performance skills.

How do you improve your fitness level? You must perform aerobic exercise three to five times a week. This includes running, particularly up and down hills to work the calves and quads, and on uneven, curvy terrain to maximize the use of ski-specific muscles; aerobics classes; swimming; serious cycling in which you ride with loose arms to help isolate the work of your gluteal muscles; cross-country skiing; endurance roller or ice skating; intense racquetball or squash; aggressive singles tennis; brisk walking or hiking, especially with a weighted pack; in general, any activity that increases your heartbeat for at least 20-30 minutes at 70-85% of your maximum heart rate (MHR): 220 minus your age = MHR.

Once your chosen activity becomes too easy, intensify the aerobic workout by performing it for a longer duration; this keeps it interesting and gives you the greatest benefit.

Make your exercises a reflection of your skiing; if you like to gun it while skiing, try the same in your off-season activities (the attitude's the same).

Tailor activities to skiing style; if you're into bumps, use activities that make you work your legs in retracted and extended positions; if you're into racing, use activities that condition your legs for lateral and vertical quickness. Overall, exercise as ski-specific as you can. Think of the muscles that are at work as both encouraging and resisting the forces inherent in skiing: hips, feet, fronts and backs of legs, abdominals, lower back, and buttocks, and work these both statically (isometrically) and dynamically

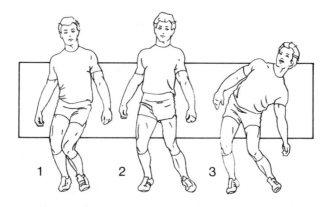

Figure 11.1 Work your ankles, knees, hips, waist, and shoulders.

(actively) to simulate how they're used in skiing. (See Figure 11.1.)

Be a tactician in your conditioning and build it up slowly, but purposefully; take several bounds to leap that building at first.

An important rule: Choose activities that are fun for you and that fit your life-style and orientation to people. Exercise usually does the most good when it's something you look forward to doing alone or with others; many persons derive considerable enjoyment and added motivation when attired in clothing and shoes that make them feel great even before exercising.

It's nice to spread your exercise time throughout the week, with easy days in between harder days. Your benefits decrease greatly if you concentrate your exercise in only one part of the week; you must allow time for rest.

Strength

Why is muscular strength important? Dynamic skiing involves diverging steps, skating, explosive reactions to terrain changes, and defensive pole plants in the steeps and in unexpected mogul situations; all of these activities necessitate resilient leg and upper body strength. Dynamic skiing also involves keeping your center of mass moving square down the fall line: a need for abdominal and pelvic-region strength. Racing and turning involves a steady and sturdy downhill leg: strong legs. Dynamic racing requires a powerful start: a strong upper body. And finally, dynamic skiing requires adaptation and recovery from errant attempts to take it to the edge: overall body strength.

Increasing Muscular Strength

Muscular strength can be increased by doing plenty of isotonic strengthening exercises for your legs and upper body; that is, exercises that make you move your legs and upper body against increasingly heavy resistances (there should be an exertion/lifting and a relaxation phase for these exercises). A program of daily abdominal, lower back, and pelvic strengthening exercises also increases strength.

The very best combination exercise is the "protective sit-up" where you lift only your shoulder blades off the floor and make small contractions of your abdominal muscles: small lifts, straight ahead with hands behind head or outstretched, or hands behind head, elbows to the sides, touching opposite elbow to opposite knee. To add pelvic and lower back work to the exercise, vary the lifting and positioning of your feet; try keeping them off the floor (e.g., fan them out as in the splits; hold them parallel to the floor, knees bent; point them to the ceiling, legs straight, etc.). (See Figures 11.2 through 11.4.)

In building strength, approach it slowly and meticulously. Here are some general guidelines I suggest for the average recreational lifter who wants to enjoy working out with weights, while increasing his or her strength and body contour. When lifting, exhale on the lift and inhale during the resting phase. If it takes

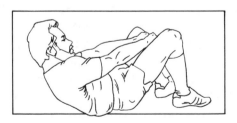

Figure 11.2   Repeatedly, but slowly, lift your shoulder blades off the floor and reach your hands through your knees.

Figure 11.3 Press your lower back against the floor and your chin to your chest as you repeatedly, but slowly, reach your hands forward two to three inches with each lift.

Figure 11.4 Start with your back on the floor, and alternately touch opposite elbow to opposite knee, returning to the floor between each contraction.

you two to three seconds to lift, take four to six seconds to bring the weight back to the starting position. Use 8 to 10 repetitions of each lift during each set. Do two to three sets for each weight workout; work out a minimum of two days a week and no more than three days on the same muscles.

When the weight feels too easy to lift, it's time to increase the weight. You should notice weekly increases in the amount of weight you're lifting during the first month of a serious weight workout. Rest 60-90 seconds between each exercise in a set, not during lifts, to reoxygenate your muscles.

As a rule, allow a day in between workouts of different muscle systems to allow for repair. The one exception is when you first get started; I advise repeating the same lifts for four to five consecutive days to acquaint your body with these new exercises and more readily get rid of the start-up muscle pain you'll experience due to neural aches and built up lactic acid. For recreational skiers, I recommend a basic, total-body, weight workout, every other day, three days a week.

Try to include dynamic expressions of strength in your program: something to give you the incentive to keep working or to modify workouts to accomplish what you're after. (These can take the form of dramatic lifts of weights, radical waterskiing, leaping-bounding against resistances, etc.) In all, you want to build dynamic strength that makes you strong when stationary and when moving or responding to stimuli!

I recommend consulting an athletic trainer, weight coach, qualified weight room staff, or any number of excellent weight training books for additional guidance that's customized to meet more competitive lifting needs. If you're going to build strength, do it in balance; a lack of balanced strength in opposing muscles contributes to injury.

Flexibility

Why is flexibility so critical to your overall physical conditions? Adding planned stretches to complement strength workouts will add versatility to your strength and power, making you agile and quick. When you work on building strength, you also work on shortening your muscles. Stretching will improve the range of motion in your muscles and joints, thus leading to the kind of flexibility that allows you to move effortlessly without strain.

Flexibility adds to your potential for getting the most out of your strength and conditioning program; this allows you to ski aggressively, in control, and in a relaxed, fluid state that uses only a minimal amount of your energy. Flexibility also provides muscle elongation for those times your body is called on to react, adapt, and contort to any number of awkward positions in order to "right" itself during an impending fall or out-of-balance move, especially common on race courses and in the bumps.

Pete expresses a keen appreciation for this aspect of training. In reflecting on his racing career and training, he speaks of changes he'd make if he were to do it over again. "A lot of times we used to do a lot, maybe too much, endurance work; just a lot of long bike rides to get really strong. I don't think we spent enough time on agility, coordination, and balance. There's a great need for these skills, and I would include more quickness and balance activities in my training by using more gymnastics, karate, and related sports that also help build strength. Going out and riding a bike is good for you, but that's not all you need to do."

How to Increase Overall Flexibility

Stretch only after your body's been warmed up; fill the muscles with blood to allow necessary flexibility and stretching movements. Once you've warmed up, be patient while stretching; press into your stretches gently at first (never bounce), gradually increasing the length and duration of the stretch with each repetition.

I encourage persons to stretch statically; that is, to press into their stretch, hold for a 5 to 10 count, the point at which the stretch begins to cause a mild tingling (not pain); then either relax the stretch for another repetition, or press further, hold, and continue as is comfortable, each time reaching those points of mild tingling. According to a panel of experts (Kent, 1983), "Unless you feel some discomfort — a sensation of tension and tingling in the stretched muscle and tendon — you will make no gain in flexibility" (p. 151). Again, stretching should not be painful.

Stretching can be fun if you find the most enjoyable way for you to execute it. This means that you must play with a variety of stretches and opportunities for stretching. Perhaps the very best overall body stretch is provided in regular (3 days a week) attendance at an aerobics class (preferrably low-impact or soft aerobics if you're primarily interested in the flexibility aspect of the aerobics).

Still, it's the everyday, at-home stretching that leads to consistent, though incremental, increases in flexibility. As experts note (Kent, 1983), "Make a habit of warming up and stretching your muscles and tendons twice daily—on arising and before going to bed—and just before you start periods of strenuous physical activity. Each routine need not take more than 15 minutes; even 10 minutes can produce significant gains in flexibility'' (p. 148).

Use stretches that increase the flexibility of parts of your body not commonly used in everyday life, yet essential to high performance skiing. Most notably, these include stretches that work on the lateral movement of your knees and ankles, the rotational movement of your femur (large bone of your thigh) in your hip socket, the movement of your trunk and arms (upper body) in the opposite direction that your knees and ankles (lower body) are moving, and the uncoiling movement of switching the upper and lower bodies to opposite sides. (See Figures 11.5 through 11.8.)

To develop your own flexibility program, perform your stretches regularly, in an organized fashion, and in the proper environment. The very worst programs are those that you feel forced to complete.

The following are the critical areas of the body for skiers with suggested stretches. (See Figures 11.9 through 11.12.)

The Trunk. Particularly in need of stretching are the external oblique muscles on the sides of your waist and rib cage. Use twisting stretches and side bends that stretch one side of your

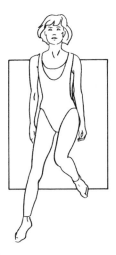

Figure 11.5 Bound from leg to leg.

Figure 11.6 Stretch long to each side.

Figure 11.7 Stretch one hip—hold—then stretch the other hip.

Figure 11.8 Slowly stretch and hold each leg for a count of ten.

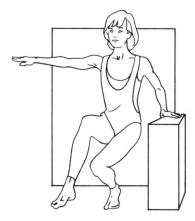

Figure 11.9 Build your balance and your quadriceps at the same time.

Figure 11.10 Hold the tuck to strengthen quadriceps and ankles.

trunk at a time. Perform these stretches either statically or with very tiny stretches beyond the already stretched position.

The Back. To increase flexibility in the lower back use stretches that encourage the gentle elongation of the spine, gently arc the back, and work the back and abdominals together. Many experts caution against stretches that strain the back, like bending at the waist while standing with knees locked.

The Knees. To gain flexibility in lateral movement, focus on activities that stretch the knees like ski pole taps: Squat with knees together and poles held in skiing position outside your knees, planted perpendicular to the ground. Swing your knees side to side to touch your poles. Stand erect and counterrotate your upper and lower body, back and forth to rhythm, with ex-

Figure 11.11 Hopping up will build overall leg strength, ankle agility, and foot sensitivity.

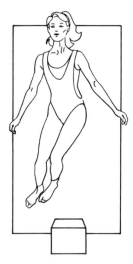

Figure 11.12 Leap side to side to acquaint hip and leg muscles with the turning pressures they must accommodate.

tension and flexion. Jump in and out to a wedge, the in jump being the placement of your feet together, the out jump being a very large wedge. This is a continuous movement stretch.

Another exercise for knee flexibility is a stretch for the outside and inside of your knee. Stand parallel to a wall, a couple of feet away. Keeping your legs together, lift your inside leg and allow your shoulder to gently fall into the wall. You will naturally angle or incline your outside leg into the wall, creating a continuous stretch of the inside and outside of your knee. Switch sides.

The Hamstring and Groin.   These muscles lie in the backs and insides of your thighs and run up into your crotch. To increase flexibility, include the following stretches: Position your upper body over your outstretched thigh while sitting on the floor. Sitting on the floor, open your legs wide and work your upper body forward between them while maintaining a flat, straight back. Focus on the inside of your legs by standing next to a counter and raising one leg up onto the counter, the inside of your foot flush against the counter top; reach down and touch the outside of the ankle of the foot on the ground for a 5 to 10 count. Your legs should form a square with the floor and side of the counter. Stretches that require you to use your inner thigh to move your leg independent of other body parts protect your hip and thigh.

The Hip.   Focus particularly on the rotational socket where the femur joins the pelvic bone. The following stretches increase flexibility in this area: Cross one leg over the other while lying on your back with arms outstretched; perform knee stretches; and get down on all fours, lifting your leg like a dog at a fire hydrant, thus isolating the action in the hip joint.

The Quadriceps.   These are your front thigh muscles that perform so much of the stability and endurance work while skiing. Stretch them with these exercises: Sit on your lower legs and heels and bend back. Stand erect and bend one leg at a time, grabbing the foot of the bent leg behind your back and pulling it to stretch the front of your thighs and your knees. Also do lunge-type stretches in which you place one foot on its toes well behind you and the other foot in front of you and flat on the ground directly beneath its knee; the stretch is the lunge.

Food and Liquid

Having written nearly a thousand newspaper and magazine articles on behavioral and nutritional research, fitness, sport, sports nutrition, and contemporary health issues, I could write a lot about this subject here. Fortunately for both of us, I won't; instead I'll share the quintessential elements of the sports nutrition plan I've developed for high performance athletes.

Food is Energy

Without food, all the oxygen in the world won't provide your body with the blood glucose it needs to fire its muscles. You must eat to be active. The foods used most readily for energy by your body are carbohydrates. In their absence, fat is used, and finally protein.

In abbreviated form, the energy-related digestive process works like this:

1. Carbohydrates are readily digested; simple carbohydrates (naturally occurring sugars like fructose, maltose, lactose, etc.) and complex carbohydrates (starches and complex arrangements of simple carbohydrates like potatoes, beans, peas, corn, and the host of common fruits, vegetables, and whole grains) are converted to glucose (and glycogen or stored glucose) for use by the body's muscles and brain.

2. Once a fit body has been pushed to a point where it requires boosts of energy (after 20 to 30 minutes of intense aerobic activity) it will naturally seek to catabolize some fat out of adipose tissue and convert it to glucose for the body's muscles. This is actually a highly efficient use of stored fat. Yet, to efficiently burn fat, the body must have a certain amount of carbohydrate-generated glucose to fuel its machinery (often in the form of stored muscle glycogen, which is converted to blood glucose as muscles dictate need). When blood glucose is lacking, inefficient and incomplete fat burning results.

3. If there is no carbohydrate-generated glucose to fire the fat-burning machinery, yet the body must call on fat for energy (just what it does when there is no carbohydrate energy available), our bodies call on protein to substitute for carbohydrates. Incredibly, we have a mechanism for converting protein to glucose; once done, the body uses protein-generated glucose just as it uses carbohydrate-

generated glucose to fire the fat-burning machinery. The irony is that unnecessarily forcing the body to use protein-generated glucose too often leads to a host of adverse factors for athletes including, but not limited to, fatigue, nausea, headaches, muscle cramping, dizziness, mental lapses, and generally low motivation.

The average recreational athlete needs at least 1,000-1,500 pure *energy calories* (calories over your basic metabolic requirement: BMR) for each day of activity (on rest days caloric need may vary); all of this energy diet, and all but 10-20% of the total calorie intake for the day, should be complex and simple carbohydrates. Look at an overview of the proportions of major nutrients you need: 80% carbohydrates ($\pm$65% complex, $\pm$15% simple); 12% lean protein; 5-8% obvious fats (butters, whole milk products, meat fat, poultry skin, oils, fried foods, etc.).

More and more, advocates of healthful diets and what is fast becoming the athletic diet abhor the excess of fats in the average athlete's eating plan. Proponents of the modern athletic diet recommend less protein, absolutely minimal fat, and an abundance of complex carbohydrates. Briefly, here are the views on fats from a number of advocates of healthful athletic diets:

Covert Bailey. "We should decrease dietary fat as much as possible. It is almost impossible to eat too little fat. I could almost urge you to try to eat no fat at all because I know you would inevitably get enough fat hidden inside your foods" (1978, p. 88). For the athletic body with a low percentage of body fat, Bailey recommends 10% daily calories from fat.

Denis Waitley and Irving Dardik. "So why eat fat at all? The primary reason is the 'essential fatty acid' linoleic acid. It is found mostly in polyunsaturated fats, which the body requires for the synthesis of other important fats. An adult's linoleic acid requirement is met by about one to two percent of their daily calories, or 30-60 calories' worth of vegetable oil for an active male" (1984, p.74). Waitley and Dardik recommend up to 20% daily calories from fat, in part to make foods taste better.

Robert Haas. "The body requires a small amount of fat which you can get from a large bowl of oatmeal . . . excess fat, like excess protein, can hamper endurance by impairing carbohydrate metabolism (resulting in poor glycogen storage in the muscles) and by limiting the amount of oxygen that blood delivers to exercising muscles'' (1983, p. 27). Haas varies fat intake from 5-20% depending on your sports and performance profile.

Julian Whitaker. ''When fat supplies over 10 to 15 percent of the calories, the human body can't handle it, and the lymphatic system dumps the excess into the bloodstream, where the fat forms coats around the red blood cells. Eventually, the red blood cells are unable to flow through the capillaries, and arteries become plugged. This stops oxygen supply, and tissues degenerate and die'' (1981, p. B-9, 10). Dr. Whitaker says the ideal nutrient balance is 10% fat, 10% protein, and 80% carbohydrate.

The American Heart Association (AHA, 1986). Not since 1978 has the AHA released dietary guidelines, but extensive study and review of the latest medical thinking ''regarding an optimum diet for so-called 'healthy American adults,' '' led to the recent issuance of new dietary guidelines that include these, among other, recommendations: Saturated fat intake should be less than 10% of calories; total fat intake should be less than 30% of calories; protein intake should be approximately 15% of calories; carbohydrate intake should comprise 50-55% or more of calories, with emphasis on increasing sources of complex carbohydrates.

Trained and conditioned athletes might well consider even more stringent guidelines than those prescribed above.

While Nathan Pritikin advocated his radical high-carbohydrate, low-protein, very low-fat diet for cardiac patients (his program for athletes advocates 5-10% calories from fat each day), I experimented with a similar dietary scheme for healthy, active athletes. Both programs led to success; with increasing refinement, my *Diaita Plan*™ (an average of 80% carbohydrates, 12% protein, and 8% fat) offers you a life-style plan of eating to ensure energy for performance and, if you like, to control your weight. Overall, it's a plan for feeling good and LIVING WELL![1]

---

[1]Dr. Yacenda offers his Diaita Plan to individuals at fitness and health facilities in California and Nevada, and through telephone and written correspondence throughout the world. To find out more about the Diaita Plan write to Health Promotion Features, P.O. Box 21076, Reno, NV 89510.

Part of the physiological beauty of concentrating on a high-carbohydrate diet is that you get plenty of fiber: an asset to performance at any level; further, because complex carbohydrates contain variable amounts of protein and the essential fatty acids, you need to add neither fats nor too much protein to your diet.

Your body requires 1-2% of its calories in the form of linoleic acid to meet the basic adult metabolic need for fat. For most recreational athletes, fats are a drag biochemically. True, we need fatty acids for hormone development and transport; for the transport of vitamins A, D, E, and K; to perk up and satisfy our acquired tastes; to help insulate the body's internal organs; to help regulate body temperature; and to give staying power to meals and thus, help curb our appetite or fill us up. Nevertheless, as noted earlier, we get plenty of fat in our diet from the carbohydrates we eat. It's more important to think of excluding rather than including fats in your diet.

Once again, the problems with fats for recreational athletes are legion. Too many fats in a meal can lead to slow reaction times, less oxygen to the working muscles, poor assimilation of needed carbohydrate-generated glucose, and an overall conflict between being mentally alert and physically tired. The less oxygen provided to the muscles, the less energy there is to move them.

You need only low-fat varieties of protein, even though you may enjoy fattier varieties, which generally carry the tastes of their fatty acids. Actually, a very small amount (10-12% of daily calories) accomplishes the regulatory functions of protein, as well as furnishing the body with enough amino acids to meet other bodily responsibilities without adding excess protein to fat stores. Protein is not considered a primary energy source! The principle functions of protein are to promote the growth and maintenance of body tissues (e.g., bone, hair, skin, muscle, cartilage, blood vessels, lymph); to serve as a building block of essential hormonal, enzyme, and antibody (immunological) activity; and to help regulate the delivery of bioenergy to, and the acid-base balance of, our bodies.

Anywhere from 35 to 60 grams of protein a day is sufficient for most persons. A handy way to calculate your performance-plan protein need is to divide your weight by 4 and by 3. The numbers will reveal your minimum and maximum protein need in grams, respectively.

What You Eat Influences Performance

The kind of food you eat as well as the time of the day or night you eat it may have a dramatic effect on your mental and physical output. Eating at the wrong time in your athletic day may foul up your performance more than if you ate the wrong kind of food. Though carbohydrates are a wonderful source of energy, in order to be used they must be digested. In other words, you can't expect a whole-grain roll or fruit juice (complex and simple carbohydrates, respectively) to give you immediate energy. Each requires a certain processing time before any of its carbohydrate-generated glucose can be used for energy.

I've always viewed total food intake, muscular tonicity, and level of present activity as codeterminants of how readily these foods are used by the body. Nevertheless, some years ago a group of researchers led by Dr. David Jenkins at the University of Toronto (1981), identified different response times to glucose production from various foods, which at face value contradict our common sense view of simple and complex carbohydrates. In sum, glucose response depends on the food; cornflakes, carrots, and parsnips are quicker to effect rises in blood sugar levels than a candy bar, for example. Conversely, apples, oranges, oatmeal, sweet potatoes and yams, skim milk, yogurt, beans, peas, and tomato soup are more slowly converted to energy than is the candy bar.

If you're like many skiers, you may want a candy bar on the slopes. Of course, not all candy bars are the same with respect to their effect on performance; those with sugar as the first ingredient have more of a need for nutritional backup. This can be accomplished by eating an apple or orange with it. By doing so, you counter the candy bar's effecting a rapid rise, then an abrupt drop in blood glucose. The fruit will kick in just as the candy bar kicks off.

Ironically, both simple and complex carbohydrates may cause adverse bodily reactions in susceptible persons. The former may lead to hypoglycemic reactions, symptoms of which are light-headedness, headaches, fatigue, anger, rage, confusion, the shakes, unbearable cravings for more sugary foods, and muscle aches. The latter may lead to such reactions as fluid retention and bloating, some mild muscular discomfort, headaches, and fatigue.

Confronting the Issue of Sweets.   The most notable of the criticisms of sweets with respect to athletic performance are that they steal water from the body, produce a false sense of energy that quickly subsides, induce hypoglycemic symptoms in susceptible athletes, and potentially inhibit the burning of fat for bioenergy.

Fortunately, most of these can be countered with other helpful, dietary practices: (a) Keep your body hydrated (drink plenty of fluids of which plain water is the best); (b) eat sweets along with more complex carbohydrates; (c) be aware of your hypoglycemic tendencies, moderate sweets consumption, and increase small snacks of low-fat protein, while still allowing sweets; and (d) unless you're an endurance athlete, the inhibition of burning fat for energy probably doesn't matter, and if you are an endurance athlete, fats-for-energy likely matters only with respect to competition of over 90-120 minutes duration.

By using just a bit of forethought and imagination, you can enjoy the tastes, textures, and pure fun of eating all kinds of foods, including sweets, without really jeopardizing a sound performance food plan. However, I do recommend that you stay away from fats and fried foods: These give you minutes of a taste high in return for hours, possibly days, of antiperformance lows.

Time the Foods You Eat.   This helps to orchestrate the flow of your blood (bioenergy) needed for performance. If you eat immediately before exertion, your body will be in the middle of digestion (i.e., blood flow to the stomach and gut) when you really need the blood to flow bioenergy to your muscles. Why create this conflict? Your body will divert the blood to your muscles if the demand is greatest there, even as it continues to try to digest the food you've eaten for use at a later time (perhaps during the exercise you're doing!).

Eat With Performance in Mind.   Plan to eat your foods at a time that allows them to be available for your mind and muscles when each are needed most: during exertion! As a rule, simple carbohydrates are used most immediately (glucose solution right away; sugars, as in table sugar, candy, fruit juice, jelly, honey, etc. in 15-45 minutes, depending on what's in the system and your level of activity). Complex carbohydrates must first be digested and are then used readily (anywhere from 45-90 minutes or more, with variability as above). There are, however, exceptions like carrots and parsnips. Other foods may quickly raise your blood glucose. Thoughtful self-experimentation with a variety of these foods eaten separately and on an empty stomach may help you to discover those that more quickly raise your blood sugar.

Eat the Foods That Work for You When You Need Them. A right food at the wrong time (e.g., a complex carbohydrate 15 minutes before a slalom race) is just as bad, if not worse, than a wrong food at the right time (e.g., a fatty steak or heavily buttered roll two hours before the race). Fatty carbohydrate foods take hours to digest; protein foods longer than carbohydrates, yet not as long as fats. Fatty protein foods that require a good deal of mastication and gastric breakdown may take a day or more to be completely assimilated. Time your eating to perform and feel better while exercising!

Rest

Rest is important, to rejuventate your mind, to relax your muscles, to stop you from injuring yourself, and to dream. There are several ways to rest. The most obvious is to sleep, but there are other ways to accomplish the relaxation and rejuvination we seek. Meditating or reflecting on fond memories, painting, drawing, craftwork, and singing are also restful activities. It is also good to assume a resting position like reclining with or without legs elevated; sitting comfortably; lounging in the sun, hot tub, or sauna; or by receiving a full-body massage. To prevent you from skiing while fatigued, the time when most injuries occur, rest midway down a run or between runs, do relaxation exercises while riding the chairlift, and shake out your arms and legs.

Rest allows messages from your inner self to emerge while asleep at night or awake during the day. Importantly, dreaming is a proven ingredient of positive mental health and high self-esteem. Dreams are often blocked by restrictive, overly judgmental personalities and by persons who continually deny themselves in their daily lives.

Do you have to follow this diet plan to become a high performance skier?

Emphatically, no! The keys to training for glory are all within yourself. All I have done in this chapter and throughout the book is give you tools to identify and realize this potential. Some of the tools will be easy to handle; others will require a tutorial to maximize their application; still others will strain your sense of the possible, even though they are sound and workable. There are many other books and articles that I encourage you to consult on conditioning, flexibility, diet, and the like. With this book and others in mind, however, remember that the one crucial element in the quest for glory is how you interpret the rules for getting there. You are the turning power in your skis.

However passionate your investigation, though, never deny the aspects of your life that provide you with pleasure, fantasy, and adventure. Enjoy these, and allow yourself to speak, feel, imagine, question, boast, admit your frailities, be proud of your accomplishments, be humble, give, and receive. Free yourself to be open to life and you will dream wonderful dreams. Some of these will be about skiing and skiing well!

Summary

1. The balance of the high performance skier includes being technically sound, physically fit, aggressive, committed to off-season and in-season training, and in possession of a psychological edge.
2. Consider the seasons of training: off-season, preseason, early season, ski season, and postseason.
3. The majority of recreational skiers don't ski frequently enough to ski themselves into shape. For these skiers, aerobic exercise and conditioning are a must!
4. Dynamic skiing requires dynamic as well as static muscu-

lar strength to skate, take step turns, react to dramatic terrain changes, utilize an effective defensive pole plant, and, in general, to be resilient.

5. Planned flexibility stretches to complement strength workouts add versatility to your strength and power, making you more agile and quick.

6. Stretching should not be painful! Nonetheless, you must create some discomfort (tension and tingling in the stretched muscle and tendon) to achieve a gain in flexibility.

7. Food is essential for energy because without food, all the oxygen in the world won't provide your body with the glucose it needs to fire its muscles; you must eat to be active.

8. In order for energy to fuel its muscles, your body uses carbohydrates first, followed by fats and then protein. Protein is not a quick energy food!

9. Eat with performance in mind; that is, plan to eat your foods at the time that makes them available to your mind and muscles during exertion.

10. Too many fats in a meal can lead to slow reaction times, poor assimilation of needed carbohydrate-generated glucose, less oxygen to the working muscles, and an overall conflict between being mentally alert and physically tired.

11. Stay away from fats and fried foods because these give you minutes of taste highs in return for hours, possibly days, of antiperformance lows.

12. Rest is important to rejuvenate your mind, relax your muscles, prevent you from injuring yourself, and give you time to dream.

High Performance Tip #16

Fluid Intake

Your body needs fluid before, during, and after strenuous skiing. By strenuous I don't mean a few cruiser runs; rather, strenuous is a morning in heavy powder and an afternoon in the bumps. A common misunderstanding is that if your body is dehydrated, you will be thirsty; on the contrary, it is possible to be close to dehydration and not even feel thirsty.

Sweating is the body's mechanism for cooling itself. The more you sweat, the more fluid you lose; the more fluid you lose, the more that must be replaced. When you lose too much fluid without replacement (3% of body weight is considered safe; 5% is borderline; 8% dangerous), you are prone to dehydration. This is especially noteworthy for spring skiing, but applies as well to full-day cold weather skiing.

There is but one essential fluid: water! The other fluids we ingest are also accompanied by undesirable effects: Caffeinated beverages are diuretic (fluid eliminating); sugar-based drinks may cause stomach cramps; alcoholic beverages are depressants (in spite of how together one feels), which lower body temperature and act as a diuretic; and finally, a number of commercial athletic drinks, as tasty and full of electrolytes as they are, may not be any better for us than water, except in giving us a psychological feeling that we're really into our sport.

All this does not mean that you have to eliminate soft drinks, teas, and coffee from your diet. Thinking of these as fluids for athletic performance, however, is a bit misguided and perhaps risky. Again, don't rely on thirst alone as an indicator of fluid need, even though it can be; thirst can also indicate that you are nervous, hot, bothered, impatient, or tense.

It's best to drink in anticipation, just as you should eat in anticipation of bioenergetic demands. First, hydrate the body's tissues with plenty of water before going skiing, regardless of whether it's hot or cold outside. Drinking small amounts of water at frequent intervals is a helpful practice, as is drinking cold water when you're in most need of fluid (after sweating); it's absorbed more quickly than warmer water.

At summer racing camp, cold water is always available in jugs at the base of the chairlifts leading to the training courses. Part of getting on the lift involves first getting a lift from drinking cold water. I find that water is the best source of fluid before and after athletic exertion; if my mouth and throat are still dry after watering down following exertion, I favor caffeine-free, sugar-free drinks over commercial athletic drinks.

We can't live without water. It's a critical component of your saliva, digestive juices, and mucous to name a few. Without water you're likely to experience a dry mouth, grumbly stomach, hard stools, and difficulty swallowing. Get hooked on water, and it will make a difference in the quality of your life. As for salt tablets, there's no place for them in alpine skiing.

Appendix

Tuning for Maximum Performance and Choosing Your Boots

Keeping your skis tuned: edges sharp, bases clean and waxed for the day's conditions, can make all the difference in the world to skiing in variable conditions. Just as you wouldn't expect a car with bald tires to perform well in a snow storm, why expect your skis to perform in conditions for which they aren't prepared?

You've heard the expression, "Ski racers take it to the edge." It could very well read, "Ski racers live for the edges of their skis." If you're not a racer and could care less about risking life and limb for a few seconds or minutes of excitement, then how about at least adding more versatility and proficiency to your skiing?

Use your thumb and forefinger or the backs of your fingers to get a sense of how your edges ride on the snow. If you can't feel a distinct edge to your skis, one that would cut into soft wood, then your edges are probably too rounded to respond to the subtle movements of your feet and ankles within your boots. This distinct edge is what high performance skiers look for on their skis.

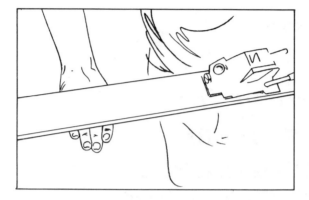

Figure A.1 Feel the sharpness of your skis' edges with the backs of your fingers.

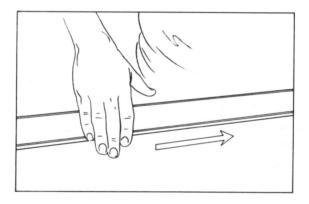

Figure A.2 Run your fingers along the length of your ski to check for a smooth but sharp edge.

At the same time you want your edges to be sharp to lateral touch or pressure, you also want them to be longitudinally smooth. To test this, Jack Rounds suggests running your fingers along the edges, tip to tail. It should be a smooth feeling, not sharp or rough. The latter suggests damaged edges and burrs. If there's a problem with your edges, you'll feel and hear it as you run the carbon stone along the edges. You can also run a carbon stone along the edges to check for hardcasing (e.g., burrs and irregularities). (See Figures A.1 and A.2.)

Consider the advantages and disadvantages of sharp edges. The advantages are responsiveness to subtle movements or angles created at slow, very slow, fast, and very fast speeds; holding power on very hard snow and ice; stability while making quick turns; carvability in various turn radii; and maneuverability in difficult situations where a quick edge set is needed to maintain control.

Some disadvantages include cutting yourself on your edges and being cut by them if you crash and they hit you just the right way. Further, they require your regular attention to stay sharp, are subject to bruising by rocks and icy conditions, and are not prone to easy skidding, so they must be turned: a chore for the skier who is more comfortable skidding from turn to turn.

Before getting together with Jack for this chapter, I detuned (rounded) the tips and tails of my inside edges (the full tip and approximately one inch back from the shovel, and an inch back from the tail of the ski). To allow for more experimentation on my skis with inside-ski steering exercises without the threat of catching an outside edge, I detuned the outside edges of my skis approximately 30 degrees back from the point at which I detuned the inside edge. Although I've since become a convert to Jack's maximum performance tune (I prefer very sharp, beveled edges, tip to tail), I believe the 30 degree angular tuning is an excellent transitional tune for skiers beginning to more seriously explore drills focusing on the inside ski.

As a rule, the further forward and back your edges are sharpened the more quickly your skis will respond to the slightest suggestion of a turn. If you're not fond of quick turns and dynamic ski responsiveness or find that your edges seem to be catching at the beginning or end of your turns, it may be that your tips and tails should be detuned back from the tips and up from the tails. This is because your skiing skills or skiing style are not well-suited to using the entire length of your ski while making short-radius turns. If, however, you prefer slower skiing, or making longer, cruising-type turns, routinely detuning your inside edges a couple of inches from tips and tails may be a blessing. It's really a matter of personal preference, but it's important to your performance.

Maximum Performance Ski Tune

Regardless of the filing technique and tools you use, or your order of filing and base preparation, Jack recommends some fundamental steps for performing a maximum performance ski tune in order to, as he says, "Get performance out of the entire length of your skis."

1. Round off the tips of your skis back to the point where the running surfaces end (the shovel); file and stone all around the tips.

2. Round off the edges of the tails that are just beyond their widest part. This point is past and within the part of the tail that is angled up from the base; you can readily see this. It is less than an inch in length. Eliminate the sharp corners on the tails, and file down the sharpness of the metal tail protector. (See Figure A.3.)

3. Assuming your bases are flat, file the running edges with a long file that allows you to bevel the edges as well. To accomplish this, place the file flat across your base at 30 to 45 degrees; put your hands outside the edges of your ski on each end of the file, pressing down as you file from tip to tail. Beveled edges accomplish two things: They get the otherwise squared edge up off the snow while your skis are gliding, thus preventing unnecessary drag, and they allow the skis to swivel more easily. (Note: With

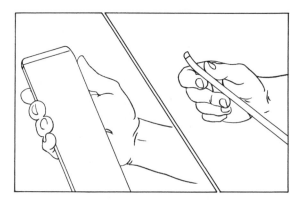

Figure A.3 Round off the metal tail piece.

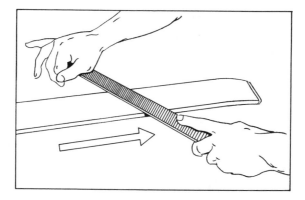

Figure A.4 File to a slight bevel, tip to tail.

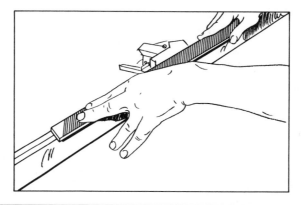

Figure A.5 Hold the file firmly and tune the sides of your edges to square off the bevel on the running surface of your edges.

cracked metal edges, file tip to tail to prevent minute particles from getting into the cracks. Also, short strokes with the file generate less heat; long strokes that generate too much heat may lead to edge irregularities). (See Figure A.4.)

4. Once the running edges are filed, lay the file lengthwise against the full sidewall of the ski, top to bottom. In that the top side of the ski is narrower than the base, this angling procedure will effect a nice 90 degree angle with the running surface of the beveled edge. Side-filing the beveled edge without creating the 90 degree angle would lead to an imprecise edge and altered performance. (See Figure A.5.)

5. Run a flat, wet stone along the running surfaces of the edges and along the sidewall, tip to tail to avoid creating any resistance. Don't use the wet stone until it has soaked a few minutes, and keep it in water when not in use. (You may wipe your edges with an emery cloth or scotch bright cloth as well.)
6. Wax accordingly and go win a race!

Get Acquainted With Your Bases

Make sure your bases are flat and flush with your edges. Make sure there are no gaping holes in them; that is, holes that go through the base into the fabric of the inner ski which, if left alone, may ruin the base of your ski. These holes should be repaired at a ski shop that does base welding. And finally, keep your bases clean!

With respect to the flatness of your bases, too low a base between the edges (concave) leads to skiing your metal edges, excessive suction between ski and snow, poor ski-snow contact, and greater chance of mishap. Too high a base between the edges (convex) leads to skis that track poorly and are quite wobbly, even though they may appear to be much easier to slide into and out of turns. Dirty, grimy bases lead to sticky skis, slower speeds, poor performance, injury, dirty gloves, and messy ski racks; who needs it?

Olympic racers and team ski technicians consider the condition of the bases of their skis and the skis' tune as an integral part of success or failure. Although you don't have to be so intense about your bases, particularly if they're slightly gouged or scraped, it's important to keep in mind the importance of well-prepared skis to high performance skiing. Don't let your imperfect bases keep you from skiing, unless they're dangerously damaged or dirty. A novel and effective way to clean your bases is to first hot wax with household parafin wax; then scrape away the debris that's pulled out by the waxing. Now you're ready to hot wax for skiing.

Get Acquainted With Your Waxes

Wax your bases at least every third time you go skiing or, ideally, every day to keep your skis in top gliding form. Consider some of the reasons why it's important to wax:

1. All snow is made of minute crystals (snowflakes). Sharp snow crystals (as in light, new-fallen snow) and cold air create more friction against your skis; in these situations your wax must be hard. Round crystals (old snow, slush, etc.) and warm air demand softer wax. We wax skis to create the atmosphere for the development of a thin film of water between the heat-producing base of your moving skis and the variable snow conditions upon which your skis are gliding.
2. Wax counters the suctioning effect of snow on the porous bases of your skis. Regular waxing helps to keep the bases responsive to changes in conditions and thereby maximizes your movement down the fall line.
3. You need less energy to push your skis when they're properly waxed.
4. Waxing protects the bases of your skis from excessive wear.
5. Waxing prevents the bases from drying out.
6. Overall, waxing enhances the performance potential of your ski; a lack of waxing diminishes it.

    (*Note*: If your wax smokes during hot waxing, it's a sign that you've broken down its molecular configuration such that it loses almost 60% of its water repellancy.)

Finally, Your Boots

Even if you have great skis and fantastic conditions, poor fitting boots mean poor or less than optimal performance. The high performance skier wants the boot to fit the foot so well, that when he or she steps into the bindings, the skis seem to be as rigidly attached to the legs as are the feet.

Think of properly fitting boots as gaskets between your feet and your skis. Different boots (top entry, rear entry, front buckle) offer a range of technologies to cant your foot, lift your heel, advance your forward lean, provide flex, stabilize your arch, and so on. Great stuff; but first the boot must fit you properly.

Here are a number of considerations modeled after those noted by a panel of experts (Kent, 1983):

1. Avoid borrowing or buying cheap or used boots. If they've been used for any appreciable time, they may not be suitable for your feet.
2. Always try boots on with the socks you use for skiing; wear them for 20 to 30 minutes while you walk around the shop and get the feel of them.
3. After fastening the buckles, press your shin forward (hard) and see if you can slip your index and middle fingers into the boot at the back of your leg. If you can't, the boot may be too small; if it's too easy the boot may be too large.
4. Fasten the buckles and try to lift your heel within the boot. If you can, the boot is too big.
5. Stand up straight; your toes should not touch the front of the boot. If you can't wiggle them, the boot is too small.
6. If you feel a pressure point in the boot, ask the shop to expand the boot for you or seek other remedial measures (e.g., spot padding of the boot bladder, shims in the boot, experimenting with boot adjustments).

Remember, your boots will stretch from a half to a full size after a few days of skiing; in high performance skiing, your boots become your ankles and feet! A tight-fitting boot at purchase will become a well-fitting boot when skied.

References

Abraham, H. (1983). *Skiing right*. San Francisco: Harper & Row.

American Heart Association. (1986, August). *Dietary guidelines for healthy Americans*. Dallas, TX: Author.

Bailey, C. (1978). *Fit or fat*. Boston, MA: Houghton Mifflin Company.

Dardik, I., & Waitley, D. (1984). *Quantum fitness*. New York: Pocket Books.

Haas, R. (1983). *Eat to win*. New York: Rawson Associates.

Jenkins, D.J., Wolever, T.M., Taylor, R.H., Ghafari, H., Jenkins, A.L., Barker, H., & Jenkins, M.J. (1981). Glycemic index of foods: A physiological basis for carbohydrate exchange. *American Journal of Clinical Nutrition*, **34**, 362-366.

Kent, J.M. (1983). Preventing winter sports injuries. *Patient Care*, **17**(20), 145-206.

Loudis, L.A., Lobitz, W.C., & Singer, K.A. (1986). *Skiing out of your mind*. Champaign, IL: Leisure Press.

Mahre, P., Mahre, S., & Fry, J. (1985). *No hill too fast*. New York: Simon & Schuster.

Twardokens, G. (1985). Skiing biomechanics. In National Alpine Staff, U.S. Ski Team (Eds.), *U.S. ski team training manual* (rev. ed., pp. 283-302). Park City, UT: U.S. Ski Team.

Whitney, H. (November, 1981). [Interview with Julian Whitaker]. *The Arizona Republic*, **92**(171), B9-10.

Index